THE
IMAGE MAKERS

A bibliography of
American presidential
campaign biographies

by William Miles

The Scarecrow Press, Inc.
Metuchen, N.J., & London 1979

072502

Library of Congress Cataloging in Publication Data

Miles, William, 1942-
  The image makers.

  Includes indexes.
  1. Presidents--United States--Election--Bibliography.
2. Presidents--United States--Biography--Bibliography.
3. Campaign biography--Bibliography. I. Title.
Z7164.R4M63   016.329'01'0973   79-19472
ISBN 0-8108-1252-5

For
Susan, Amy, and Jennifer

TABLE OF CONTENTS

v

ACKNOWLEDGMENTS

A work of this scope could not have been completed but for the assistance and collective efforts of many people. Initially, I would like to express my appreciation to John Cumming, director of the Clarke Historical Library of Central Michigan University, for not only introducing me to and stimulating my interest in campaign biographies, but also for encouraging me to compile this bibliography. His support of my work never wavered, although I suspect his patience often did.

I am also grateful to the many dealers, collectors, and librarians who willingly answered my queries for bibliographic assistance and advice, and to those members of the American Political Items Collectors who kindly responded to my initial survey letter, thus sharing with me information about their collections of presidential campaign biographies. Had such response not been received, I fear this work would still remain in its infancy.

Special thanks are also due to Tom and Brenda Huston who opened their home to me and assisted in this compilation far beyond that which any researcher could reasonably expect. I only hope that this book justifies their efforts and support.

Richard Maxson also permitted me to examine his personal collection and James Hart shared his with me through correspondence extending over several years. Similarly, Dr. Edmund Sullivan, curator of the DeWitt-Hartford Collection at the University of Hartford, patiently uncovered for me numerous rare and obscure volumes included in that magnificent collection of political Americana. Without his help, this book would not have been published.

The staffs of the American History Division of the New York Public Library and the Divisions of Rare Books and Stack and Read-

ers' Services of the Library of Congress were also most helpful.
No one ever flinched at the innumerable requests for materials I submitted, and all willingly assisted me with any query I might have
had.   Research trips to these and other collections were made possible by financial assistance granted me by the Central Michigan
University Faculty Research and Creative Endeavors Committee.   To
that group, I am most grateful, as I am also to Brian and Constance
Miles who made my research trips to Washington, D. C., comfortable
and pleasant experiences.   While never really sure of exactly what
I was doing, they were, nevertheless, generous in their encourage-
ment and patience.   So also were Tim Curry and Richard O'Brien
and without their help, the typing of the manuscript would not have
been realized.

More than anyone else, however, this book could not have
been completed were it not for the assistance of my wife Susan.
She was most understanding in enduring my absences and listening to
the problems I encountered during the years I spent in researching
and compiling this volume.   Always a perceptive critic, she also
helped in establishing the final arrangement of the work, in proof-
reading, and in all else that is necessary in the preparation of a
manuscript.   More important, she prepared the indexes for the volume, and it can be truthfully said that this is as much her book as
it is mine.

Yet, while I am pleased to acknowledge the many contributors
to this work, I alone am responsible for all omissions and errors in
fact and judgment which may appear herein.

INTRODUCTION

For over 150 years, the campaign biography has been a staple of American presidential elections. Written by the famous as well as the unknown, these works attempt, through a recounting of the lives of candidates or would-be candidates, to assist in the process of persuading the electorate to nominate and elect contenders for the presidency. As such, there is a quality of sameness about them as each biographer seeks to present the favorable characteristics of those who would lead the nation through emphasis upon their subjects' family, circumstances of birth, the republican qualities of their parents, an education generally befitting a man of the people, and engagement in occupations often described as beneficial to the American people as a whole. If such works seem to stretch reality or overlook fact at times, it is only because their sole purpose is to promote.

To expedite this process of promotion, biographers create, as William Burlie Brown argues in The People's Choice: The Presidential Image in the Campaign Biography (Baton Rouge: Louisiana State University Press, 1960), a symbol which combines all of those features and ideals most appealing to the American electorate. In short, they bring forth "out of the raw material of the candidate's real life the biography of the ideal citizen of the Republic" (p. xiii). That such often borders on the mythical is of no concern for if nothing else, campaign biographers are image makers, and if this is true in favorable terms for those whom they support, it is equally true in the unfavorable for those whom they oppose; the image of the "ideal citizen" being reversed and replaced by an exposition of negative characteristics designed to dissuade the electorate in their choice of a particular candidate.

And yet, despite the longevity and popularity of this genre in the American political process, little of a substantive nature has been written about it. Indeed, with the exception of James D. Hart's article, "They All Were Born in Log Cabins, " appearing in the August, 1956, issue of American Heritage, and Brown's previously mentioned book, studies which investigate and analyze this aspect of our political life are few. Even fewer are bibliographic investigations of the campaign biographies themselves, for discounting the non-descriptive listing of selected works in Brown's volume or the scattered references in such standard tools as Sabin and Howes, only Ernest James Wessen's Campaign Lives of Abraham Lincoln, 1860, which was reprinted in 1938 from the Papers in Illinois History and Transactions for the Year 1937, qualifies as the one serious bibliographic study of but a small part of this voluminous area of political Americana.

What follows then is an initial attempt to bring some bibliographic control to this genre. As such, however, it suffers from all of the inadequacies which plague initial ventures, not the least of which is that it is by no means complete. Considering that some 48 presidential campaigns are treated herein, the total of 1283 entries, not including variant editions and printings mentioned in the notes, seems slim indeed. Yet, while this work may rightfully be termed preliminary, it is hoped that it will, nevertheless, prove useful to librarians, scholars and collectors for reference and identification purposes, as well as stimulate interest in this field and thus help to uncover additional volumes, whether they be titles not listed or different printings of items cited herein.

The bibliography itself includes books, pamphlets, magazines, almanacs, speeches, political compendia and the like which are or in which appear what I have judged to be campaign biographies, both favorable and unfavorable, dating from 1796 to 1976. Specific campaign newspapers, the majority of which devote an issue or at least part of one to the lives of the candidates have been purposely excluded. This decision has been made primarily because this area is as vast as that of the campaign biography itself and inclusion of

a few titles would only render the work even more incomplete. To
do justice to the campaign newspaper necessitates a separate such
bibliography and one is currently in preparation. Similarly, because
almanacs and political compendia are included, it should not be assumed that complete runs of these volumes will be found in this compilation. Not all contain biographical sketches, thus only those
which do and were examined are entered. Unless reissued for subsequent campaign purposes, reprints of cited biographies are also
excluded.

The subjects of the biographies themselves are not restricted
to the nominated candidates of all official parties, but also include
those who sought the nominations only to encounter defeat. Inclusions here, as in the titles described, are thus a matter of personal
judgment, although I was aided in my final decision through frequent
reference to the four-volume History of American Presidential Elections, 1789-1968 (New York: Chelsea House Publishers, 1971),
edited by Arthur M. Schlesinger, Jr., and Fred L. Israel, and the
two helpful research reports of the association of American Political
Items Collectors: Presidential and Vice Presidential Candidates of
All Parties, 1789-1960 issued in 1963, and their Presidential Hope-
fuls, 1789-1960, published in 1965.

It should also be noted that the following bibliography begins
with the year 1824, which is often recognized as being the campaign
in which the first true campaign biography was published. The addendum, however, opens with 1796 and also includes several items
published for the campaigns of 1808 and 1812. The whole period
prior to 1824, with its mass of political campaign pamphlets, needs
to be studied more fully than the consideration given to it here and
elsewhere, for while I am willing to admit that the 1796 John Adams
item does not completely exemplify the characteristics of a "campaign biography, " I also have no doubts that the George Clinton work
(entry 1263) and that relating to Charles C. Pinckney (entry 1265)
do. The year 1824 seems to be a convenient if not an arbitrary
date in this branch of Americana. Again, however, all inclusions
in this work are based upon personal judgment which I am willing to
admit may well have been faulty at times.

The Arrangement of the Bibliography

The bibliography itself is initially arranged chronologically according to campaigns. Within, the successful candidate is entered first, followed by the defeated opponent. Official candidates of third parties appear next while after those, all potential or aspiring candidates for the office appear in strict alphabetical order. Party affiliations are cited with the candidates' names, and all entries under each are listed alphabetically by author or title.

Entries themselves provide author, title, and imprint information, although titles have frequently been shortened in the interest of space. Special attention has been given to providing complete pagination in order that volumes can be readily identified. Definite divisions of a work have thus been indicated as have blank pages, advertisements, and the like. The use of the term "cover title" is broad and includes title pages in sewn copies which do not enfold all of the signatures as well as wrapper titles. Binding descriptions which follow are complete only if a work is described as in wrappers, and unless otherwise noted, all wrappers should be assumed to be printed. For volumes issued in cloth, only color is given, notations relating to decorative effects being excluded.

An attempt has likewise been made to be as complete as possible in describing illustrative matter, particularly in terms of the number of inserted plates. Here also, broad use is made of the term "title vignette," for while the actual vignette is not indicated, one can assume that it ranges from either a full illustration or a portrait, to merely a cut. The process by which illustrations were created, however, is generally excluded, although differences in title vignettes or plates which might appear in the same title, but variant printings of a work, are so noted. Such differences are identified in the brief notes accompanying entries, which are designed to distinguish between printings and variant bindings as well as to describe salient features of the work in question. Establishment of priority among editions, states, variants, etc. has not been attempted. Except for broadsides, where it is given in inches, the size of described volumes has been omitted. An asterisk preceding an entry number indicates that that item was not personally examined, although enough peripheral information was discovered to warrant my assumption that the work is a campaign biography. In the majority of such cases, references have been cited.

Concluding the volume are two indexes, one of authors and candidates, the other of short titles. The first includes only authors of presidential sketches; those who may have written vice-presidential lives or political articles appearing in any of the works listed are excluded, as are other personal names which may be cited on title pages of examined volumes. Since many candidates ran more than once and some had frequent presidential aspirations, "candidates" have been included in this index in order to assist users in discovering the various campaigns in which they were or desired to be involved. As candidates, such names are entered in capital letters, although should they also prove to be authors, those particular entries follow that of the candidate in lower case. References in both indexes are to entry numbers cited in the bibliography and addendum.

As noted earlier, it is more than probable that during the preparation of this work many items were overlooked or unknown to me. This may prove particularly true of ephemeral sketches, locally or state produced party publications, and items issued on a subscription basis with variant imprints for local publishers or booksellers. Likewise, it is also probable that this bibliography contains volumes of a questionable nature. Should users find such to be true, correspondence relating to these as well as omitted items would be most appreciated.

William Miles
Clarke Historical Library
Central Michigan University
August 1978

ABBREVIATIONS

adv(s).	advertisement(s)	ℓ.	leaf
bds.	boards	$\ell\,\ell$.	leaves
biog.	biography/biograph-ical	ltd.	limited
		misc.	miscellaneous
biogs.	biographies	ms.	manuscript
bl(s).	blank(s)	n. d.	no date
cld.	colored	n. p.	no place
col(s).	column(s)	orig.	original
dbl.	double	p.	page
div. t.	divisional title	pf.	portrait frontispiece
dj	dust jacket	pl(s).	plate(s)
doc.	document	port(s).	portrait(s)
ed.	edition	pp.	pages
eng.	engraved	pr.	printed
enlg.	enlarged	pub.	publisher('s)
f.	frontispiece	pub. cat.	publisher's catalog
fac.	facsimile	pubs.	publishers
fld.	folded	sig(s).	signature(s)
illus.	illustration(s)/ illustrated	sm.	small
incl.	including	t.	title page
intro.	introduction	tbls.	tables
		wrp(s).	wrapper(s)

REFERENCES

BAL

Blanck, Jacob. Bibliography of American Literature. 6 vols. New Haven and London: Yale University Press, 1955- .

Brown

Brown, William Burlie. The People's Choice: The Presidential Image in the Campaign Biography. Baton Rouge: Louisiana State University Press, [1960.]

Drake

Drake, Milton. Almanacs of the United States. 2 vols. New York: Scarecrow Press, 1962.

Howes

Howes, Wright. U.S.iana (1650-1950): A Selective Bibliography.... Rev., enlgd. ed. New York: R. R. Bowker, 1962.

Martin

Martin, Dorothy V. "William Henry Harrison and the Campaign of 1840: A Check List of Books and Pamphlets," Annual Report of the Historical and Philosophical Society of Ohio (1940), 7-21.

Monaghan

Monaghan, Jay. Lincoln Bibliography, 1839-1939. 2 vols. Springfield: Illinois State Historical Library, 1943-1945.

Sabin

Sabin, Joseph. Bibliotheca Americana: A Dictionary of Books Relating to America, from Its Discovery to the Present Time. 29 vols. 1868-1936. Reprint (29 vols. in 15). Amsterdam: N. Israel, 1961-1962.

Thompson

Thompson, Peter G. A Bibliography of the State of Ohio. Being a Catalogue of Books and Pamphlets Relating to the History of the State. Cincinnati: Published by the Author, 1880.

Wessen

Wessen, Ernest James. Campaign Lives of Abraham Lincoln, 1860. [Springfield:] Reprinted from the Papers in Illinois History and Transactions for the Year 1937 [1938.]

1824

(All Candidates Were Democratic-Republicans)

ADAMS, JOHN QUINCY

1 Sketch of the Life of John Quincy Adams; Taken from the Port Folio of April, 1819. To Which Are Added, the Letters of Tell: Originally Addressed to the Editor of the Baltimore American ... [N. p.] 1824.

Cover title [1], bl. [2], [3]-11, [12]-52. Sewn. Text of Sketch differs from 1827 and 1828 works of same title.

CALHOUN, JOHN C.

2 An Address to the Citizens of North-Carolina, on the Subject of the Presidential Election. [Raleigh: Bell & Lawrence, Printers, 1823.]

Caption title. [1]-20, signed "Carolina, November 1823." Sewn. Printer's imprint at foot of p. 20. Pro-Calhoun, anti-Crawford.

3 An Address to the Citizens of North-Carolina, on the Subject of the Presidential Election. [N. p., 1823.]

Caption title. [1]-15, bl. [16], signed "Carolina, November 1823." Sewn. Lacks printer's imprint; different typeface and ornament employed in caption title.

4 An Address to the People of Maryland, on the Subject of the Presidential Election. [N. p., n. d., 1824.]

Caption title. [1]-17, bl. [18], bl. ℓ. Sewn. Essentially a biographical sketch of the personal and public career of Calhoun.

5 Measures, Not Men. Illustrated by Some Remarks upon the Public Conduct and Character of John C. Calhoun.... By a Citizen of New-York. New York: Printed by E. B. Clayton, 1823.

    T. [1], bl. [2], [3]-49, bl. [50]. Brown coated wrps.

6 Presidential Election. The Following Pieces, Copied from the Richmond Enquirer, Having Been Published at Different Periods of the Year 1823, Are Now Imbodied [sic] in the Pamphlet Form, and Submitted to the Calm Consideration of the People. [Richmond? 1823.]

    Caption title. Cover title [1], bl. [2], [3-11], 12-64. Sewn. Cover title reads Presidential Election. Pp. [3-11] signed "Wythe"; pp. 12-25, "Roanoke." Pro-Calhoun, anti-Crawford.

CRAWFORD, WILLIAM H.

7 [Butler, Benjamin Franklin.] Sketches of the Life and Character of William H. Crawford. By Americanus. Albany: Printed by Packard & Van Benthuysen, 1824.

    Cover title [1], bl. [2], [3]-4, [5]-39, bl. [40]. Sewn. Intro. pp. [3]-4, dated October 20, 1824. Originally published in the Albany Argus, September-October, 1824.

JACKSON, ANDREW

8 Address of the Committee Appointed by a Republican Meeting in the County of Hunterdon, Recommending Gen. Andrew Jackson, of Tennessee, to the People of New-Jersey, as President of the United States. Trenton: Sept. 1824.

    Cover title [1], bl. [2], [3]-4, [5]-16, [17]-21, bl. [22], [23]-24. Life of Jackson, pp. [17]-18, from the Richmond Enquirer, March, 1815; extracts from nominating address at Harrisburgh convention, March 4, 1824, pp. 18-21.

9 An Address to the People of Ohio, on the Important Subject of the Next Presidency; by the Committee ... Assembled at Columbus, on Wednesday, the 14th Day of July, 1824. Cincinnati: Looker & Reynolds, Printers [1824.]

    Cover title [1], [2], [3]-16. Sewn. "This brief sketch of the life of Gen. Jackson, has been principally digested from Mr. Waldo's memoirs of that officer."

10 Eaton, John Henry. The Life of Andrew Jackson, Major-General in the Service of the United States: Comprising a History of the War in the South, from the Commencement of the Creek

Campaign, to the Termination of Hostilities Before New Orleans. Philadelphia: Published by Samuel F. Bradford, Jesper Harding, Printer, 1824.

Pf., t. [i], [ii], [iii]-vii, bl. [viii], [9]-442, [443]-468.   3/4
marbled bds.   Pf. inserted.   Notes, pp. [443]-468.   Second
edition, the first, 1817, reading, Commenced by John Reid
... Completed by John Henry Eaton.

11 The Letters of Wyoming, to the People of the United States, on
    the Presidential Election, and in Favour of Andrew Jackson.
    Originally Published in the Columbian Observer.   Philadelphia:
    Published by S. Simpson & J. Conrad, 1824.

    T. [i], bl. [ii], [1-2], [3]-104.   All copies examined rebound.

12 Memoirs of General Andrew Jackson, Together with the Letter
    of Mr. Secretary Adams, in Vindication of the Execution of
    Arbuthnot and Ambrister, and the Other Public Acts of Gen.
    Jackson, in Florida.   New York: Published at the Office of
    the National Union, 1824.

    T. [1], [2], [3]-40.   Brown wrps.

13 Memoirs of General Andrew Jackson....   Bridgeton, N. J.:
    Printed by Simeon Siegfried, 1824.

    As in entry 12.   Sewn.

1828

JACKSON, ANDREW (Democratic)

14 Address of the Republican Committee of Correspondence of Phila-
    delphia, to the People of the United States.   Philadelphia:
    Printed by William Stavely, 1828.

    Cover title [1], bl. [2], [3]-6, [7]-12.   Self wrps.   Letters,
    pp. [3]-6, captioned "Pennsylvania"; p. 12 dated July 26,
    1828.

15 Address of the Republican General Committee of Young Men of
    the City and County of New-York, Friendly to the Election of
    Gen. Andrew Jackson to the Presidency, to the Republican
    Electors of the State of New-York.   New York: Alexander
    Ming, Jr., Printer, Stereotyped by James Connor, 1828.

    Cover title [1], bl. [2], [3]-48.   Sewn.

16   Address of the State Convention Delegates from the Several
     Counties of the State of New-York to the People, on the Sub-
     ject of the Approaching Presidential Election.   Albany:
     Printed by Beach, Denio & Richards, at the Office of the Al-
     bany Morning Chronicle, 1828.

     Cover title [1], bl. [2], [3]-16.   Sewn.   Text pr. in dbl.
     cols.   Anti-Jackson.

17   An Address, to the People of the United States, on the Subject
     of the Presidential Election: With a Special Reference to the
     Nomination of Andrew Jackson, Containing Sketches of His
     Public and Private Character.   By a Citizen of the United
     States.   [N. p.]   Printed for the Proprietor, 1828.

     Cover title [1], [2], [3]-40 [41]-48.   Sewn.   Appendix, pp.
     [41]-48.   Anti-Jackson, pro-John Quincy Adams.

18   Eaton, John Henry.   The Life of Major General Andrew Jack-
     son: Comprising a History of the War in the South. . . .   Ad-
     denda: Containing a Brief History of the Seminole War and
     Cession and Government of Florida.   Third Edition.   Revised
     and Corrected by the Author.   Philadelphia: Published by
     M'Carty & Davis, 1828.

     Pf., t. [i], [ii], [iii]-iv, [5]-317, bl. [318], [319]-335, bl.
     [336].   Calf, black leather label on backstrip.   Pf. inserted.
     Notes, pp. [319]-335.   Also noted with imprint: Cincinnati:
     Hatch & Nichols, 1827.

19   _____ .   Memoirs of Andrew Jackson, Late Major-General
     and Commander in Chief of the Southern Division of the Army
     of the United States.   By a Citizen of Massachusetts.   Bos-
     ton: Published by Charles Ewer, 1828.

     Half title [1], bl. [2], pf., t. [3], [4], [5]-7, bl. [8], [9]-
     12, [13]-334.   3/4 marbled bds., leather backstrip.   Pf. in-
     serted.   Preface, pp. [5]-7, dated March 15, 1828.   Binding
     also noted in calf.

20   Hill, Isaac.   An Address, Delivered at Concord, N. H. January
     8, 1828, Being the Thirteenth Anniversary of Jackson's Vic-
     tory at New-Orleans.   Concord: Printed by Manahan, Hoag
     & Co., 1828.

     T. [1], [2], [3]-31, bl. [32], [33]-35, [36]-44.   Orange
     wrps.   Hill's address, pp. [3]-31.

21   _____ .   Brief Sketch of the Life, Character and Services of
     Major General Andrew Jackson.   By a Citizen of New-Eng-
     land.   Concord: Printed by Manahan, Hoag & Co. for Isaac
     Hill, 1828.

Pf. , t. [1], bl. [2], [3]-46, [47]-51, bl. [52]. Rose wrps. ,
adv. on outer back.   Notes, pp. [47]-51.

22   A History of the Life and Public Services of Major General An-
     drew Jackson.   Impartially Compiled From the Most Authentic
     Sources.   [N. p.] 1828.

     Cover title [i], bl. [ii], [1]-37, bl. [38].   Sewn.   Caption
     title: An Impartial and True History of the Life and Services
     of Major General Andrew Jackson.   Anti-Jackson.

23   An Impartial and True History of the Life and Services of Major
     General Andrew Jackson.   [N. p. , n. d. , 1828.]

     Caption title.   1-36.   Sewn.

24   An Impartial and True History. . . .   [Portsmouth, N. H. ?   Feb-
     ruary, 1828?]

     Caption title.   [1]-16.   Sewn.   At head of title: Read the
     Following Facts, and Lend to Your Neighbour.   Imprint in-
     formation taken from ms. note.   Anti-Jackson.

25   [Kane, John Kintzing?]   A Candid View of the Presidential Ques-
     tion, by a Pennsylvanian.   Philadelphia: Printed by William
     Stavely, 1828.

     Cover title [1], bl. [2], [3]-22, bl. ℓ. Sewn.

26   [Lee, Henry.]   A Vindication of the Character and Public Ser-
     vices of Andrew Jackson; in Reply to the Richmond Address,
     Signed by Chapman Johnson, and to Other Electioneering
     Calumnies.   Originally Published in the Nashville Republi-
     can. . . .   Boston: True and Greene, Printers, 1828.

     Cover title [1], bl. [2], [3]-4, 4-51, bl. [52].   Sewn.   Let-
     ters signed "Jefferson. "

27   Loughborough, Preston S.   Speech . . . Delivered by Request,
     Near Frankfort on the 10th of September, 1827, at the Cele-
     bration of Perry's Victory on Lake Erie; and of the Success
     of the Cause of Andrew Jackson. . . .   Frankfort: Printed for
     the Author by A. G. Hodges, 1827.

     Cover title [1], bl. [2], [3]-24.   Sewn.

*28 Reflections on the Character and Public Services of Andrew
     Jackson . . . By a Native American.   New York: Printed and
     Sold by Geo. F. Hopkins, 1828.

     Cover title [1], bl. [2], [3]-48.   Sabin 35387.

29   Some Account of General Jackson, Drawn Up From the Hon. Mr.
     Eaton's Very Circumstantial Narrative, and Other Well-Estab-

lished Information Respecting Him. By a Gentleman of the
Baltimore Bar. Baltimore: Published by Henry Vicary,
Matchett, Print., 1828.

Pf., t. [i], [ii], [iii-iv], [v-vi], [7]-272, ℓ. adv. All copies
examined rebound. Pf. inserted. Prolegomena, pp. [v-vi],
dated February 4, 1828, with notation regarding first impression; p. [vi] missigned viii.

30 [Van Ness, William Peter.] A Concise Narrative of General
Jackson's First Invasion of Florida, and of His Immortal De-
fence of New-Orleans: With Remarks.... By Aristides.
New York: February, 1827.

Cover title [1], bl. [2], [3]-5, bl. [6], [7]-39, [40]-48. Self
wrps. Appendix, pp. [40]-48.

31 _____. A Concise Narrative .... Second Edition With Ad-
ditions. By Aristides. Published by Order of the General
Committee of Republican Young Men of New-York. New
York: Printed by E. M. Murden & A. Ming, Jr., 1827.

Cover title [1], bl. [2], [3]-4, [5]-32, div. t. [33], bl. [34],
[35]-40. Self wrps. Appendix, pp. [35]-40.

32 _____. A Concise Narrative.... Fifth Edition. Albany:
Printed at the Argus Office by Order of the Republican General Committee, 1828.

Cover title [1], [2], [3]-20, [21]-24. Self wrps. Preface,
p. [2]; appendix, pp. [21]-24.

33 _____. A Concise Narrative.... Sixth Edition. [N. p.,
1828.]

Cover title [1], [2], [3]-19, [20]-24. Self wrps. Preface,
p. [2]; appendix, pp. [20]-24. Library of Congress copy
extra-illustrated, pf. and 11 pls. inserted.

34 A Voice From the Interior. Who Shall Be President? The
Hero of New-Orleans, or John the Second, of the House of
Braintree. By a Republican of the Jefferson School. Boston:
True and Greene, Printers, 1828.

Cover title [1], bl. [2], [3]-20. All copies examined bound
with other pamphlets.

35 [Waldo, Samuel Putnam.] Memoirs of the Illustrious Citizen and
Patriot, Andrew Jackson, Late Major-General in the Army of
the United States; and Commander-In-Chief of the Division of
the South.... By a Citizen of Hagers-Town, Md. Chambers-
burg: Printed for Subscribers, 1828.

Pf. , t. [i], bl. [ii], [iii], bl. [iv], [v]-x, [11]-20, [21]-306.
Calf, red leather label on backstrip.   Pf. inserted.   To the
Reader, p. [iii], dated February, 1828.

36   [Walsh, Robert.]   Biographical Sketch of Andrew Jackson.   [Al-
      bany: 1828.]

      Caption title.   [1]-16.   Sewn.   Pp. [1]-8, in dbl. cols. , 9-
      16 single; To the People of New York, pp. 15-16; p. 16
      signed, "General Republican Corresponding Committee of the
      City of Albany ... May 15, 1828. "

37   _____ .   Biographical Sketch of the Life of Andrew Jackson,
      Major-General of the Armies of the United States, the Hero
      of New-Orleans. ...   Hudson: Published by William E. Nor-
      man, 1828.

      Bl. [i], pf. [ii], t. [iii], bl. [iv], [v]-vi, [7]-65, bl. [66].
      Brown pr. paper bds.   Pf. inserted.

ADAMS, JOHN QUINCY (National Republican)

38   Commentator Extra.   June 21, 1828.   Two Sheets; Containing a
      Sketch of the Life and Public Services of John Quincy Adams,
      President of the United States. ...   [Frankfort, Ky. : Com-
      mentator, 1828.]

      Cover title [1], bl. [2], [3]-[47], bl. [48].   Sewn.   P. num-
      ber 42 omitted; p. 43 cited as 42, 44 as 43, and 47 as 48.

39   A Sketch of the Life and Public Services of John Quincy Adams,
      President of the United States, and Commander In Chief of
      the Army and Navy, &c. &c. [N. p. , 1827.]

      Caption title.   Broadside, $20\frac{1}{2}$ x 12 3/4, pr. in 5 cols. , on
      both sides of sheet.   At foot of col. 5, p. [2], "Plutarch.
      Fayette Co.   July 31, 1827. "

40   A Sketch of the Life and Services of John Quincy Adams, Presi-
      dent of the United States of America. ...   New York: Sickels,
      Printer, 1828.

      Cover title [1], bl. [2], [3]-16.   Sewn.

41   A Sketch of the Life and Services of John Quincy Adams. ...
      [N. p.] 1827.

      Cover title (?) [1], bl. [2], [3]-31, bl. [32], bl. ℓ .   All
      copies examined disbound.

42   Sketch of the Life of John Quincy Adams.   [N. p.]   1827.

Cover title [1], [2], [3]-11, bl. [12]. Sewn. To the Public, p. [2]; text, pp. [3]-11, in dbl. cols. This and entry 41 based, in part, upon a sketch of Adams which appeared in the Port Folio, April, 1819.

1832

JACKSON, ANDREW (Democratic [Democratic-Republican])

43 Eaton, John Henry. Leben Des General-Majors Andreas Jackson. ... Von Johann Heinrich Eaton. ... Reading: Johann Ritter und Comp. , 1831.

Pf. , t. [i], [ii], [iii]-iv, [v]-vi, [7]-419. 3/4 orange paper bds. , leather backstrip. Pf. and fld. cld. map inserted. Title vignette.

44 Goodwin, Philo A. Biography of Andrew Jackson, President of the United States, Formerly Major General in the Army of the United States. Hartford: Published by Clapp and Benton, 1832.

Pf. , t. [i], [ii], [iii]-vi, [vii]-xi, bl. [xii], 1-422. Calf. Pf. inserted. Preface, pp. [iii]-vi, dated October 1, 1832.

45 [Snelling, William Joseph.] A Brief and Impartial History of the Life and Actions of Andrew Jackson, President of the United States. ... By a Free Man. Boston: Stimpson and Clapp, 1831.

Pf. , t. [i], [ii], [iii]-iv, [5]-202, [203]-216. 3/4 brown paper bds. , cloth backstrip with pr. paper label. Pf. inserted. Copyright notice with printer's imprint on label tipped to p. [ii]; appendix, pp. [203]-216.

CLAY, HENRY (National Republican [Whig])

46 Prentice, George D. Biography of Henry Clay. Hartford: Samuel Hanmer, Jr. and John Jay Phelps, Publishers, 1831.

Pf. , t. [i], [ii], [iii]-v, bl. [vi], [7]-276, [277]-300, 301-304. Calf. Pf. inserted. Appendix, pp. [277]-300; index, pp. 301-304.

47 _____ . Second Edition, Revised. Biography of Henry Clay. New York: Published by John Jay Phelps, 1831.

Pf. , t. [i], [ii], [iii]-v, bl. [vi], [7]-284, [285]-308, [309]-312. Calf. Pf. inserted. Appendix, pp. [285]-308; index, pp. [309]-312.

1836

VAN BUREN, MARTIN (Democratic)

48 Crockett, David. The Life of Martin Van Buren, Heir-Apparent
to the "Government," and the Appointed Successor of General
Andrew Jackson. Containing Every Authentic Particular by
Which His Extraordinary Character Has Been Formed....
Philadelphia: Robert Wright, 1835.

Bl. [i], adv. [ii], t. [1], [2], 3-21, bl. [22], 23-209, bl.
[210], bl. ℓ., adv. [1]-26. Maroon cloth with pr. paper
label on backstrip. Pub. cat., pp. [1]-26, dated June, 1835.
Copies also noted with pub. cat., pp. [1]-6. Burlesque life;
also attributed to A. S. Clayton.

49 _____. The Life of Martin Van Buren.... Tenth Edition.
Philadelphia: Robert Wright, 1836.

As in entry 48, but lacking opening adv. and concluding pub.
cat.

50 [Emmons, William.] Biographies of Martin Van Buren and
Richard M. Johnson. New York: Published and for Sale
Wholesale and Retail by Childs and DeVoe [c1833.]

Caption title. [1]-12, 13-16. Self wrps. Title vignette.
Newspaper format, text in triple cols.; at head of title:
Van Buren [vignette] Johnson.; at foot of p. 16, copyright
notice by William Emmons.

51 _____. Biography of Martin Van Buren, Vice President of
the United States. With an Appendix.... Washington:
Printed by Jacob Gideon, Jr., 1835.

T. [i], [ii], [iii]-vi, bls. [vii-viii], [1]-44, [45]-196. Blue
paper bds., cloth backstrip; pr. paper label on front. Appendix, pp. [45]-196. Also noted in green paper bds.

52 _____. Biography of Martin Van Buren.... Second Edition.
Washington: Printed by Jacob Gideon, Jr., 1835.

As in entry 51, but green paper bds.

53 Grund, Franz J. Martin Van Buren als Staatsmann und künsti-
ger Präsident der Vereinigten Staaten von Nord-Amerika.
[New York?] 1835.

Half title [i], bl. [ii], t. [iii], bl. [iv], [v], bl. [vi], [vii]-
viii, 1-29, bl. [30], bl. ℓ. Buff wrps.

54 Holland, William M. The Life and Political Opinions of Martin
    Van Buren, Vice President of the United States. Hartford:
    Belknap & Hamersley, 1835.

    Flyleaf [i-ii], pf. [iii], bl. [iv], t. [v], [vi], [vii]-x, [xi]-xiv,
    div. t. [xv], bl. [xvi], [13]-364. Purple cloth. Pf. inserted.
    Copies also noted with blindstamped statue and eagle on front
    and back covers; others with pub. cat., 1-11, [12] pp.

55 _____. The Life ... of Martin Van Buren.... Second Edi-
    tion. Hartford: Belknap & Hamersley, 1836.

    Pf., t. [i], [ii], [iii]-vi, [vii]-ix, bl. [x], [xi]-xvi, div. t.
    [xvii], bl. [xviii], [13]-372, [373], bl. [374], 5 ℓ ℓ. Calf.
    Pf. inserted. Preface to second ed., pp. [vii]-ix; terminal
    5 ℓ ℓ., notices of first ed. Copies also noted in green cloth.

56 Jackson Almanac. 1836. New York: Elton [1835.]

    Cover title [1], 2-[35], adv. and illus. [36]. Self wrps.
    Title vignette. Illus. in text. Erratic pagination; biography
    of Van Buren, pp. 6-7.

*57 Sketches of the Life and Public Services of Martin Van Buren.
    Comprehending the Principal Events in the History of His Il-
    lustrious Career. Albany: A. J. Bready, 1836.

    Pf., 12 pp. Sabin 98425 (note).

HARRISON, WILLIAM HENRY (Whig)

58 A Biographical Sketch of the Life and Services of Gen. William
    Henry Harrison, Together With His Letter to Simon Boli-
    var.... Montpelier, Vt.: Printed at the Watchman Office,
    1836.

    T. [1], bl. [2], [3]-30. Blue wrps. Letter to Bolivar, pp.
    17-30.

*59 A Brief History of the Public Services of Gen. William H. Har-
    rison, Commander-In-Chief of the Northwestern Army in the
    War of 1812.... By the Editor of the Penna. Intelligencer.
    Harrisburg: 1836.

    16 pp. Thompson, p. 150; Martin (lists as 1835).

60 A Brief Sketch of the Life and Public Services of William Henry
    Harrison, As Secretary of the North Western Territory....
    Compiled From Official Documents.... New-York: Pub-
    lished by T. & C. Wood, Stationers, 1835.

    T. [1], [2], [3], [4], [5]-31, [32]. Green wrps. Preface,
    p. [3], dated September 1, 1835; appendix, p. [32]. Based

in part on the sketch of Harrison which appeared in the Port Folio, 1814.

61 Hall, James. A Memoir of the Public Services of William Henry Harrison, of Ohio. Philadelphia: Edward C. Biddle, 1836.

Pf. , t. [i], [ii], [iii], bl. [iv], [v]-vi, [7]-323, bl. [324]. Brown cloth. Copies also noted in green cloth with pr. paper label on front, and imprint: Philadelphia: Key & Biddle, 1836. Sabin 29790 also notes earlier printing: Philadelphia: Key & Biddle, 1835.

*62 [Jackson, Isaac Rand.] Narrative of the Civil and Military Services of William H. Harrison. Compiled From the Most Authentic Authorities. With Engravings. Cincinnati: Printed by Ormsby H. Donogh, 1836.

72 pp. , f. , pls. Martin notes that the main body of the text is the same as the New York and Philadelphia eds. , but the New York printing has three introductory paragraphs not found in the Cincinnati or Philadelphia eds. Philadelphia has one introductory paragraph not in either of the others, while Cincinnati includes two lengthy quotes from Dawson's Life (1824) not included in New York or Philadelphia.

63 _____ . A Sketch of the Life and Public Services of William Henry Harrison. Columbus: Printed by Scott & Wright, Journal Office, 1836.

Cover title. [1]-28, [29]-36. Blue wrps. Appendix, pp. [29]-36; concludes with extract from Johnson's speech.

64 _____ . A Sketch. ... Philadelphia: Jan. 1836.

T. [1], bl. [2], [3]-36. Blue wrps. For differences in introductory paragraphs between this and entry 66, see entry 62.

65 _____ . A Sketch of the Life and Public Services of William Henry Harrison, Commander-In-Chief of the Northwestern Army During the War of 1812, &c. Albany: From the Power Press of Hoffman & White, 1836.

T. [1], bl. [2], [3]-24. Brown wrps.

66 _____ . A Sketch of the Life ... of William Henry Harrison. ... New York: Printed by Harper & Brothers, Stereotyped by F. F. Ripley, MDCCCXXXVI.

T. [1], bl. [2], [3]-32. Green wrps. , outer back with "Col. Richard M. Johnson's Opinion [of] General Harrison. " Copies also noted lacking wrps. , sewn.

67   _____. William Henry Harrison. [N. p., 1836.]

>Caption title. 1-28, [29]-36. All copies examined disbound. Concludes, p. 36, with Johnson's testimonial; pp. [29]-36, appendix on why Van Buren should not be elected.

68 Proceedings of a State Convention of Delegates Friendly to the Election of William Henry Harrison, for President, and Francis Granger, for Vice President, Assembled at the Capitol, Feb. 3, 1836. Albany: Printed by Hoffman and White, 1836.

>Cover title (?) [1], bl. [2], [3]-16. All copies examined disbound. Address by William Parmalee, pp. 8-16, primarily biographical.

69 Sketch of the Life of Major General William Henry Harrison. Comprising a Brief Account of His Important Civil and Military Services; Including a Description of the Victories of Tippecanoe, Fort Meiggs [sic], and the Thames. [N. p.] 1836.

>Pf., t. [1], bl. [2], [3]-39, bl. [40]. Copy examined in Xerox form only.

70 Speech of Mr. Storer, in Defence of Gen. William Henry Harrison. To Which Is Annexed, a Short Sketch of the Principal Events of His Life. Baltimore: Printed by Sands & Neilson, 1836.

>Cover title [1], bl. [2], [3]-25, [26]-32. Sewn. Title vignette. Speech, pp. [3]-25; Life, pp. [26]-32.

1840

HARRISON, WILLIAM HENRY (Whig)

71 Abstract of the Public Services of William Henry Harrison. Boston: E. Tappan & A. C. Warren, 1840.

>Caption title. Broadside, pr. in single col. and surrounded by ornaments and 4 illus.

72 Badger, George E. Speech Delivered at the Great Whig Meeting, in the County of Granville, on Tuesday, the Third Day of March, 1840 ... and Published at the Request of His Fellow Citizens. Raleigh: Printed at the Office of the Raleigh Register, 1840.

Cover title [1], bl. [2], [3]-18, 19-24.   Sewn.   Appendix, pp. 19-24.

*73   Bayard, Samuel J.   A Short History of the Life and Services of Gen. William Henry Harrison.   [Seneca Falls: Fuller & Bloomer, Printers, 1840?]

1 ℓ., 20 pp.   Half title.   Martin.

*74   Burnet, Jacob.   Araeth y Barnwr Burnett [sic], o Dalaeth Ohio. Yn Nghenhedledig Eistedelfod y Whigiaid, a Gyfarfw yn Harrisburg, Pa., yn Rhoddi byr Hanes o Fywyd y Cadg.   William Henry Harrison.   Agr a Gyfieuthwyd ir Iaith Gymraeg, Gan H. R. Price.   Columbus: Angraffwyd gan Chas. Scott, 1840.

8 pp.   Thompson, p. 152; Martin.   Burnet's speech in Welsh.

75   _____.   Notices of the Public Services of General William Henry Harrison.   [N. p., 1839?]

Caption title.   [1]-7, bl. [8].   Sewn.   Intro., p. [1], in single col., signed "Editor Cincinnati Gazette"; Burnet's speech, pp. [1]-7, in dbl. cols.

76   _____.   Proceedings of the Democratic Whig National Convention, Which Assembled at Harrisburg, Pennsylvania, on the Fourth of December, 1839, for the Purpose of Nominating Candidates for President and Vice President of the United States.   Harrisburg: Printed by R. S. Elliott & Co., 1839.

Cover title [1], bl. [2], [3]-42, bl. ℓ.   Sewn.   Burnet's speech, pp. 34-42.

77   _____.   Speech of ... in the Whig National Convention, Giving a Brief History of the Life of Gen. William Henry Harrison.   Washington: Printed at the Madisonian Office, 1839.

Cover title [1], bl. [2], [3]-8.   Sewn.

78   Burr, Samuel Jones.   The Life and Times of William Henry Harrison.   New York: L. W. Ransom; Philadelphia: R. W. Pomeroy, 1840.

Pf., t. [i], [ii], [iii]-iv, [v]-viii, [9]-266, [267]-300, [301]-304.   Green cloth.   Pf. inserted.   Appendix, pp. [267]-300; adv., pp. [301]-304.   Also noted in purple cloth, gold cloth, and cream wrps., outer back with "Opinions of the Press."

79   _____.   The Life ... of William Henry Harrison.   Eighth Edition.   New York: L. W. Ransom; Philadelphia: R. W. Pomeroy, 1840.

As in entry 78, but lacking adv. Brown cloth. Also noted in wrps.

80 The Civil Services of William Henry Harrison, With Extracts From His Addresses, Speeches, and Letters, and a Sketch of His Life. [Philadelphia: Published by C. Sherman & Co. , 1840?]

Caption title. [1]-3, 3-48. Sewn. Title vignette. Intro. , pp. [1]-3, in single col. , text in dbl. cols. ; imprint, in single col. , at foot of p. 48, with additional 6 booksellers' imprints.

*81 A Condensed Memoir of the Public Services of William H. Harrison, From the Time of His Entering the Public Service in 1792 to the Present Time, and Showing That in Every Emergency He Has Been Ready to Peril His Life and Fortune in the Service of His Country. [N. p. , 1840?]

32 pp. Sabin 30576; Martin.

*82 Cooke, Eleutheros. An Address in Commemoration of the Brilliant and Glorious Defence of Fort Meigs ... in 1813: Embracing a Sketch of the Civil and Military Services of Gen. William H. Harrison.... Perrysburg: H. T. Smith, 1840.

21 pp. Martin.

*83 [Cushing, Caleb.] Brief Sketch of the Life and Public Services, Civil and Military of William Henry Harrison, of Ohio.... Augusta, Me. : Severance and Dorr, 1840.

32 pp. Appendix, pp. [27]-32, contains Harrison's letter to Bolivar, and Governor Shelby's opinion. New York Public Library (Eames Indian Collection), unexamined.

84 _____. Outline of the Life and Public Services Civil and Military, of William Henry Harrison, of Ohio.... Newark: Printed at the Daily and Sentinel Office, 1840.

T. [1], [2], [3]-32. Buff illus. wrps. , songs on outer back. Title vignette. "Tippecanoe Songs, " pp. 29-32.

85 _____. Outlines of the Life and Public Services, Civil and Military, of William Henry Harrison. Boston: Eastburn's Press, 1840.

Cover title [1], [2], [3]-24. Sewn.

86 _____. Outlines of the Life.... Boston: Weeks, Jordan and Company, 1840.

Half title [1], pf. [2], t. [3], [4], [5]-6, [7]-63, bl. [64],

[65]-71, bl. [72].   Brown wrps., adv. on outer back.   Statement of terms, p. [4]; Burnet's speech, incomplete, pp. [65]-
71.   Also noted in green wrps., adv. on outer back, and
pagination as above except, p. [1] bl., pf. [2].

87 _____ . Outlines of the Life.... Boston: Weeks, Jordan
and Company, 1840.

As in entry 86, except p. [4] an adv. for Law Reporter
and The Boston Atlas.   Sewn.

88 _____ . Outlines of the Life.... Boston: Weeks, Jordan
and Company, 1840.

As in entry 87, except p. [72] an adv. for Cushing's forthcoming Extracts From the Speeches and Writings of General
Harrison.   Light green wrps.

89 _____ . Outlines of the Life ... of William Henry Harrison,
of Ohio.... Washington: Published by Thomas Allen, Madisonian Office, 1840.

Cover title [1], [2], 3-21, bls. [22-24].   Sewn. P. [2] begins "To the People of the Third District of Massachusetts."
Copies also noted with text, pp. 3-24.

90 _____ . Outlines of the Life ... of William Henry Harrison,
of Ohio.... Washington: Published by Thomas Allen, Madisonian Office, 1840.

As in entry 85, but lacking "To the People ... "; caption title:
Life of William Henry Harrison, by Hon. Caleb Cushing.
Sewn.   Copies also noted with caption title: Life of William
Henry Harrison.

91 Dana, Edmund P. A Voice From Bunker-Hill, and the Fathers
of the Revolutionary War, in Favor of the Hero of North
Bend, Being a Few Candid Remarks and Observations on the
Approaching Presidential Election, and Subjects Connected
Therewith....   Second Edition.   Copy Right Secured.   Bunk-
er-Hill: 1840.

Cover title [1], bl. [2], [3]-18, [19]-[26].   Sewn. Text concludes: "Bunker-Hill, Charlestown, July 4, 1840.   First
Edition."

*92 Garrard, Daniel. Address to the Young Men of Kentucky, Com-
prising a Brief Review of the Military Services of General
William Henry Harrison, During the Late War Between Great
Britain and the United States.   Frankfort: Robinson & Adams, 1840.

29 pp.   Martin.

93   General Harrison in Congress. [N. p. , Washington? n. d. , 1840?]

   Caption title. [1]-32. Sewn.

94   General Harrison in Congress. Originally Compiled for and
   Published in the National Intelligencer. [Washington: 1840.]

   Caption title. [1]-32. Sewn. At foot of p. 32: "Published
   at the Office of the National Intelligencer, May, 1840. "

95   Grund, Franz J.   General Harrison's Leben und Wirken.   Philadelphia: Gedruckt bei C. J. Stollmeyer, 1840.

   Pf. , t. [1], [2], [3]-30.   Blue wrps. , outer back with
   quotes by Richard Johnson and Simon Schneider.   Pf. and 2
   pls. inserted.   At head of title, Aufruf an die deutschen
   Wähler.

96   Hard Cider and Log Cabin Almanac for 1841.   Harrison and
   Tyler.   Philadelphia: Turner & Fisher [c1841.]

   Unpaged, 12 ℓ ℓ . Cover title [1], [2-23], illus. [24].   Sewn.
   Title vignette.   Illus. in text.   Also noted with the following
   imprints: Baltimore: H. A. Turner [1840]; Boston: James
   Fisher [1840] (Drake 4219); St. Louis: Dinnies & Radford
   [1840] (Drake 4583); and Washington City: John Kenedy
   [1840] (Drake 1548).

97   The Harrison Almanac.   1841.   New York: Published by
   James P. Giffing [c1840.]

   Unpaged, 18 ℓ ℓ . Cover title [1], [2-34], adv. [35], illus.
   [36].   Title vignette.   Illus. in text.   Biography, pp. [4-5].
   Also noted: pub. prospectus being an oblong sheet fld. to
   4 pp. , interior 2 bl.

98   The Harrison Almanac.   1841.   Improved Edition.   New York:
   Published by J. P. Giffing [c1840.]

   As in entry 97, except different title vignette and on p.
   [12]: "Harrison's Kindness to an Irishman in Distress. "
   On p. [12], entry 97: "Harrison's Treatment of an Old
   Fellow Soldier. " Sewn.

99   Harrison Calender auf das Jahr, 1841.   Philadelphia: Georg
   W. Menz und Sohn [1840.]

   Cover title [1], 2-35, illus. [36].   Sewn.   Title vignette.
   Illus. in text.   Life of Harrison, pp. 4-35; text generally
   in dbl. cols.

100 Hero of Tippecanoe; or the Story of the Life of William Henry
   Harrison.   Related By Captain Miller to His Boys.   New
   York: Published by J. P. Giffing [c1840.]

F. [1], bl. [2], t. [3], [4], [5]-8, [9]-12, [13]-121, adv.
[122], 3 ℓ ℓ. adv. All copies examined with wrps. added.
Title vignette. Illus. in text.

101 [Hildreth, Richard.] The Contrast: Or William Henry Harrison Versus Martin Van Buren.... Boston: Weeks, Jordan
& Company, 1840.

T. [1], [2], [3]-4, [5]-64, adv. [65]-72. Green illus.
wrps., adv. on outer back.

102 _____. The People's Presidential Candidate; or the Life of
William Henry Harrison, of Ohio. Boston: Weeks, Jordan
and Company, 1839.

Flyleaf [1-2], t. [3], [4], adv. [5]-8, 9-11, bl. [12], [13]-
211, bl. [212]. Brown cloth. First ed., concluding with
letter to Denny. Also noted in green cloth with pr. paper
label on backstrip.

102a _____. The People's Presidential Candidate.... Boston:
Weeks, Jordan and Company, 1840.

T. [1], [2], adv. [3]-4, [5]-6, [7]-126. Green illus. wrps.,
adv. on outer back, front also noting Second Edition. Text
concludes with letter to Denny.

103 _____. The People's Presidential Candidate.... Boston:
Weeks, Jordan and Company, 1840.

As in entry 102a. Green illus. wrps., noting Third Edition, adv. on outer back. Text concludes with letter to
Denny.

104 _____. The People's Presidential Candidate.... Fourth
Edition. Boston: Weeks, Jordan and Company, 1840.

Pf., t. [1], [2], adv. [3]-4, [5]-6, [7]-126. Green cloth.
Pf. inserted. Text concludes with Burnet's speech,
incomplete. Also noted in buff illus. wrps., adv.
on outer back.

105 _____. The People's Presidential Candidate.... Seventh
Edition. Boston: Weeks, Jordan and Company, 1840.

Bl. [1], pf. [2], t. [3], [4], adv. [5]-6, [7]-126. All
copies examined disbound. Text concludes as in entry 104.

106 Incidents in the Life of William Henry Harrison, the People's
Candidate for the Presidency. Albany: Printed at the Sun
Office, 1839.

Cover title [1], [2], [3]-24. Sewn.

107 [Jackson, Isaac Rand.] General William Henry Harrison, Candidate of the People for President of the United States. Baltimore: Published at the Office of the "Baltimore Patriot"; Printed by Samuel Sands, 1840.

Cover title [1], bl. [2], [3]-15, 16. Sewn. Title vignette. Illus. in text. Text in dbl. cols.; Harrison's record, p. 16.

108 _____ . General William Henry Harrison.... Philadelphia: Published by Jesper Harding; Stereotyped by L. Johnson, 1840.

Cover title [1], [2]-15, 16. Sewn. Title vignette. Illus. in text. Text in dbl. cols.

109 _____ . Lebensgeschichte des Generals Harrison, des Candidaten des Volkes, für die Präsidentschaft. Aus dem Englischen des I. R. Jackson. Philadelphia: Marschall [sic], Williams, und Butler; Stereotypirt bei John Fagan, 1840.

T. [1], bl. [2], [3]-32. Yellow illus. wrps., outer back with 2 illus.

110 _____ . The Life of William Henry Harrison, (Of Ohio,) the People's Candidate for the Presidency. With a History of the Wars With the British and Indians on Our North-Western Frontier. Philadelphia: W. Marshall & Co., 1840.

Half title [i], bl. [ii], t. [iii], 4, 5-ix, bl. [x], 11-xiii, bl. [xiv], 15-212. Maroon cloth. First ed., based upon entry 115.

111 _____ . The Life.... Second Edition. Philadelphia: W. Marshall & Co., 1840.

As in entry 110, except text, pp. 15-218. Brown cloth. Section on Harrison's intellectual and literary attainments added, pp. 199-205.

112 _____ . The Life.... Third Edition. Philadelphia: Marshall, Williams & Butler, 1840.

As in entry 111. Brown cloth.

113 _____ . The Life.... By Isaac R. Jackson. Fourth Edition. Philadelphia: Marshall, Williams & Butler, 1840.

Flyleaf [i-ii], t. [iii], [iv], 5-vii, 8-x, 15-222. Brown cloth. Copies also noted in maroon cloth with goldstamped port. on front.

114 _____ . The Life.... Fifth Edition. Philadelphia: Marshall, Williams & Butler, 1840.

As in entry 113.   Green cloth.

115 _____ .   The Life of William Henry Harrison, the People's
Candidate for the Presidency.   Philadelphia: [W. Marshall
& Co.] 1840.

T. [1], [2], [3]-5, bl. [6], [7]-60.   Brown wrps.

*116 _____ .   A Sketch of the Life and Public Services of General
William Henry Harrison, Candidate of the People for President of the United States.   New Orleans: Young Men's Tippecanoe Association of New Orleans, 1840.

Cited in Brown, p. 149.

117 _____ .   A Sketch of the Life and Public Services of General
William Henry Harrison, Candidate of the People for Presi-
dent of the United States, to Which Is Annexed an Appendix.
Washington City: Printed by Jacob Gideon, Jr. , 1840.

Cover title [1], [2]-13, 14-15, [16].   Sewn.   Title vignette.
Illus. in text.   Harrison's Record, p. [16].

118 _____ .   A Sketch of ... William Henry Harrison ... to
Which Is Appended an Appendix.   Washington City: Printed
by Jacob Gideon, Jr. , 1840.

As in entry 117.

119 _____ .   A Sketch of the Life and Public Services of William
Henry Harrison.   Commander In Chief of the North Western
Army, During the War of 1812, &c.   [N. p. , n. d.]

Caption title.   [1]-16.   Sewn.

120 _____ .   A Sketch. . . .   Detroit: Printed by Dawson & Bates,
1840.

Cover title [1], bl. [2], [3]-32.   Sewn.   "An Eloquent Record, " pp. 30-32.

121 _____ .   A Sketch. . . .   Hartford: Printed by J. B. Eldredge,
1840.

T. [1], bl. [2], [3]-30, 31-32.   Brown wrps. , Johnson's
opinion on outer back.   Letter from Nathaniel G. Pendleton, pp. 30-32.

122 _____ .   A Sketch. . . .   New York: Printed at the Office of
the New York Express, 1839.

Cover title [1], bl. [2], [3]-32.   Sewn.   Title, incl. ornamental rule, set in 12 lines.

123 _____ . A Sketch.... New York: Printed at the Office of the New York Express, 1839.

As in entry 122, except that title, incl. diamond rule and leaders, set in 13 lines.

124 _____ . A Sketch.... Providence: Printed by Knowles and Vose, 1840.

Cover title [1], bl. [2], [3]-32. Sewn. Copies also noted in green and in blue wrps., Johnson's opinion on outer back.

125 _____ . A Sketch of the Life and Public Services of General William Henry Harrison, of Ohio. St. Louis: Churchill & Harris, Printers, 1840.

Cover title [1], bl. [2], [3]-40. Sewn.

126 _____ . A Sketch of the Life and Public Services of William Henry Harrison, With an Appendix Containing the Letters of His Aids-De-Camp John Chambers, John Speed Smith, Charles S. Todd and John O'Fallon.... Columbus: Published by I. N. Whiting, 1840.

Cover title [1]-29, [30]-[50]. Lemon wrps., entire back being pp. 49-[50]. Appendix, pp. [30]-[50].

*127 _____ . Eine Skizze des Lebens und der öffentlichen Dienste von William H. Harrison. Nebst einem Anhang enthaltend die Brief von seinen Adjutaten John Chambers, John Speed Smith, Charles S. Todd und John O'Fallen [sic]. Columbus: Herausgegeben von J. S. Weistling, 1840.

Cover title. 40 pp. German translation of entry 126. Martin.

128 The Life and Public Services of William Henry Harrison. [N. p., 1840.]

Caption title. Broadside, 24 x 19, pr. in three cols. surrounded by ornaments and nine illus.

129 The Life and Public Services of William Henry Harrison. Philadelphia: Designed, Engraved, and Published by Croome, Meignelle & Minot, J. Crissy Printer, 1840.

Caption title. Broadside, 24 x 31, pr. in three cols. surrounded by ornaments and ten illus.

130 Life in a Log Cabin, With Hard Cider.... Philadelphia: Published by M. B. Roberts, 1840.

Cover title [1], [2]-8. Self wrps. Title vignette.

131 The Life of Major-General William Henry Harrison: Compris-
     ing a Brief Account of His Important Civil and Military Ser-
     vices, and an Accurate Description of the Council at Vin-
     cennes With Tecumseh. . . .   Philadelphia: Published by
     Grigg & Elliot, and T. K. & P. G. Collins, 1840.

     Pf. , t. [1], [2], 3-93, bl. [94].   Green coated wrps. , adv.
     on outer back.   Pf. and 3 pls. inserted.

132 The Life of Major-General William Henry Harrison: Compris-
     ing a Brief Account of His Important Civil and Military Ser-
     vices. . . .   Philadelphia: Published by Grigg & Elliot, and
     T. K. & P. G. Collins, 1840.

     Pf. , t. [1], [2], 3-96.   Green paper bds.   Pf. and 4 pls.
     inserted.   Text concludes with Harrison's letter to Denny.
     Also noted in green wrps. , "Homage to Justice" on outer
     back.

133 The Life of Major-General William Henry Harrison. . . .   Phila-
     delphia: Published by Grigg & Elliot, and T. K. & P. G.
     Collins, 1840.

     As in entry 132 except text concludes with Harrison's letter
     to Bolivar.   Green paper bds. , "Homage to Justice" on out-
     er back.   Illus. in text.   Copies also noted with pf. and 2
     pls. inserted.

134 "Log Cabin Anecdotes. " New York: Published by J. P. Gif-
     fing at the Office of the Harrison Almanac, 1840.

     Caption title.   Broadside, 25 x 19, pr. in 2 cols. sur-
     rounded by ornaments and 12 illus.   Text pr. in red and
     captioned, Illustrated Incidents in the Life of Gen. William
     Henry Harrison.

*135 The Log Cabin Almanack for 1841.   Columbus: E. Glover
     [1840.]

     24 ℓℓ. Drake 9240.

136 [Montgomery, John C.] Montgomery's Tippecanoe Almanac, for
     the Year 1841.   Fourth Edition, Enlarged and Improved.
     Containing a Short History of the Life and Services of Gen-
     eral William Henry Harrison; With Testimonials of His Con-
     duct and Character by Officers and Soldiers Who Fought
     Under Him and With Him. . . .   Philadelphia: M'Carty &
     Davis; Thomas Cowperthwait & Co. ; Marshall, Williams &
     Butler; G. W. Mentz & Son; Hogan & Thompson; Grigg &
     Elliot; Kay & Brother.   Stereotyped by L. Johnson [1840.]

     Cover title [1], 2, 3-4, 5-16, 17-26, 27-71, 72-79, illus.
     and adv. [80].   Sewn.   Title vignette.   Illus. in text.   Life

of Harrison "from the 8th No. of Huddy & Duval's U. S. Military Magazine," pp. 17-26; pp. 27-79 in dbl. cols.; preface to 4th ed., p. 72; continuation of almanac and additional matter on Harrison, pp. 72-79.

137 _____. The Tippecanoe Almanac, for the Year 1841. Containing a Short History of the Life and Services of General Henry Harrison.... Philadelphia: M'Carty & Davis [etc., 1840.]

Cover title [1], 2, 3, 4-16, 17-26, 27-71, illus. [72]. Sewn. Title vignette. Illus. in text. Life of Harrison as in entry 136; pp. 27-71 in dbl. cols. First edition?

138 [Moore, Jacob Bailey.] The Contrast: Or, Plain Reasons Why William Henry Harrison Should Be Elected President of the United States, and Why Martin Van Buren Should Not Be Re-elected. By an Old Democrat. New York: Published by J. P. Giffing [c1840.]

Caption title. [1]-16. All copies examined disbound. Copyright notice at foot of p. [1].

139 Niles, William Ogden. The Tippecanoe Text-Book, Compiled From Niles' Register and Other Authentic Records ... and Respectfully Dedicated to the Young Men of the United States. Baltimore: Published by Duff Green, Editor of "The Pilot," 1840.

Cover title [1], 2, 3-92, 93-95, bl. [96]. Sewn. Title vignette. 4 pls. in text, not counted in pagination. Imprint of stereotyper and printer at foot of p. 95; life based upon sketch in the Port Folio and Jackson's Life.

140 _____. The Tippecanoe Text-Book.... Baltimore: Published by Duff Green, Editor of the "Pilot," and Cushing & Brother; Philadelphia: Hogan & Thompson and T. K. & P. G. Collins, 1840.

As in entry 139.

*141 Ogle, Charles. Speech ... (Part III) on the Character and Services of General William H. Harrison ... in the House ... April 16, 1840. [Washington: 1840.]

32 pp. Martin.

142 The People's Presidential Candidate! Worcester: Published by Dorr, Howland & Co. [1840?]

Caption title. Broadside, 22 x 17, pr. in 4 cols. within ornamental box, port. at head. Col. 1 captioned: Brief Sketch of the Life and Public Services of Gen. William Henry Harrison.

143 Russell, John B. The Log Cabin Almanac. 1841. ... Cincinnati: Published by Truman & Smith [1840.]

>   Cover Title. Unpaged, 24 ℓℓ. Sewn. Title vignette. Il-
>   lus. in text. Life of Harrison, pp. [28-31]; adv., p. [47],
>   illus. p. [48].

144 Sprague, Peleg. Remarks of ... at Faneuil Hall, Before the
Citizens of Boston and Its Vicinity, Upon the Character and
Services of Gen. William Henry Harrison, of Ohio, the
Whig Candidate for the Presidency of the United States.
Boston: Published by the Whig Republican Association of
Boston, John H. Eastburn, Printer, 1839.

>   Cover title [1], bl. [2], [3]-16, [17]-20. Sewn. Report of
>   the meeting, pp. [17]-20. Also noted in brown green wrps.

145 Todd, Charles S. Sketches of the Civil and Military Services
of William Henry Harrison. By Charles S. Todd, Late an
Inspector-General in the U. S. Army, and Benjamin Drake,
Author of the Life of Black Hawk, &c. ... Cincinnati: Published by U. P. James, 1840.

>   T. [iii], [iv], [v]-vi, vii-x, 11-165, bl. [166]. All copies
>   examined rebound. Preface, pp. [v]-vi, dated March, 1840.
>   First edition.

146 The Various Charges Against General W. H. Harrison Briefly
Stated and Refuted, and Some of the Objections to the Present Administration Enumerated. Jonesborough: Brownlow
and Garland Publishers, 1840.

>   Cover title. [1]-40. Buff wrps. Text in dbl. cols.; is-
>   sued by the Whig Party, Washington County, Tennessee and
>   signed June 1, 1840; at head of title, Facts for the People.

147 Züge aus dem öffentlichen Leben des Generals William Henry
Harrison. [N. p., 1840.]

>   Caption title. Broadside, 24 x 19, pr. in 3 cols. sur-
>   rounded by ornaments and 9 illus. German translation of
>   entry 128.

VAN BUREN, MARTIN (Democratic)

148 A Brief Account of the Life and Political Opinions of Martin
Van Buren, President of the United States: From the Most
Authentic Sources. [N. p.] May, 1840.

>   T. [1], bl. [2], [3]-23, bl. [24]. Yellow wrps. Anti-Van
>   Buren.

*149   The Claims of Martin Van Buren to the Presidency Fairly Rep-
       resented, in a Sketch of the Chief Political Transactions of
       His Life. [N. p. , 1840.]

       12 pp. Anti-Van Buren.

*150   Dawson, Moses. Sketches of the Life of Martin Van Buren,
       President of the United States. Cincinnati: J. W. Ely,
       1840.

       [3]-216 pp. , pf. Sabin 18957.

151   The Democrat's Almanac and People's Register for 1841. Con-
       taining, in Addition to the Usual Calendar Pages, a Brief
       Sketch of the Life of Martin Van Buren.... Boston: Pub-
       lished by E. Littlefield [1840.]

       Cover title [1], 2-36. Sewn. Life of Van Buren, pp. 34-
       36; p. 36 concludes with adv.

152   [Mayo, Robert.] A Word in Season; Or Review of the Political
       Life and Opinions of Martin Van Buren. Addressed to the
       Entire Democracy of the American People.... Dedicated to
       the Tippecanoe Clubs of the Union, by a Harrison Democrat.
       Washington: Published by W. M. Morrison, 1840.

       Cover title [1], [2], [3]-46, [47], bl. [48]. Sewn. P. [47],
       table of contents with "Printed at the Intelligencer Office, "
       at foot. Anti-Van Buren.

153   . A Word in Season.... Second Edition.... Wash-
       ington: Published by W. M. Morrison, 1840.

       As in entry 152.

154   . A Word in Season.... Third Edition. Washington:
       Published by W. M. Morrison, 1840.

       Cover title [1], [2], [3]-47, 48. Sewn. Reviews of the
       work, p. 47; contents, p. 48.

*155   Sketch of the Life of Martin Van Buren. Columbus: 1840.

       16 pp. Sewn. Supplement to the Ohio Statesman.

CLAY, HENRY (Whig)

156   The Beauties of the Hon. Henry Clay. To Which Is Added, a
       Biographical and Critical Essay.... New York: Edward
       Walker, 1839.

Adv. [i-iv], half title [v], bl. [vi], t. [vii], [viii], [ix-x], [11]-13, bl. [14], [15]-16, [17]-39, bl. [40], [61 sic]-235, bl. [236]. All copies examined rebound. Life of Clay, pp. [17]-39; selections from his work, pp. [61]-235; adv., pp. [11]-13.

157 Flournoy, John James. An Essay on the Eminent Services and Illustrious Characters of Henry Clay.... Athens, Ga.: Printed at the Whig Office, MDCCCXL.

Cover title [1], bl. [2], [3]-46. Sewn. Errata, p. 46.

1844

POLK, JAMES K. (Democratic)

158 Biographical Sketches of the Democratic Candidates for the Presidency and Vice Presidency. James K. Polk, of Tennessee. From the Democratic Review for May, 1838. [N. p., n. d., 1844?]

Caption title. [1]-8. Self wrps. Polk, pp. [1]-5; Dallas, pp. 5-8, from the Democratic Review, February, 1842; text pr. in dbl. cols.

159 [Hickman, George H.] The Life and Public Services of the Hon. James Knox Polk, With a Compendium of His Speeches on Various Public Measures. Also, a Sketch of the Life of the Hon. George Mifflin Dallas. Baltimore: Published by N. Hickman, 1844.

T. [1], [2], [3]-40. Grey green wrps., inner wrps. with "George M. Dallas and the United States Bank," outer back with opinions on the tariff, front with 8 additional pubs. listed. Title vignette. Life of Polk, pp. [3]-17; Dallas, pp. [18]-24; appendix, pp. 24-40.

160 _____. The Life ... of the Hon. James Knox Polk.... Baltimore: Published by N. Hickman, 1844.

As in entry 159 except appendix, pp. 24-47, Young Hickory, p. [48]. Grey green wrps., noting Second Edition, with "United States Bank and Distribution" on outer back.

161 _____. The Life ... of the Hon. James Knox Polk.... Baltimore: Published by N. Hickman, 1844.

As in entry 160 except wrp. notes Third Edition.

*162 The Political and Public Character of James K. Polk, of Ten-
      nessee. [Boston, 1844.]

      20 pp. Also noted: 2nd and 4th eds., [Boston: Eastburn's
      Press, 1844.] Sabin 63841.

163 Political Biography: Polk, Dallas, & Shunk. Philadelphia:
     Printed by Mifflin & Parry, Office of "The Pennsylvanian,"
     September, 1844.

     Cover title [1], [2], [3]-15, [16]. Self wrps. Life of Polk,
     pp. [3]-7; Dallas, pp. [8]-12; Shunk, pp. [13]-15; tables,
     p. [16]. Text pr. in dbl. cols. Authorized by the Demo-
     cratic Committee of Correspondence for the City of Phila-
     delphia. Sabin 63840 calls for 12 pp. (another ed. omitting
     life of Shunk?).

CLAY, HENRY (Whig)

164 Brownlow, William G. A Political Register, Setting Forth the
     Principles of the Whig and Locofoco Parties in the United
     States, With the Life and Public Services of Henry Clay.
     Also an Appendix Personal to the Author; and a General
     Index. Jonesborough: Published at the Office of the "Jones-
     borough Whig," 1844.

     T. [i], bl. [ii], [iii]-vi, [vii-viii], [9]-13, bl. [14], [15]-
     240, [241]-322, [323]-343, bl. [344], [345]-349, bl. [350].
     All copies examined rebound. Illus. in text. P. number
     [viii] listed as vii; life of Clay, pp. [241]-322; appendix,
     pp. [323]-343; index, pp. [345]-349.

165 Clay and Frelinghuysen Almanac Compiled by F. B. Graham.
     1845. New York and Philadelphia: Turner & Fisher [1844].

     Cover title. 18 ℓℓ., pp. with textual matter numbered.
     Sewn. Title vignette. One illus. in text, p. [24, i.e.
     36].

166 [Collins, George C.] Fifty Reasons Why the Honorable Henry
     Clay Should Be Elected President of the United States. By
     an Irish Adopted Citizen.... Baltimore: Printed for the
     Author, 1844.

     T. [1], [2], [3]-43, bl. [44]. Yellow illus. wrps., quotes
     on outer back. Text, pp. [3]-43, in dbl. cols.

167 _____. Fifty Reasons.... Baltimore: Printed for the
     Author, 1844.

     As in entry 166 except green illus. wrps. noting Third Edi-
     tion Revised.

168 [Colton, Calvin.] The Junius Tracts. No. IV. Sept. ...
1843. Life of Henry Clay. By Junius. Author of "The
Crisis of the Country," and Other Tracts of 1840.... New
York: Published by Greeley & McElrath, 1844.

T. [1]/49, 2/50-16/64. All copies examined disbound with
other numbers in the Junius Tracts. Double pagination,
[1]-16 at head, 49-64 at the foot of each p.

169   . Life of Henry Clay. By Junius. Author of "The
Crisis of the Country," and Other Tracts of 1840. New
York: Published and for Sale by Greeley & McElrath; Phi-
ladelphia: Godey & McMichael, 1843.

Cover title [1], 2-16. Self wrps.

170 The Henry Clay Almanac, for the Year of Our Lord 1843....
Containing Songs and Anecdotes and a Biographical Sketch
of Henry Clay.... Philadelphia: Grigg & Elliot; Thomas,
Cowperthwait & Co.; Hogan & Thompson; G. W. Mentz &
Son; Kay & Brother; M'Carthy & Davis; Carey & Hart.
Printed and Published by T. K. & P. G. Collins [c1842.]

Cover title [1], 2, 3-16, [17]-32. Sewn. Title vignette.
P. 2, memoranda and imprints for stereotyper and printer;
life of Clay, pp. [17]-32; text in dbl. cols.

171 The Henry Clay Almanac.... Philadelphia: Grigg & Elliot
[etc., c1843.]

As in entry 170, but p. [2] prints eclipses, feasts, etc.
Postage information at head of title as in entry 170.

172 The Henry Clay Almanac, for the Year of Our Lord 1844....
Philadelphia: Grigg & Elliot [etc., c1843.]

Cover title [1], [2], 3-[16], [1]-16. Sewn. Title vignette.
Life of Clay, pp. [1]-16; texts in dbl. cols.; postage infor-
mation at head of title. Also noted with the following im-
prints: Boonville: E. Hart [1843] (Drake 4589); New York:
Turner & Fisher [1843] (Drake 8070); and Philadelphia:
Thomas, Cowperthwait & Co. [1843] (Drake 12334).

173 The Life and Public Services of Henry Clay. [N. p., 1844.]

Caption title. Broadside, $12\frac{1}{2}$ x 10, pr. in 2 cols., surrounded by ornaments and illus. Title vignette.

174 Life of Henry Clay. [Washington: Expositor, n. d.]

Caption title. [81]-88. Self wrps. At head of title, Tract
No. 18; at foot of p. 88, col. 2, "Address Expositor, Washington, D. C."; text in dbl. cols.

175 [Littell, John S.] The Clay Minstrel; Or, National Songster.
To Which Is Prefixed a Sketch of the Life, Public Services,
and Character of Henry Clay.... Philadelphia and New
York: Turner & Fisher, 1842.

Bl. [i], f. [ii], t. [iii], [iv], [v-vi], [vii]-viii, [9]-70, div.
t. [71], [72], [73]-167, [168]. Yellow coated illus. wrps.
Illus. in text. P. number [vi] pr. as iv; life of Clay, pp.
[9]-70; text of Minstrel, pp. [73]-167.

176 _____ . The Clay Minstrel ... By John S. Littell, President of the Clay Club of Germantown. Second Edition; Enlarged. New York: Greeley & M'Elrath; Philadelphia:
Thomas, Cowperthwait and Co., 1844.

Pf. [i-ii], t. [iii], [iv], [v], [vi], [vii-viii], 9-147, bl. [148],
div. t. [149], [150], bl. [151], illus. 152, 153-378, 379-
380, 381-384. Wrps. as in entry 175. Illus. in text.
Life of Clay, pp. 9-147; text of Minstrel, pp. 153-378; "To
the Reader," pp. 379-380; index, pp. 381-384. Inserted
pf. noted in 2 states, one an engraving, the other a wood-
cut. Also issued in 1844, but lacking the biography and
noting that a "new and seventh edition of the 'Minstrel' including the biography of Mr. Clay ... " was ready.

177 Mallory, Daniel, ed. The Life and Speeches of the Hon. Henry
Clay, in Two Volumes.... New York: Robert P. Bixby &
Co., 1843.

Vol. I: Pf., pl., t. [i], [ii], [iii]-iv, [v]-viii, [9]-193, bl.
[194], [195]-606. Vol. II: F., pl., t. [i], [ii], [iii]-iv,
[5]-600. Blue cloth. Pf., f., and pls. inserted. Life of
Clay, I [9]-193, speeches, pp. [195]-606; speeches, II [5]-
600. Also noted in brown cloth.

178 _____ . The Life and Speeches.... Fourth Edition. New
York: Van Amringe and Bixby, 1844.

As in entry 177, except speeches, I [195]-634; II, speeches,
pp. [5]-600, index, pp. [601]-607, bl. [608]. Purple cloth.
Also noted, but unexamined, 3d, 5th, and 6th eds.

179 [Sargent, Epes?] Life and Public Services of Henry Clay.
New York: The New World [c1842.]

Column title. [1]-16. Newspaper. Text in 4 cols., except p. [1], with port. Special issue of the newspaper,
The New World.

180 Sargent, Epes. The Life and Public Services of Henry Clay....
New Edition, Revised, Enlarged and Brought Down to the
Year 1844, By the Author. New York: Greeley & McEl-
rath, 1844.

Pf., t. [1], [2], [3]-80. Pale green wrps., adv. on entire
back. Pf. inserted. Preface, p. [2], dated March 1844;
pr. in dbl. cols. Also noted in salmon wrps. as above.

181 [Sargent, Nathan.] Brief Outline of the Life of Henry Clay.
By Oliver Oldschool.... Washington: John T. Towers
[1844.]

Caption title. [1]-16. All copies examined either bound or
disbound.

182 _____. Life of Henry Clay. [Philadelphia: R. G. Bedford,
1844?]

Caption title. [17]-32. Self wrps. Pr. in dbl. cols.

183 _____. ...Life of Henry Clay. By N. Sargent, (Oliver
Oldschool.)... Philadelphia: R. G. Berford, 1844.

Cover title. [17]-32. Green illus. wrps., adv. on entire
back. Title vignette. Pr. in dbl. cols. At head of title:
Berford's Cheap Edition., followed by prices.

184 _____. ...Life of Henry Clay.... Philadelphia: R. G.
Berford, 1844.

Cover title. [1]-16. All else as in entry 183.

185 _____. A Sketch of the Life and Public Services of Henry
Clay. By "Oliver Oldschool," (N. Sargeant [sic], Esq. of
Philadelphia.). [Baltimore: Printed at the Office of the
"American Whig," by Samuel Sands, 1844?]

Caption title. 1-16. Sewn. Title vignette. Pr. in dbl.
cols.; imprint and price information at foot of p. 16.

186 [Swain, James B., ed.] The Life and Speeches of Henry Clay,
Volume I. [II.] New York: Greeley & McElrath, 1843.

Vol. I: pf., pl., t. [i], [ii], [iii], bl. [iv], [v]-vi, [7]-198,
[3]-307, bl. [308], [i]-xxvi; Vol. II: pl., fac. letter, [i],
[ii], [iii], bl. [iv], [9]-597, bl. [598]. Brown cloth. Pf.,
pls. and fac. letter inserted. Life of Clay, I [7]-198,
speeches, pp. [3]-307, appendix, pp. [i]-xxvi; speeches, II
[9]-597. Also noted in brown coated illus. wrps., adv. on
outer back of both vols.

187 _____, ed. The Life and Speeches of Henry Clay, Volume
I. [II.] New York: Greeley & McElrath, 1844.

As in entry 186 except pf. only in I, and f. only in II. Vol.
I notes "McElrath" and "Tribune Buildings" in imprint, while
II employs a different typeface on t.p. and notes "M'Elrath"
and "Tribune Office" in imprint.

188   Vandenhoff, G. , ed. The Clay Code; Or, Text-Book of Elo-
      quence, a Collection of Axioms, Apothegms, ... Gathered
      From the Public Speeches of Henry Clay....   New York:
      C. Shepard, 1844.

         T. [i], [ii], [iii]-viii, [ix], bl. [x], div. t. [xi], bl. [xii],
         [13]-144, [147 sic]-[151], bl. [152], [153], bl. [154], adv.
         [155], bl. [156], adv. [157], bl. [158].   Maroon cloth.   In-
         dex, pp. [147]-[151]; errata, p. [153].

189   The Whig Almanac and United States Register for 1843.   New
      York: Greeley & McElrath [1842?]

         Cover title [1], [2-18], [19]-24, [25]-30, [31]-49, [50]-64.
         Sewn.   Title vignette.   Essay by Greeley, pp. [19]-24; life
         of Clay by Henry J. Raymond, pp. [31]-49.

BIRNEY, JAMES G. (Liberty [Abolitionist])

190   Green, Beriah.   Sketches of the Life and Writings of James
      Gillespie Birney.   Utica: Published by Jackson & Chaplin,
      1844.

         T. [i], [ii], [iii], bl. [iv], [1]-119, bl. [120].   All copies
         examined rebound.   Preface, p. [iii], dated July 1844.

191   Tucker, J. N. T.   The Liberty Almanac....   No. Two.
      1845....   Syracuse: Tucker & Kinney, Publishers [1844.]

         Cover title [1], 2, [3], 4, [5-16], 17-32, adv. 32-[36].
         Sewn.   Title vignette.   Life of Birney, pp. 19-23.

TYLER, JOHN (Federal Officeholders [Rump])

192   [Abell, Alexander Gurdon.] Life of John Tyler, President of
      the United States ... Including Some of His Most Important
      Speeches....   New York: Harper & Brothers, 1843.

         Pf. [i-ii], t. [iii], [iv], [v], bl. [vi], [vii]-viii, [9]-247,
         [248]-256.   Pale blue wrps. , adv. on inner front and entire
         back.   Pf. inserted.   Appendix, pp. [248]-256.

193   _____ . Life of John Tyler....   New York: Harper &
      Brothers, 1844.

         As in entry 192.   Buff wrps. as above but with different
         adv. matter.

194   John Tyler: His History, Character, and Position.   With a
      Portrait.   New York: Harper & Brothers, 1843.

Pf. , t. [1], [2], [3]-40. Light green wrps. , adv. on inner
front and entire back. Pf. inserted.

195 Political Tracts for the Times. No. II. Who and What Is
John Tyler? By Anti-Junius. ... New York: J. & H. G.
Langley, 1843.

Cover title [1], [2]-16. Sewn. Preface, p. [2], dated December, 1843; p. 16 concludes with adv.; postage information at foot of title.

CALHOUN, JOHN C. (Democratic)

196 The Calhoun Text Book. ... New York: Herald Office; Phila-
delphia: G. B. Zieber & Co.; Boston: Redding & Co.;
Charleston: Babcock & Co. , Samuel Hart Sr.; New Orleans:
Bravo and Morgan; Mobile: J. M. Sumwalt and Co. [1843].

Cover title. 1-36. Yellow wrps. , intro. dated Nov. 15,
1843 and copyright notice on inner front, adv. on entire
back.

197 Life and Character of the Hon. John C. Calhoun, With Illustrations: Containing Notices of His Father and Uncles, and
Their Brave Conduct During Our Struggle for Independence,
in the American Revolutionary War. New York: J. Win-
chester, New World Press, 1843.

T. [1], bl. [2], [3], bl. [4], [5]-24. Wrps. , adv. on inner
front and entire back; imprint lists 6 additional publishers.
Preface, p. [3], dated November, 1843.

198 Life of John C. Calhoun. Presenting a Condensed History of
Political Events From 1811 to 1843. New York: Harper
& Brothers, 1843.

Pf. , t. [1], [2], [3]-74, [75]-76, 2 ℓ ℓ. adv. Salmon wrps. ,
adv. on inner front and entire back. Pf. inserted. List
of speeches by Calhoun, pp. [75]-76; adv. dated variously
January and February, 1843.

199 Life of John C. Calhoun, Presenting a Condensed History of
Political Events From 1811 to 1843. Together With a Se-
lection From His Speeches, Reports, and Other Writings
Subsequent to His Election as Vice-President of the United
States, Including His Leading Speech on the Late War Deli-
vered in 1811. New York: Harper & Brothers, 1843.

Pf. , t. [i], [ii], [1], bl. [2], [3]-74, bl. ℓ . , div. t. , bl. ,
contents, bl. , [9]-554. Brown cloth. Pf. inserted. Life
of Calhoun, pp. [3]-74; speeches, pp. [9]-554.

CASS, LEWIS (Democratic)

200 Biography of General Lewis Cass. Including a Voice From a
     Friend. New York: J. Winchester, New World Press,
     1843.

     T. [1], bl. [2], [3]-10, [11]-36, bl. ℓ., 5 ℓℓ. adv. Wrps.,
     adv. on inner front and entire back; imprint lists 8 addi-
     tional publishers. Life of Cass, pp. [3]-10; "A Voice," pp.
     [11]-36.

201 Sketch of the Life and Services of General Lewis Cass, of
     Ohio. Harrisburg: January 9th, 1842.

     T. [1], bl. [2], [3]-24. Yellow wrps., noting January 9,
     1843.

JOHNSON, RICHARD MENTOR (Democratic)

202 A Biographical Sketch of Col. Richard M. Johnson, of Kentucky.
     By a Kentuckian. New York: Published by Saxton & Miles,
     1843.

     Bl. [1], f. [2], t. [3], [4], [5]-46. All copies examined
     disbound. One illus. in text. Supposed author, Asahel
     Langworthy.

STEWART, CHARLES (Democratic)

203 To the Democratic Party of the United States on the Presiden-
     tial Election. To Which Is Appended, a Biographical Sketch
     of Commodore Charles Stewart. Philadelphia: Printed for
     the Committee, 1844.

     Cover title [1], [2], [3]-12, [13]-24, 24-27, bl. [28]. Self
     wrps. Speech by Anthony Wayne, pp. [3]-12; life of Stewart,
     pp. [13]-24; Old Ironsides Club, pp. 24-27; text pr. in dbl.
     cols.

VAN BUREN, MARTIN (Democratic)

204 Bancroft, George. Martin Van Buren to the End of His Politi-
     cal Career. New York: Harper & Brothers, 1889.

     T. [i], [ii], [iii]-iv, [v], bl. [vi], 1-239, bl. [240]. Brown
     cloth. Written specifically for the campaign of 1844, but
     issued in 1889 with additions.

205 Democratic Almanac for 1844. Containing a Life of Martin Van
     Buren, and Various Political Information.... Philadelphia:
     Printed and for Sale by Mifflin & Parry, 1844.

Cover title [1], 2-8, 6 ℓℓ., [1]-15, bl. [16].   Sewn.   Title
vignette.   Illus. in text.   Political information, pp. 2-8;
life of Van Buren, pp. [1]-15; texts pr. in dbl. cols.

1848

TAYLOR, ZACHARY (Whig)

206   A Brief Review of the Career, Character & Campaigns of Zach-
      ary Taylor.   Washington: Printed and Sold by J. & G. S.
      Gideon [1848.]

      Cover title [1], bl. [2], [3]-16.   Self wrps.   Title vignette.
      At foot of caption title, p. [3], "Republished from the North
      American and United States Gazette, Philadelphia. "

207   A Brief Review. . . .   Washington: Printed and Sold by J. & G.
      S. Gideon [1848.]

      As in entry 206, but p. [2] begins "Please Circulate" and
      also includes Taylor's acceptance of the Whig nomination.

208   A Brief Review. . . .   Washington: Printed and Sold by J. & G.
      S. Gideon [1848.]

      As in entry 206, but p. [2] begins with Taylor's acceptance
      of the nomination and Governor Morehead's letter with Tay-
      lor's reply to it.

209   A Brilliant National Record.   General Taylor's Life, Battles,
      and Despatches, With the Only Correct Portrait Yet Pub-
      lished; Including Highly Important Letters. . . .   Accounts of
      the Glorious Battles. . . .   Compiled From Authentic Sources.
      Illustrated. . . .   Philadelphia: T. C. Clarke, for Sale also
      by King & Baird, Printers, 1847.

      Bl. [1], f. [2], t. [3], map [4], [5]-70.   Brown illus. wrps.
      Illus. in text.   Pr. in dbl. cols.   Also noted in yellow il-
      lus. wrps. , outer back with port. of Santa Anna and vital
      statistics.

210   [Frost, John.]   The Life of General Taylor, the Hero of Okee
      Chobee, Palo Alto, Resaca de la Palma, Monterey, and
      Buena Vista.   With Numerous Illustrative Anecdotes and
      Embellishments.   Philadelphia: Lindsay and Blakiston,
      1847.

Pf. , t. [i], 2, iii-vi, vii-viii, 9-214, adv. 215-216.   Illus.
wrps.   Pf. and 7 pls. inserted.   Same as the Pictorial Life
of General Taylor (see entry 213).

211 _____ .   Life of Major General Zachary Taylor; With Notices
of the War in New Mexico, California, and in Southern
Mexico; and Biographical Sketches of Officers Who Have
Distinguished Themselves in the War With Mexico, by John
Frost. ...   New York: D. Appleton & Co. ; Philadelphia:
G. S. Appleton, 1847.

Pf. , t. [1], [2], 3-6, 7-8, 9-12, [13]-273, bl. [274], div.
t. [275], bl. [276], 277-346.   All copies examined rebound.
Title vignette.   Pf. and 18 pls. inserted, other illus. in
text.   Appendix, pp. 277-346.

212 _____ .   The People's Life of General Zachary Taylor, the
Hero of Palo Alto, Monterey, and Buena Vista.   With Numerous Illustrative Anecdotes.   Also, a Biography of Millard
Fillmore.   Illustrated.   Philadelphia: Lindsay and Blakiston, 1848.

F. , eng. t. , t. [i], 2, iii-vi, vii-viii, 9-217, bl. [218],
div. t. 219, bl. [220], 221-228.   Brown illus. wrps. , adv.
on outer back.   F. , eng. t. and 6 pls. inserted.   Life of
Taylor, pp. 9-217; Life of Fillmore, pp. 221-228.

213 _____ .   Pictorial Life of General Taylor, the Hero. ...
Philadelphia: Lindsay and Blakiston [c1847.]

See entry 210.   Brown cloth.

214 _____ .   Pictorial Life. ...   Philadelphia: Lindsay and Blakiston, 1847.

See entry 210.   All copies examined rebound and lacking
adv. , pp. 215-216.   Copies also noted with pls. hand col-
ored.

215 Fry, J. Reese.   A Life of Gen. Zachary Taylor; Comprising a
Narrative of Events Connected With His Professional Career,
Derived From Public Documents and Private Correspondence
... and Authentic Incidents of His Early Years, From Ma-
terials Collected by Robert T. Conrad. ...   Philadelphia:
Grigg, Elliot & Co. , 1847.

Pf. , t. [i], 2, 3, 4, 5-x, bl. [xi], map [xii], 13-325, 326-
332, pub. cat. 1-12.   Brown cloth.   Pf. and 7 pls. inserted; 3 maps in text not figured in pagination.   Anecdotes
of Taylor, pp. 326-332.   Variant binding: Brown cloth
with different blindstamping; goldstamped eagle on front;
goldstamped military motifs on backstrip.

216 _____. A Life of Gen. Zachary Taylor.... Philadelphia: Grigg, Elliot & Co., 1848.

As in entry 215, but p. [xi] a map and [xii] an illus. F., pf., and 5 pls. inserted. All copies examined rebound.

217 _____. A Life of Gen. Zachary Taylor.... Philadelphia: Grigg, Elliot & Co., 1848.

As in entry 215. Grey illus. wrps., adv. on inner front and entire back; imprint lists one additional publisher. Pf. and 7 pls. inserted.

218 _____. A Life of Gen. Zachary Taylor.... Philadelphia: Grigg, Elliot & Co., 1848.

As in entry 215, but postscript, pp. 326-337, anecdotes, pp. 338-344, pub. cat., pp. 25-46. Brown cloth. Pf. and 7 pls. inserted. Postscript brings life down to nomination at Whig Convention.

219 Gales, Joseph. A Sketch of the Personal Character and Qualities of General Zachary Taylor. [Washington: Towers, printer, 1848.]

Caption title. [1]-8. Self wrps. At foot of p. [1], "From the National Intelligencer of September 16, 1848"; at foot of p. 8, "Towers, printer, Washington"; pr. in dbl. cols.

220 _____. A Sketch.... From the National Intelligencer of September 16, 1848. [N. p., J. & G. S. Gideon, Printers, 1848.]

Caption title. [1]-8. All copies examined disbound. At foot of p. [1], "J. & G. S. Gideon, Printers."; pr. in dbl. cols.

*221 The General Taylor Almanac for 1848. Philadelphia: Griffith & Simon; King & Baird, Printers [1847?]

18 ℓℓ. Drake 12585.

222 The General Taylor Almanac for 1849. Or Rough and Ready Text Book. Philadelphia: For Sale by King & Baird [1848.]

Cover title [1], [2], [3]-[14], 15-30. Sewn. Title vignette. Illus. in text. Life of Taylor, pp. [3]-[14]; life of Fillmore, pp. 15-17; texts pr. in dbl. cols. Drake 12667 cites this as 16 ℓℓ.

223 Gen. Taylor, and the Mexican War. Including the Particulars of the Last Battles, Names of the Killed and Wounded, Anecdotes, &c. New York: N. H. Blanchard [c1847.]

Cover title [1], [2], [3]-[20].   Dark yellow illus. wrps.
Title vignette.   Life of Taylor, pp. [3]-6.

224   General Taylor and His Staff: Comprising Memoirs of Generals
Taylor, Worth, Wool, and Butler: Colonels May, Cross,
Clay, Hardin, Yell, Hays, and Other Distinguished Officers
Attached to General Taylor's Army ... Compiled From Pub-
lic Documents and Private Correspondence....   Philadelphia:
Grigg, Elliot & Co. , 1848.

F. , pf. , t. [i], 2, iii-iv, 5-vi, 11-284, pub. cat. 1-12.
Cloth.   F. , pf. , and 10 pls. inserted, other illus. in text.

*225   The General Taylor Or, "Rough and Ready" Almanac for 1848.
Philadelphia: Griffith & Simon; King & Baird, printers
[1847?]

18 ℓ ℓ. Drake 12586.

*226   General Taylor's Calendar für 1849.   Philadelphia: King &
Baird [1848.]

35, [1] pp. , illus.   Drake 12668 also cites as 16 ℓ ℓ. German translation of entry 222.

227   Gen. Taylor's Moral, Intellectual, & Professional Character
... and Anecdotes Illustrative of His Republican Habits, and
Simplicity of Manners....   [N. p. , J. & G. S. Gideon,
Printers, 1848?]

Caption title.   [1]-8.   Self wrps.   At foot of p. [1], "J. &
G. S. Gideon, Printers. "; pr. in dbl. cols.

228   General Taylor's Rough and Ready 1848 Almanac.   Philadelphia:
R. Magee [1847?]

Cover title [1], [2-35], adv. [36].   Sewn.   Title vignette.
Illus. in text.   Life and anecdotes of Taylor throughout, pp.
[2-35].   Also noted with the following imprints: Lancaster:
S. Beates [1847] (Drake 12587); Philadelphia: Grigg, Elliot
& Co. [1847] (Drake 12588); Philadelphia: Turner & Fisher
[1847] (Drake 12590); Philadelphia [and] New York: Turner
& Fisher [1847] (Drake 12591); and Pittsburgh: C. Yeager
[1847] (Drake 12593).

229   Gen. Zachary Taylor's Old Rough & Ready 1848 Almanac.
Baltimore: Samuel E. Smith [1847?]

Cover title.   Unpaged, 16 ℓ ℓ.   Sewn.   Title vignette.   Illus.
in text.   Also noted with imprint: New York & Philadelphia: Turner & Fisher [1847] (Drake 8571).

230   Kurze Lebensgeschichte des Generals Z. Taylor.   Philadelphia:
Zu Haben bei King und Baird [1848.]

Cover title. 1-16. Lemon illus wrps., inner front and
back with anecdotes of Taylor; outer back with campaign
adv. Title vignette. Illus. in text. Life of Taylor, pp.
1-15; life of Fillmore, pp. 15-16; texts pr. in dbl. cols.
Caption title: Leben des Generals Zacharias Taylor. Volks-
kandidat für die nächste Präsidentschaft. Copies also noted
with above caption title and sewn.

231 Life and Public Services of Gen. Z. Taylor: Including a Minute
Account of His Defence of Fort Harrison, in 1812.... With
Numerous Illustrations. To Which Is Added, Sketches of
the Officers Who Have Fallen in the Late Contest. Edited
by an Officer of the U. S. A. New-York: H. Long &
Brother, Publishers, 1846.

Pf., fld. fac. letter, t. [1], [2], [3], bl. [4], fld. map, 5-
52, [53]-56. Buff wrps., list of contents on inner front and
back; adv. outer back; and noting on front, Long's Illustrated Edition. Pf., fld. fac. letter, and 2 fld. maps inserted.

232 Life and Public Services of Gen. Z. Taylor.... New York:
H. Long & Brother, Publishers, 1846.

As in entry 231, but p. [2] lists only copyright notice and
omits notice which appears in the above. Fld. map which
in 231 is inserted between pp. [4]-5 here precedes pf.
Brown wrps., inner front and back bl., outer back with
list of contents.

233 Life and Public Services of Gen. Z. Taylor.... New York:
H. Long & Brother, Publishers, 1846.

As in entry 231, but half title [i], bl. [ii], t. [1] ... [53]-
56, pub. cat. [1]-[16].

234 Life and Public Services of Gen. Z. Taylor.... With Fifteen
Illustrations.... New York: E. Hutchinson, J. J. Reed,
Printer, 1848.

Pf. [i], illus. [ii-iv], t. [1], [2], [3], illus. [4], 5-52, [53]-
61, 62-69, bl. [70], 81 [sic]-96. Cream illus. wrps., adv.
on inner front; entire back being pp. 95-96; and noting on
front, Illustrated Edition. Illus. in text. Treaty of Mexico, pp. [53]-61; sketches, pp. 62-69; list of killed, etc.,
pp. 81-96.

235 The Life and Public Services of Major General Zachary Taylor,
With Graphic Accounts of the Battles.... Illustrated. With
All His Letters and Despatches. Philadelphia: G. B. Zieb-
er & Co., 1847.

Bl. [1], f. [2], t. [3], 4, 5-60. Blue illus. wrps., inner
front and back bl., outer back with illus. Illus. in text.

236 The Life and Public Services of Major General Zachary Tay-
     lor. . . . Philadelphia: Turner & Fisher, Publishers [1847?]

     As in entry 235. Pink illus. wrps. , inner front and back
     bl. , outer back with illus.

237 The Life of Gen. Zachary Taylor. And a History of the War
     in Mexico. . . . Illustrated With a Portrait of General Tay-
     lor, and Views of the Battles. New York: Wm. H. Grah-
     am, 1847.

     Bl. [1], pf. [2], t. [3], [4], [5]-62. Cream illus. wrps. ,
     adv. matter on outer back. Title vignette. Illus. in text.
     Pr. in dbl. cols.

*238 The Life of General Zachary Taylor, Embracing His Military
     and Civil Career. . . . To Which Is Added a Biographical
     Sketch of Hon. Millard Fillmore. . . . New York: Dewitt
     & Davenport, 1848.

     64 pp. incl. pf. , illus.

239 Montgomery, Henry. The Life of Major General Zachary Tay-
     lor. With Illustrations. Auburn: J. C. Derby & Co. ,
     Publishers; Buffalo: Derby & Hewson, 1847.

     Pf. , t. [i], [ii], [iii]-iv, [v]-xiv, [17]-360. Calf. Pf. and
     4 pls. inserted. Preface, pp. [iii]-iv, dated June, 1847.

240 _____ . The Life of Major General Zachary Taylor. . . .
     Buffalo: Derby & Hewson, Publishers; Auburn: J. C.
     Derby & Co. ; Geneva: Derby, Wood & Co. , 1847.

     Bl. [i], pf. [ii], t. [iii], [iv], [v]-vi, [vii]-xii, [13]-360.
     Brown cloth. Pf. and 5 pls. inserted.

241 _____ . The Life of Major General Zachary Taylor. . . .
     Second Edition. Auburn: J. C. Derby & Co. , Publishers;
     Buffalo: Derby & Hewson; Geneva: Derby, Wood & Co. ,
     1847.

     As in entry 240. Brown cloth.

242 _____ . The Life of Major General Zachary Taylor. . . .
     Second Edition. Auburn: J. C. Derby & Co. , Publishers;
     Buffalo: Derby & Hewson; Geneva: Derby, Wood & Co. ,
     1848.

     As in entry 240. Calf.

243 'Old Rough and Ready, ' Or Taylor and His Battles. The Life
     of Gen. Zachary Taylor, Compiled From Authentic Sources,
     Together With Sketches. . . . New York: Published by Wil-
     liam Applegate, 1847.

T. [1], [2], illus. [3], bl. [4], 5-32. Light green illus.
wrps. , adv. on outer back; front captioned Taylor and His
Battles. Pr. in dbl. cols.

244 Poore, Benjamin Perley. Life of Gen. Zachary Taylor, the
Whig Candidate for the Presidency.... [Boston: Stacy,
Richardson & Co. , Printers, 1848.]

Caption title. [1]-16. Sewn. At foot of p. 16, col. 2:
"Stacy, Richardson & Co. , Printers, Boston. "; pr. in dbl.
cols.

245 Powell, C. Frank. Life of Major-General Zachary Taylor;
With an Account of His Brilliant Achievements on the Rio
Grande, and Elsewhere.... With Sketches.... New York:
D. Appleton & Company; Philadelphia: Geo. S. Appleton,
MDCCCXLVI.

Pf. , t. [1], [2], [3]-4, [5]-6, [7]-96, pub. cat. [i-ii], 1-38.
Brown wrps. , adv. on inner front and entire back; front
notes Appleton's Library of Popular Reading. No. 4.
Price 25 Cents. Pf. inserted.

246   . Life of Major General Zachary Taylor; With an Ac-
count of His Early Victories, and Brilliant Achievements in
Mexico Including the Siege of Monterey and Battle of Buena
Vista. Also Sketches of Maj. Ringgold, Maj. Brown, Col.
Cross, Capt. Montgomery, Capt. May, Capt. Walker,
Lieuts. Ridgeley, Blake, Jordan, etc.... Illustrated With
a Portrait of General Taylor. New York: D. Appleton &
Company; Philadelphia: Geo. S. Appleton, 1847.

As in entry 245, but text being pp. [7]-121, bl. [122]. All
copies examined rebound. Second enlarged ed.

247 A Review of the Life, Character and Political Opinions of Zachary Taylor. Boston: Eastburn's Press, 1848.

Cover title [1], bl. [2], [3]-16. Sewn. Title vignette.
Title set in 10 lines.

248 A Review of the Life, Character, and Political Opinions of
Zachary Taylor. Boston: Eastburn's Press, 1848.

As in entry 247, but title set in 12 lines and lacking vignette.

249 The Rough and Ready Almanac, for 1847. Containing a Com-
plete Life of General Taylor, and Sketches of the Battles of
Palo Alto, Resaca de la Palma, and Monterey. Cincinnati:
Robinson & Jones [1846?]

T. [1], [2-14], [15]-32, 33-38, [39]-43. Blue illus. wrps. ,
adv. on inner front and back, illus. on outer back. Life

of Taylor, pp. [15]-32; reports, pp. 33-38; appendix, pp. [39]-43.

250 Rough and Ready Almanac for the Year 1848.   New York: For Sale at Wholesale at the Tribune Buildings [1847?]

Cover title [1], [2-14], [15]-24, [25]-26, [27]-28, [29]-30, [31], adv. [32-40]. Sewn. Title vignette. Illus. in text. Life of Taylor, pp. [15]-24; Calhoun, pp. [25]-26; Scott, pp. [27]-28; McLean, pp. [29]-30.

251 The Rough and Ready Annual; Or Military Souvenir.   Illustrated With Twenty Portraits and Plates.   New York: D. Appleton & Co.; Philadelphia: Geo. S. Appleton, MDCCCXLVIII.

Pf., t. [1], [2], [3]-4, [5]-7, bl. [8], [9], bl. [10], div. t. [11], bl. [12], [13]-262, l. adv. All copies examined rebound. Pf. and 19 pls. inserted. First issued in 1848 under the title, The American Gift Book; Or, Military Souvenir.

252 A Sketch of the Life and Character of Gen. Taylor, the American Hero and People's Man; Together With a Concise History of the Mexican War....   By the One-Legged Sergeant. Boston: Published by J. B. Hall, 1847.

Cover title [1], songs [2], [3]-[36]. Buff illus. wrps., back being pp. [35-36]. Title vignette. Illus. in text. Also noted in lemon wrps.

253 A Sketch ... of Gen. Taylor....   By the One-Legged Sergeant. New York: S. French, 1847.

As in entry 252, but pp. [35-36] pr. in dbl. cols. Salmon illus. wrps. as above.

254 A Sketch ... of Gen. Taylor....   By the One-Legged Sergeant. New York: N. H. Blanchard; Boston: J. B. Hall, 1847.

As in entry 252. Blue illus. wrps. as above.

255 A Sketch of the Life and Public Services of General Zachary Taylor, the People's Candidate for the Presidency.   [Washington: J. T. Towers, 1848.]

Caption title. [1]-32. Sewn. At foot of p. [1], "Printed by J. T. Towers, Washington, D. C." followed by 1 line of price information; at foot of p. 32, "Washington, July 4, 1848. Printed by Jno. T. Towers, Washington, D. C."; at head of title, Please Circulate., followed by a 5 line warning against postmasters.

256 A Sketch of the Life and Public Services of General Zachary Taylor....   [New Orleans: Evening National, 1848.]

Caption title. [1]-29, [30]-32. Sewn. At foot of p. [1],
"Printed at the Office of the 'Evening National,' New Orleans, La."; life of Taylor, pp. [1]-29; life of Fillmore,
pp. [30]-32.

257 A Sketch of the Life and Public Services of General Zachary
     Taylor ... With Considerations in Favor of His Election.
     [Washington: Printed by Jno. T. Towers, 1848.]

     Caption title. As in entry 255, except price information at
     foot of p. [1] in 2 lines.

258 Sketch of the Lives and Public Services of Gen. Zachary Tay-
     lor, and Millard Fillmore. [New York: Appleton, 1848.]

     Caption title. [1]-26, [27]-32. Sewn. Illus. in text. Life
     of Taylor, pp. [1]-26; life of Fillmore, pp. [27]-32; imprint
     from note at foot of p. 32.

259 Sketch of the Lives of Taylor and Fillmore, the People's Can-
     didates for President and Vice President of the United
     States. Boston: Benjamin Adams [1848?]

     T. [1], [2], [3]-12, [13]-16. Yellow illus. wrps., songs
     on inner front, adv. on entire back. Life of Taylor, pp.
     [3]-12; life of Fillmore, pp. [13]-16.

260 Stearns, Charles. Facts in the Life of General Taylor; the
     Cuba Blood-Hound Importer, the Extensive Slave-Holder,
     and the Hero of the Mexican War. Boston: Published by
     the Author, 1848.

     T. [1], [2], [3]-35, [36]. Buff wrps., For Sale by Bela
     Marsh, 25 Cornhill added to outer front imprint. Imprint
     of Abner Forbes, printer, p. [2]; postscript, p. [36].
     Anti-Taylor.

261 Sumpter, Arthur. The Life of Major-General Zachary Taylor,
     the Whig Nominee for President of the United States. With
     a Brief Biographical Sketch of the Hon. Millard Fillmore....
     Illustrated By Numerous Engravings. New York: Published
     by Ensign & Thayer, 1848.

     [1], f. [2], t. [3], [4] [5], port. [6], [7]-31, [32]. All
     copies examined rebound. Illus. in text. Votes of the
     delegates, p. [1]; illus. and copyright notice, p. [4]; life
     of Fillmore, p. [32].

262 _____. The Lives of General Zachary Taylor and General
     Winfield Scott: To Which Is Appended an Outline History
     of Mexico ... and a Brief History of the Mexican War....
     Illustrated by a Map of Mexico, and Twelve Other Spirited
     Engravings. New York: H. Phelps & Co., 1848.

Bl. [1], pf. [2], illus. [3-4], t. [5], [6], [7], [8], [9]-62, [63-64]. Cream illus. wrps. pr. in blue, adv. on outer back. Illus. in text. Life of Taylor, pp. [9]-30; Scott, pp. [31]-51; Mexico, pp. [52]-62; appendix, pp. [63-64].

*263   . The Lives of General Zachary Taylor and General Winfield Scott.... New York: H. Phelps & Co., 1848.

2 ℓℓ., [1], 10-102 pp., ℓ., 1 pl., 1 port. Listed in the New York Public Library but unexamined.

264   Taylor and Fillmore. Life and Public Services of Major-Gen. Zachary Taylor. Also, the Life and Services of the Hon. Millard Fillmore. Embellished With Numerous Engravings. Hartford: Belknap & Hamersley, 1848.

Bl. [1], pf. [2], t. [3], [4], 5-54, bl. [55], port. [56], 57-64. Blue illus. wrps. Title vignette. Illus. in text. Life of Taylor, pp. 5-54; life of Fillmore, pp. 57-64.

265   Taylor and Fillmore. Life of Major-General Zachary Taylor, With Characteristic Anecdotes and Incidents. Also Life of the Honorable Millard Fillmore. Philadelphia: Published by T. K. & P. G. Collins, 1848.

Cover title [1], illus. [2], [3]-27, port. [28], 29-32. Sewn. Title vignette. Illus. in text. Life of Taylor, pp. [3]-27; life of Fillmore, pp. 29-32.

266   Taylor and His Campaigns. A Biography of Major-General Zachary Taylor, With a Full Account of His Military Services. With 27 Portraits and Engravings. Philadelphia: Published by E. H. Butler & Co., 1848.

Bl. [1], pf. [2], t. [3], [4], [5], bl. [6], [7], bl. [8], [9]-128. Brown illus. wrps., adv. on inner front and entire back. Title vignette. Illus. in text.

267   Taylor and His Generals. A Biography of Major-General Zachary Taylor; and Sketches of the Lives of Generals ... Together With a History of the Bombardment of Vera Cruz, and a Sketch of the Life of Major-General Winfield Scott. Embellished With Portraits and Engravings. Philadelphia: Published by E. H. Butler & Co., 1847.

Pf., t. [i], [ii], [iii]-iv, [v]-vi, [13]-215, bl. [216], [217]-268, div. t. [269], bl. [270], [271]-318. All copies examined bound with other pamphlets. Title vignette. Pf. and 5 pls. inserted, other illus. in text. Life of Taylor, pp. [13]-215; of other generals, pp. [217]-268; of Scott, pp. [271]-318.

268   Taylor and His Generals.... Philadelphia: Published by E. H. Butler & Co., 1847.

As in entry 267 but concluding with pub. cat. [1]-[8]. Brown
illus. wrps. , adv. on inner front and entire back; at head
of title on front, Butler's Cheap Edition.

269   Taylor and His Generals.... Philadelphia: Published by E.
H. Butler & Co.; New York: Burgess, Stringer & Co. ,
1847.

As in entry 267 except the life of Taylor is pp. [13]-214,
while the remainder of the text consists of pp. [215]-325,
adv. [326]. Brown wrps. as in entry 268.

270   Taylor and His Generals.... Philadelphia: Published by E.
H. Butler & Co.; New York: Burgess, Stringer & Co. ,
1847.

As in entry 267 except the life of Taylor is pp. [13]-214,
while the remainder of the text consists of pp. [215]-326,
pub. cat. [1]-[8]. All copies examined rebound.

271   Taylor and His Generals.... Hartford: Silas Andrus & Son,
1848.

Pf. , t. , t. [i], [ii], [iii]-iv, [v]-vi, port. , [13]-204, bl.
ℓ. [205-206], [207]-264, [265]-326. Brown cloth. Title
vignette. Pf. , 1st t. , and 10 pls. inserted. Life of Taylor, pp. [13]-204; of other generals, pp. [207]-264; of
Scott, pp. [265]-326.

272   Taylor Meeting. [Lexington: Scrugham & Dunlop, Printers,
1848.]

Caption title. [1]-12. Sewn. At foot of p. 12, "Scrugham
& Dunlop, Printers, Lexington"; meeting of citizens of Lexington, Ky.; 1,000 copies printed.

273   The Taylor Text-Book, Or Rough and Ready Reckoner. Baltimore: Printed and Published by Samuel Sands, 1848.

T. [1], [2]-7, [8]-58. Illus. wrps. , inner front being index, all copies examined lacking entire back. Sketch of
Taylor, pp. [2]-7; additional information throughout remainder of text; pr. in dbl. cols.

*274   Thistle, T. Rough and Ready Rhymes: A Democratic Epic
Poem.... Philadelphia, 1848.

74 pp.

275   [Thorpe, Thomas B.] The Taylor Anecdote Book. Anecdotes
and Letters of Zachary Taylor. By Tom Owen, the Bee-
Hunter. With a Brief Life. Illustrated With Engravings.
New York: D. Appleton & Company; Philadelphia: Geo. S.
Appleton, MDCCCXLVIII.

T. [3], [4], [5], [6]-8, [9]-12, [13]-138, 139-150. All
copies examined rebound (wrps. ? pp. [1-2]). Illus. in text.
Life of Taylor, pp. [9]-12; appendix, pp. 139-150.

*276   Zach Taylor Almanac for 1848.   Baltimore: Armstrong &
       Berry [1847?]

       16 ℓℓ. Drake 2799 (Drake 2800, Baltimore: Isaac P.
       Cook.)

CASS, LEWIS (Democratic)

277   The Cass and Butler Almanac, for 1849.   Compiled by the
      Democratic Committee of Publication of the City and County
      of Philadelphia.   Philadelphia: John B. Perry [1848?].

      Cover title [1], [2], 3-35 [36].   Sewn.   Title vignette.   Il-
      lus. in text.   Cut and song, p. [36].

278   Cass and Butler.   The Life and Public Services of Gen. Lewis
      Cass: Comprising His Services in the War of 1812....   To
      Which Is Added, the Military and Civil Life of Gen. William
      O. Butler....   Embellished with Numerous Engravings.
      Hartford: Belknap & Hamersley, 1848.

      Bl. [1], pf. [2], t. [3], [4], 5, bl. [6], 7-40, port. 41, bl.
      [42], 43-64.   All copies examined disbound.   Illus. in text.
      Half title, p. 5; life of Cass, pp. 7-40; life of Butler, pp.
      43-64; page number 5 lacking in p. 51.

279   [Hickman, George H.]   The Life of General Lewis Cass, With
      His Letters and Speeches on Various Subjects.   Baltimore:
      Published by N. Hickman, 1848.

      T. [1], [2], [3], bl. [4], [5], bl. [6], [7]-72. Wrps. , with
      additional publishers listed.   Introduction, p. [5], dated
      May 1848 and signed "G. H. H. "   Copies also noted with an
      inserted pf.

280   Life and Public Services of Gen. Lewis Cass, Democratic Can-
      didate for the Presidency.   Together With a Sketch of the
      Life and Services of Gen. William O. Butler, Democratic
      Candidate for the Vice Presidency.   Boston: J. B. Hall,
      1848.

      Cover title [1], bl. [2], [3]-34, bl. [35], illus. and adv.
      [36].   Yellow illus. wrps. , back being pp. [35-36]; p. [35]
      bl. , illus. p. [36].   Title vignette.   Illus. in text.

281   Life of General Lewis Cass: Comprising an Account of His
      Military Services in the North-West During the War With
      Great-Britain, His Diplomatic Career and Civil History.

To Which Is Appended, a Sketch of the Public and Private
History of Major-General W. O. Butler, of the Volunteer
Service of the United States. With Two Portraits. Phila-
delphia: G. B. Zieber & Co. , 1848.

Pf. , t. [i], [ii], div. t. v, bl. [vi], iii-iv, vii-viii, 11-210,
adv. [211-215], bl. [216]. Brown wrps. , adv. on inner
back; front notes Zieber & Co. 's Standard Edition. Pf. and
1 pl. inserted. Life of Cass, pp. 11-160; of Butler, pp.
165-210. Copies noted with pp. v-[vi] placed correctly.
Howes N144 cites author as C. A. P. Nicholson.

282 [Schoolcraft, Henry Rowe.] Outlines of the Life and Character
of Gen. Lewis Cass. Albany: Joel Munsell, Printer, 1848.

Cover title [1], bl. [2], [3]-64. All copies examined rebound. Title vignette. Illus. in text. At head of title,
Albany Argus.

283 Sketch of the Life and Public Services of Gen. Lewis Cass.
[Washington: Printed at the Congressional Globe Office,
1848.]

Caption title. [1]-8, bl. ℓ. Self wrps. P. 8 dated "Washington, March, 1848. " and also noting "Printed at the Congressional Globe Office, Jackson Hall, Washington, D. C. ";
pr. in dbl. cols.

284 Sketch of ... Gen. Lewis Cass. [Washington: Printed at the
Congressional Globe Office, 1848.]

As in entry 283, but p. 8 concludes with "... Washington,
D. C. [dash] Price 50 Cents per Hundred Copies. "

285 Sketch of ... Gen. Lewis Cass. [Washington: Printed at the
Congressional Globe Office, 1848.]

As in entry 283, but p. 8 dated June, 1848.

286 Sketch of ... Gen. Lewis Cass. [Boston:] For Sale at the
Boston Daily Times Office [1848.]

Cover title [1], bl. [2], [3]-15, bl. [16]. Self wrps. At
head of title, Boston Daily Times Extra, No. 1; at foot of
p. 15, "Washington, March, 1848. "; pr. in dbl. cols.

287 Skizze des Lebens und Wirkens des Generals Ludwig Cass von
Michigan, und des Generals Wilhelm O. Butler von Kentucky. ... Washington: Druckerei des "Nationalen Demo-
kraten, " 1848.

Cover title [1], bl. [2], [3]-14, 15-23, bl. [24]. Sewn.
Title vignette. Life of Cass, pp. [3]-14; of Butler, pp. 15-
23.

288   To the People of Pennsylvania. Every Citizen, Who Cherishes
      and Values the Prosperity and Permanency of His Country
      and Her Institutions, As He Values His Own and His Chil-
      dren's Prosperity and Happiness, "Read! Pause!! Re-
      flect!!!" [N. p., n. d., 1848?]

         Caption title. [1]-15, bl. [16]. Self wrps. Primarily bio-
         graphical, recounting in brief paragraphs the public and
         private life of Cass.

VAN BUREN, MARTIN (Free Soil [Democratic])

289   Crockett, David. The Life of Martin Van Buren, Heir-Appar-
      ent to the "Government," and the Appointed Successor of
      General Andrew Jackson. Containing Every Authentic Par-
      ticular By Which His Extraordinary Character Has Been
      Formed.... New York: Wm. H. Graham, 1848.

         2 f., t. [i], [ii], 23-209, bl. [210]. Brown wrps. 2 f. and
         2 pls. inserted. See also entry 48. Burlesque life.

CLAY, HENRY (Whig)

290   Colton, Calvin. The Life and Times of Henry Clay.... In
      Two Volumes, Vol. I. [II.] New York: Published by A. S.
      Barnes & Co., 1846.

         Vol. I: pf., t. [i], [ii], [iii], bl. [iv], [5]-13, [14]-16,
         [17]-504; Vol. II: f., t. [i], [ii], [3]-4, [5]-8, [9]-488,
         [489]-504. Brown cloth. Pf. [I] and f. [II], inserted.

291   _____. The Life and Times of Henry Clay.... Second Edi-
      tion. New York: Published by A. S. Barnes & Co., 1846.

         As in entry 290.

292   Das Leben des amerikanischen Staats-Mannes Heinrich Clay.
      [Philadelphia, n. d.]

         Caption title. [1]-16. Self wrps.

293   Sergent, Epes. The Life and Public Services of Henry Clay.
      New Edition, Revised, Enlarged, and Brought Down to the
      Year 1848, by the Author. New York: Published by
      Greeley & McElrath, 1848.

         Pf., t. [1], [2], [3]-120. Brown cloth. Pf. inserted.
         Preface, p. [2], dated March 1848; text pr. in dbl. cols.
         Also noted in brown wrps., inner front and entire back
         with adv.

DALLAS, GEORGE MIFFLIN (Democratic)

294 Life of George Mifflin Dallas, Vice President of the United
     States. Prepared and Published in September, 1844, by
     the Democratic Committee of Publication ... Extended to
     the Present Time, and Reprinted Nov. 1847. Philadelphia:
     Times and Keystone Job Office, 1847.

         T. [1], bl. [2], [3]-20. Pink wrps. Title vignette.

SCOTT, WINFIELD (Whig)

295 Egelmann, Charles F. The General Scott Almanac, for the
     Year of Our Lord 1848.... Philadelphia: Griffith & Simon;
     King & Baird, Printers [1847?]

         T. [3], [4], adv. [5], 6-33, 34-35, adv. [36]. Illus. wrps.,
         front being pp. [1-2]; inner front, explanatory notes; back
         being pp. 35-[36]. Illus. in text. Court schedules, pp.
         34-35.

296 General Scott and His Staff: Comprising Memoirs of Generals
     Scott ... and Other Distinguished Officers.... Compiled
     From Public Documents and Private Correspondence. With
     Accurate Portraits, and Other Beautiful Illustrations. Phi-
     ladelphia: Grigg, Elliot & Co., 1848.

         F., pf., t. [i], [ii], iii-iv, 5, bl. [vi], 11-224, pub. cat.
         1-12. Brown cloth. F., pf. and 10 pls. inserted, other
         illus. in text. Life of Scott, pp. 11-77.

297 Illustrated Life of General Winfield Scott, Commander-in-Chief
     of the Army in Mexico. Illustrated by D. H. Strother.
     New York: Published by A. S. Barnes & Co., 1847.

         T. [1], map [2], [3]-144. Peach illus. wrps., list of con-
         tents on inner front, adv. on entire back; imprint on front
         lists one bookseller and 2 additional publishers. Illus. in
         text. Wrps. also noted with different adv. on back: inner
         back with Mansfield's Life, outer with illus. of Scott's resi-
         dence. Above has adv. for "Valuable Library and School
         Books" on inner and illus. of residence and adv. for Mans-
         field on outer back.

298 Illustrated Life of General Winfield Scott.... New York: Pub-
     lished by A. S. Barnes & Co., 1847.

         T. [1], map [2], [3]-156, 2 bl. ℓℓ. Brown illus. wrps.,
         as in first mentioned in entry 297. Illus. in text.

299 The Life and Military Character of Maj. Gen. Scott, Illustrated
     With Numerous Anecdotes and Spirited Engravings. Together

With His Views Upon the Principal Moral, Social and Political Topics of the Age.... Boston: Published by John B.
Hall, 1847.

Cover title [1], illus. [2], [3]-36. Blue illus. wrps., at
head of title, The Most Entertaining Book of the Season!;
the back being pp. 35-36. Title vignette. Illus. in text.

300   The Life and Military Character of Maj. Gen. Scott.... New
York: Published by S. French, 1847.

As in entry 299. Pink illus. wrps. as above. Also noted
in green illus. wrps., but lacking line at head of title.

*301   Life of General Scott. Columbus: For Sale by Scott & Bas-
com [1848?]

32 pp. Sewn.

302   Mansfield, Edward D. The Life of General Winfield Scott....
New York: Published by A. S. Barnes & Co., 1846.

Pf., t. [i], [ii], [iii]-vi, [vii]-x, bl. [xi], illus. [xii], [13]-
362, 363-366 [i. e. 368]. Brown cloth. Pf. and 4 pls.
inserted, other illus. in text. P. numbered 155* and full
p. illus. not numbered occur between pp. 155-156, thus
368 pp.

303   _____. The Life of General Winfield Scott, Embracing His
Campaign in Mexico.... New York: Published by A. S.
Barnes & Co., 1848.

Pf., t. [i], [ii], [iii]-vi, [vii]-x, bl. [xi], illus. [xii], [13]-
414. Brown cloth. Pf. and 15 pls. inserted, other illus.
in text.

304   Scenes in the Life of General Scott. [N. p., n. d., 1848?]

Caption title. Broadside $32\frac{1}{2}$ x $22\frac{1}{2}$, pr. in 4 cols. surrounded by ornaments and 18 illus. Also cited as [1847?]
and [1852?].

305   The Scott & Taylor Almanac for the Year 1848: Calculated
for Boston and New York. Embellished With Numerous Engravings. Boston and New York: For Sale by Hall, 1848.

Cover title [1], [2], [3-14], [15], [16-24]. Sewn. Title
vignette. Illus. in text. The Scott medal, p. [15]; text
deals entirely with Scott.

WEBSTER, DANIEL (Whig)

306   An Appeal to the Whig National Convention, in Favor of the

Nomination of Daniel Webster to the Presidency. By a
Whig From the Start. New York: R. Craighead, Printer,
1848.

Cover title [1], bl. [2], [3]-5, bl. [6], [7]-50. Brown
wrps., adv. on entire back.

1852

PIERCE, FRANKLIN (Democratic)

307 [Bartlett, David Vandewater Golden.] The Life of Gen. Frank.
       Pierce, of New-Hampshire, the Democratic Candidate for
       President of the United States. By D. W. Bartlett. Au-
       burn: Derby & Miller; Buffalo: Geo. H. Derby & Co.;
       Geneva: Derby, Orton & Co., 1852.

       Pf., t. [i], [ii], [iii], bl. [iv], [v]-vii, bl. [viii], [ix]-x,
       div. t. [xi], bl. [xii], [13]-300. Silver blue cloth. Pf.
       inserted. Also noted in brown, green, red, and brownish
       red cloths.

308 _____. Ninth Thousand. The Only Authentic Edition. The
       Life of Gen. Franklin Pierce.... Auburn: Derby & Mill-
       er; Buffalo: George H. Derby & Co.; Geneva: Derby, Or-
       ton & Co.; Cincinnati: H. W. Derby & Co.; Hartford:
       Cleveland & Jewett, Agents, 1852.

       As in entry 307. All copies examined rebound.

309 _____. Thirteenth Thousand. The Only Authentic Edition.
       The Life of Gen. Franklin Pierce.... Auburn: Derby &
       Miller; Buffalo: George H. Derby & Co.; Geneva: Derby,
       Orton & Co.; Cincinnati: H. W. Derby & Co.; Hartford:
       Cleveland & Jewett, Agents, 1852.

       As in entry 307. Brown cloth.

310 Biographical Sketch of General Franklin Pierce, of New Hamp-
       shire, a Citizen in Peace, a Soldier in War, and a States-
       man in Both.... Published Under the Direction of the
       Democratic State Central Committee of Ohio, August, 1852.
       Columbus: Printed at the Office of the Ohio Statesman,
       1852.

       Cover title. [1]-16. Lemon wrps. Pr. in dbl. cols.
       Another copy noted, disbound, but including 2 ports.

311 A Brief Chapter in the Life of General Franklin Pierce.   From
     the National Era of June 17.   Mr. Pierce and the Anti-
     Slavery Movement.   [Washington: Buell & Blanchard, Print-
     ers, 1852.]

        Caption title.   [1]-8.   All copies examined disbound.   At
        foot of p. 8, "Buell & Blanchard, Printers, Washington,
        D. C. "; pr. in dbl. cols.   Anti-Pierce.

312 The Democratic Text-Book, Containing the Lives of Pierce and
     King, With Illustrations of the Whig and Democratic Prin-
     ciples and Candidates.   Philadelphia: Printed by James
     Fullerton, and Sold at the Offices of the Pennsylvanian...
     [1852?].

        T. [1], bl. [2], [3]-48.   All copies examined disbound.
        Title vignette.   Pr. in dbl. cols.

313 Hawthorne, Nathaniel.   Life of Franklin Pierce.   Boston: Tick-
     nor, Reed, and Fields, MDCCLII.

        Pf. , t. [1], [2], [3]-4, [5-6], [7]-138, [139]-144.   Buff
        wrps. , adv. on inner front and entire back.   Pf. inserted.
        For variant forms of wrps. , binding cloth, backstrip im-
        print, and inserted pub. cat. , see BAL, vol. 4, entry 7612.

314 Life and Services of Gen. Pierce, Respectfully Dedicated to
     Gen'l Lewis Cass.   Concord: Gazette Press, 1852.

        T. [1], [2], [3], 4-14, bl. ℓ. [15-16].   Bl. green wrps.
        Miniature book, 1 7/16 x 1.   Intro. , p. [3], signed "Sykes. "
        Humorous, anti-Pierce.

315 The Life of Gen. Frank. Pierce, the Granite Statesman: With
     a Biographical Sketch of Hon. William Rufus King, Vice
     President of the United States.   By Hermitage.   Tenth
     Thousand.   New York: Published by Cornish, Lamport &
     Co. , 1852.

        T. [1], [2], [3]-4, [5]-59, [60]-75, 76-96.   Greenish buff
        wrps. , adv. on inner front and entire back; imprint on front
        adds one additional publisher.   Introduction, pp. [3]-4,
        dated June 9, 1852; life of Pierce, pp. [5]-59; of King, pp.
        [60]-75; historic sketches, pp. 76-96.

316 Life of Gen. Franklin Pierce, the Democratic Candidate for
     President.   Trenton: Printed by Morris R. Hamilton, 1852.

        Cover title [1], bl. [2], [3]-48.   Sewn.

317 Lives of Gen. Franklin Pierce, and William R. King, Demo-
     cratic Candidates for President and Vice President.   Issued
     Under the Authority and Sanction of the National Democratic

Committee at Washington. Boston: Published at the Boston Daily Times Office; George Roberts [1852.]

Cover title. [1]-32. Yellow illus. wrps. Title vignette. Copy also noted with wrps. listing Second Edition of 20,000! Price info. at head of title.

318 Sketches of the Lives of Franklin Pierce and Wm. R. King, Candidates of the Democratic Republican Party for the Presidency and Vice Presidency of the United States. [N. p., National Democratic Executive Committee, 1852.]

Caption title. [1]-36. Sewn.

319 Vindication of the Military Character and Services of General Franklin Pierce, By His Companions in Arms in Mexico. (Called Out by the Aspersions and Innuendoes of a Portion of the Whig Press.). [N. p., n. d., 1852.]

Caption title. [1]-16. Sewn. At head of title, Please Read and Circulate. Pr. in dbl. cols.

SCOTT, WINFIELD (Whig)

320 Conrad, Robert T. The Career and Claims of Winfield Scott, the Hero, Statesman, Philanthropist and Patriot. As Contained in the Remarks of ... of Philadelphia, Before the Great Whig Mass Convention, Held at Harrisburg, August 20th, 1852. Philadelphia: King & Baird, Printers, 1852.

Cover title [1], bl. [2], [3]-16. Sewn.

321 The Contrast; the Whig and Democratic Platforms, the Whig and Democratic Candidates for the Presidency. [N. p., n. d., 1852.]

Caption title. Cover title [1], bl. [2], [3]-40. Sewn. At head of title, Please Read and Circulate; cover title reads The Contrast; pr. in dbl. cols. Pro-Scott.

322 Events and Incidents in the History of Gen. Winfield Scott.... Washington: Printed by Kirkwood & McGill, 1852.

Cover title [1], [2], [3]-23, 24. All copies examined rebound. Preface, p. [2], signed "C. B. A."; poem, p. 24. Title vignette.

323 The Gen. Scott Almanac, for the Year 1853. Philadelphia: Published by King & Baird [1852?]

Cover title [1], [2], [3]-34, [35], adv. [36]. Illus. wrps., the back being pp. [35-36]. Title vignette. Illus. in text.

Life and anecdotes of Scott throughout pp. [3]-34; sittings
of Pa. courts, p. [35]; at head of title, Among Living Men,
"First in War, First in Peace, and First in the Hearts of
His Countrymen. "

324   The Gen. Scott Almanac.... Philadelphia: T. B. Peterson
      [1852?]

      As in entry 323 except different port. on p. [3].

325   General Winfield Scott. [New York: Druck bei "New-Yorker
      Allegemeinen Zeitung, " 1852.]

      Caption title.   [1]-32.   Sewn.   Title vignette.   Illus. in
      text.   At head of title, Heil dem Führer!   Heil der Union!,
      at foot of p. 32, "Illustrationen von A. H. Jocelyn.   Druck
      bei 'New-Yorker Allegemeinen Zeitung. '"; pr. in dbl. cols.
      German translation of entry 331.

326   Headley, Joel Tyler.   The Lives of Winfield Scott and Andrew
      Jackson.   New York: Charles Scribner, 1852.

      Half title [i], bl. [ii], pf. , t. [iii], [iv], [v]-vii, bl. [viii],
      [ix-xi], bl. [xii], [13]-202, div. t. , bl. , port., [203]-341,
      bl. [342], bl. ℓ. , 4 ℓℓ. adv. Dark brown cloth.   Pf. and
      pl. inserted.   Life of Scott, pp. [13]-202; of Jackson, pp.
      [203]-341.

327   [Johnston, Edward William.]   Anecdotes of Winfield Scott as
      Soldier and as Citizen.   [Washington: Daily American Tele-
      graph, 1852?]

      Caption title.   [1]-15, bl. [16].   All copies examined dis-
      bound.   Pr. in dbl. cols.

*328 Kurze Lebensbeschreibung des General-Majors Winfield Scott.
      Philadelphia: King & Baird [1852.]

      8 ℓℓ. Sabin 78404.

329   Life and Exploits of Gen.   Scott Respectfully Dedicated to His
      Commander, Gen. Bil. Seward.   Unabridged Edition.   New
      York: 1852.

      T. [1], [2], 3-16.   Bl. blue wrps.   Miniature book, 1 3/4
      x 1 1/8.   Preface, p. [2], signed "Soup. "   Humorous, anti-
      Scott.

330   Life and Public Services of Winfield Scott, General-in-Chief of
      the Army of the United States.   Comprising His Early Life,
      His Services in the War of 1812....   With Numerous Illus-
      trations.   From the Most Authentic Documents.   Philadel-
      phia: Lippincott, Grambo & Co. , 1852.

F., pf., t. [i], [ii], [9]-10, 11-78, pub. cat. 16-17 and 21-
30, 32. Blue illus. wrps., inner front paged 31, inner
back p. 32, adv. outer back; front also notes Nomination
for the Presidency. F., pf., and 5 pls. inserted. Preface, pp. [9]-10, dated June 1852.

331 Life of General Scott. [New York: C. A. Alvord, 1852.]

Caption title. [1]-32. Sewn. Title vignette. At head of
title, "Hail to the Chief Who in Triumph Advances."; at
foot of col. one, p. 32, "C. A. Alvord Printer, 29 Gold-
Street." set in 2 lines; pr. in dbl. cols.

332 Life of General Scott. [New York: C. A. Alvord, 1852.]

As in entry 331, but adds under col. 2, p. 32, "A. H.
Jocelyn, Engraver and Electrotyper of Woodcuts, 64 John-
Street, New York." set in 3 lines.

333 Life of General Scott. [New York: C. A. Alvord, 1852.]

As in entry 332, with added reference to Mansfield's 536
pp. Life.

334 Life of General Scott. [N. p., 1852.]

As in entry 331, but lacking both imprints on p. 32.

335 [Mansfield, Edward D.] Incidents Taken From Mansfield's
Life of General Scott. Life of General Winfield Scott,
Commander-In-Chief of the United States Army. With
Illustrations. New York: A. S. Barnes & Co.; Boston:
Redding & Co.; Philadelphia: Peterson & Co.; Baltimore:
Burgess, Taylor & Co.; Cincinnati: H. W. Derby & Co.;
New Orleans: J. B. Steel, 1852.

Pf., t. [1], map [2], [3]-191, [192]-202. Buff illus. wrps.,
inner front with list of contents and reference to Mansfield's
536 pp. Life; outer front noting A. S. Barnes & Co.'s
Pamphlet Or Campaign Edition; entire back lacking in all
copies examined. Illus. in text. At head of title, A. S.
Barnes & Co.'s Pamphlet Edition.; appendix, pp. [192]-202.

336   . Incidents ... of General Scott.... New York: A.
S. Barnes & Co. [etc.] 1852.

As in entry 335 except appendix, p. [192] only. Green illus. wrps. as above, adv. on entire back.

337   . Life and Services of General Winfield Scott, Including the Siege of Vera Cruz.... With Engravings. New
York: Published by A. S. Barnes & Co., 1852.

Pf., t. [i], [ii], [iii]-vi, [vii]-xi, illus. [xii], [13]-514,
[515]-536. Bluish green cloth. Pf. and 15 pls. inserted,
other illus. in text. Opening and terminal endpapers are
decoratively blue coated on white with adv.; appendix, pp.
[515]-536.

338   . Life ... of General Winfield Scott. ... New York:
Published by A. S. Barnes & Co.; Boston: Redding & Co.;
Philadelphia: Peterson & Co.; Baltimore: Burgess, Tay-
lor, & Co.; Cincinnati: H. W. Derby & Co.; New Orleans:
J. B. Steele, 1852.

As in entry 337, but adding pp. [537]-538 on the National
Whig Convention. At head of title, The Only Authentic Edition. Noted in green and red cloths as above. Copy also
noted with terminal 2 ℓℓ. adv., blue cloth with orange
coated endpapers as above. Copy also noted with green
cloth, pink endpapers as above.

339 Memoir of General Scott. From Records Contemporaneous
With the Events. Washington: C. Alexander, Printer, 1852.

Cover title [1], bl. [2], [3]-32. Sewn. At head of title,
Please Read and Circulate; pr. in dbl. cols. Anti-Scott.

340 Die Präsidentschaft--Winfield Scott--Franklin Pierce; ihre Fähig-
keit und Thätigkeit zu diesem hohen Amte. [N. p., 1852.]

Caption title. [1]-15, bl. [16]. Sewn. At head of title,
Zur gefälligen Durchlesung und Weiterverbreitung. German
translation of entry 341 with p. 15 adding "Das Leben General Scott's in einer Nuttshale" ("General Scott's Life in a
Nutshell").

341 The Presidency: Winfield Scott--Franklin Pierce; Their Quali-
fications and Fitness for That High Office. [N. p., Towers, Printer, 1852.]

Caption title. [1]-16. All copies examined disbound. At
head of title, Please Read and Circulate; at foot of p. 16,
"Towers, Printer, Price $1 00 per Hundred."; pr. in dbl.
cols. Pro-Scott. Another copy noted in which different
punctuation marks are employed: e. g., first line in paren-
theses rather than brackets as above, and Presidency sep-
arated from Winfield by 3 hyphens rather than colon as
above.

342 Vie Du Général Scott. [New York: Imprimerie du Phare de
New-York, 1852.]

Caption title. [1]-32. All copies examined disbound. Title
vignette. Illus. in text. At foot of p. 32, "Imprimerie du
Phare de New-York, 305, Broadway, et 122, Leonard

Street, N. Y. "; pr. in dbl. cols.   French translation of entry 331.

343 Winfield Scott und Seine Verläumder.   Washington: 1852.

Cover title [1], bl. [2], [3]-7, bl. [8].   All copies examined
disbound.

CASS, LEWIS (Democratic)

344 Young, William T.   Sketch of the Life and Public Services of
General Lewis Cass.   With the Pamphlet on the Right of
Search, and Some of His Speeches on the Great Political
Questions of the Day.   Detroit: Published by Markham &
Elwood, 1852.

Half title [i], bl. [ii], pf. , t. [iii], [iv], [v], bl. [vi], [vii]-
viii, div. t. [ix], bl. [x], [xi]-xv, bl. [xvi], [17]-420.
Black cloth.   Pf. inserted.   Copies noted in brown and purple cloths, pf. lacking.

345 Young, William T.   Sketch of the Life ... of General Lewis
Cass.... Second Edition.   Detroit: Published by Alexander
Mc'Farren, 1852.

As in entry 344, but lacking pf.   All copies examined rebound.

WEBSTER, DANIEL (Whig)

346 March, Charles W.   Daniel Webster and His Contemporaries.
Fourth Edition.   New York: Charles Scribner, 1852.

Pf. , t. [i], [ii], [i], bl. [ii], [iii]-v, bl. [vi], [vii]-viii, 1-
295 bl. [296].   Green cloth.   Pf. inserted.   Preface to
4th ed. , 2nd p. [i].   The work is entirely devoted to Webster; earlier title Reminiscences of Congress.

1856

GENERAL WORKS

347 Wells' National Hand-Book: Embracing Numerous Invaluable
Documents ... Lives and Portraits of the Nominees for
President and Vice-President ... Fifty-Two Illustrations.
New York: John G. Wells, Publishing Agent, 1856.

Bl. [1], f. [2], t. [3], [4], 5-142, 143-144. Brown cloth.
Illus. in text. Table of contents, pp. 143-144; list of illus.
p. 144. Ports. and brief biogs. of the candidates of the
American, Democratic, and Republican Parties, pp. 121-
141.

BUCHANAN, JAMES (Democratic)

348 Buchanan and Breckinridge. Lives of James Buchanan, and
John C. Breckinridge, Democratic Candidates for the Presi-
dency and Vice-Presidency of the United States, With the
Platforms of the Three Political Parties in the Presidential
Canvass of 1856. Cincinnati: H. W. Derby & Co., Pub-
lishers, 1856.

Half title [i], bl. [ii], bl. [iii], pf. [iv], t. [1], [2], 3-76,
port., 77-88, adv. [89], bl. [90]. Buff illus. wrps., Er-
ratum on inner front, port. on outer back; front notes,
Cheapest and Best Edition. Pf. and 1 pl. in text. Life of
Buchanan, pp. 3-76; of Breckinridge, pp. 77-88.

349 Horton, R. G. Authorized Edition. The Life and Public Services of James Buchanan ... Including the Most Important
of His State Papers. With an Accurate Portrait on Steel.
New York: Derby & Jackson; Cincinnati: H. W. Derby &
Co., 1856.

Half title [i], bl. [ii], pf., t. [iii], [iv], 5-viii, 9-xi, bl.
[xii], 13-428, 2 ℓ ℓ. adv. Brown cloth with brown coated
endpapers. Pf. inserted. Copies also noted in gold cloth
with yellow endpapers; maroon cloth, pink endpapers; green
cloth, green endpapers; and brown cloth, blue coated endpapers.

*350 Jerome, C. Life of James Buchanan. Claremont, N. H.:
Tracy Kenney & Co., 1856.

48 pp., pf.

351 The Life and Public Services of Hon. James Buchanan of Pennsylvania. Twentieth Thousand. New York: Published by
Livermore & Rudd, 1856.

Pf., t. [1], [2], [3]-118. Yellow illus. wrps., adv. on inner front and entire back; front notes The Authorized Campaign Edition, and adds local (Rock Island, Ill.: F. H.
Warren) imprint. Copies also noted in green illus. wrps.,
lacking local imprint, and in 3/4 black cloth, leather backstrip.

352 The Life of the Hon. James Buchanan, As Written by Himself,
and Set to Music by an Old Democrat, to the Tune of "Poor

Old Horse Let Him Die!" Price--"Half a Jimmy!" Copy-
Right Secured. Lancaster, near Wheatland: 1856.

Cover title [1], [2]-8. Self wrps. Burlesque life in verse.
Anti-Buchanan.

353 Plain Facts and Considerations: Addressed to the People of
the United States, Without Distinction of Party, in Favor of
James Buchanan, of Pennsylvania, for President, and John
C. Breckinridge, of Kentucky, for Vice-President. By an
American Citizen. Boston: Brown, Bazin, and Company,
1856.

Cover title [1], [2], [3]-32. All copies examined bound with
other pamphlets. At head of title, 3 line note to Editors
and Clubs; author's note, p. [2].

354 Sheridan, James B. Proceedings of the Pennsylvania Democratic State Convention, Held at Harrisburg, March 4th,
1856. Reported By.... Philadelphia: Wm. Rice, Penn-
sylvanian Office, Printer, 1856.

T. [1], bl. [2], [3]-90. Salmon wrps., entire back lacking
on all copies examined. "Memoir of James Buchanan, of
Pennsylvania," pp. [69]-86.

355 Short Answers to Reckless Fabrications, Against the Democratic
Candidate for President, James Buchanan. Philadelphia:
William Rice, Book and Job Printer, 1856.

T. [1], bl. [2], [3]-32. All copies examined disbound.

FREMONT, JOHN CHARLES (Republican)

356 Bigelow, John. Memoir of the Life and Public Services of
John Charles Fremont, Including an Account of His Explora-
tions, Discoveries and Adventures ... and Full Reports of
His Principal Speeches in the Senate of the United States.
With Spirited Illustrations, and an Accurate Portrait on
Steel. New York: Derby & Jackson; Cincinnati: H. W.
Derby & Co., 1856.

Pf., t. [i], [ii], [iii], bl. [iv], [v]-vi, vii-x, [11]-466, 467-
480. Purple cloth. Pf. and 8 pls. inserted. Appendices,
pp. 467-480. Also noted in green cloth with spine citing,
"Only Complete Edition," and brown cloth.

357 [Burleigh, George Shepard.] Signal Fires on the Trail of the
Pathfinder. New York: Dayton and Burdick, 1856.

T. [i], [ii], [iii]-iv, [v], bl. [vi], [vii]-viii, [9]-162. All
copies examined rebound. Major events in Fremont's life
presented in 27 poems.

358 Hall, Benjamin F. The Republican Party and Its Presidential
     Candidates: Comprising an Accurate Descriptive History of
     the Republican Party.... With Biographical Sketches and
     Portraits of Fremont and Dayton. New York and Auburn:
     Miller, Orton & Mulligan, 1856.

     2 pf., t. [i], [ii], [iii]-iv, [v]-xii, [13]-512. Light purple
     cloth. 2 pf. inserted. Biographical sketches, pp. [473]-
     512. Also noted in green cloth.

359 Das Leben des Obersten Fremont. [New York: Greeley &
     M'Elrath, c1856.]

     Caption title. [1]-32. Sewn. Title vignette. Illus. in
     text. At foot of p. [1], "Entered According to Act of Con-
     gress, in the year 1856, by Greeley & M'Elrath, in the
     Clerk's Office of the District Court of the United States,
     for the Southern District of New York."; pr. in dbl. cols.
     German translation of entry 362.

360 The Life, Explorations, and Public Services of John Charles
     Fremont. New York: Livermore & Rudd, 1856.

     Bl. [i], pf. [ii], t. [1], [2], [3]-5, bl. [6], [7]-115, adv.
     [116-118]. Yellow illus. wrps., adv. on inner front and
     entire back; front noting The Authorized Campaign Edition.

361 The Life ... of John Charles Fremont. New York: Livermore
     & Rudd, 1856.

     As in entry 360, but adv. p. [116] only. Peach wrps. as
     above.

362 Life of Col. Fremont. [New York: Greeley & M'Elrath,
     c1856.]

     Caption title. [1]-32. Sewn. Title vignette. Illus. in
     text. Copyright notice as in entry 359 at foot of p. [1]; pr.
     in dbl. cols. Copies also noted with "New York, Aug. 1st,
     1856" at foot of col. 2, p. 32. Also noted in buff illus.
     wrps., map on outer back.

363 [Life of Col. John Charles Fremont.] In New York Weekly
     Tribune, Vol. XV, No. 771, Saturday, June 21, 1856.

     8 pp. pr. in 6 cols. Newspaper. Report of the nomina-
     tion, platform and proceedings of Republican Convention,
     port. of Fremont, p. [1]; biog. of Fremont, p. 4, cols.
     2-3.

364 Life of Col. John Charles Fremont, "The Pathfinder of the
     Rocky Mountains." Middleboro: Pratt & Beals, 1856.

T. [1], bl. [2], [3]-36.   Blue wrps. , all copies examined
lacking entire back.

365 The Life of Fremont. Only Unauthorised Edition.   [New York:]
     Published by Levison & Haney; Ross & Tousey, Agents
     [1856.]

     Cover title [1], bl. [2], [5 sic]-17, adv. [18].   Sewn.   Title
     vignette.   Cartoon illus. in text.   Anti-Fremont.

366 Reminiscences of Past and Present Times.   The Old Demo-
     cratic Party, the Present Parties, Gen. Andrew Jackson
     ... Life of Col. John C. Fremont.   New York: J. Gros-
     venor, Agent, 1856.

     T. , [1], [2], [3]-48.   Buff wrps. , with lengthy note on front
     and outer back from pub.   Life of Fremont, pp. 37-40,
     "Written for the New York Sun, by Hon. Horace Greeley. "

367 Republican Campaign Edition for the Million.   Containing the
     Republican Platform, the Lives of Fremont and Dayton,
     With Beautiful Steel Portraits of Each, and Their Letters
     of Acceptance....   Boston: Published by John P. Jewett
     and Company; Cleveland: Jewett, Proctor and Worthington;
     New York: Sheldon, Blakeman and Company, 1856.

     2 pf. , t. [1], [2], 3-36, div. t. [1], bl. [2], 3-32, [33-36].
     Brown wrps. , electoral vote on inner front; reaction against
     Van Buren and Pierce on inner back; adv. on outer back.
     2 pf. inserted.   Biog. sketches, pp. 3-36; addenda, pp.
     [33-36] in 2nd half of work; quote by Fremont, p. [2].

368 Republican Campaign Edition for the Million....   Boston [etc.],
     1856.

     As in entry 367, but p. [2] reading: "Cambridge: Allen and
     Farnham, Stereotypers and Printers.   Press of Geo. C.
     Rand, Wood Cut and Book Printer, Cornhill, Boston. " set
     in 5 lines.

369 Republican Campaign Edition for the Million....   Boston [etc.],
     1856.

     As in entry 367, but p. [2] bl.

370 Republikanisches Handbuch für die millionen Deutsche in den
     Verein.   Staaten.   Enthalden die republikanische Platform,
     Biographien von Fremont und Dayton....   Boston: Heraus-
     gegeben von John P. Jewett u. Co. ; Cleveland: Jewett,
     Proctor u. Worthington; New York: Sheldon, Blakeman u.
     Co. , 1856.

     As in entry 367, but part II, 3-34, 35-36.   Burnt orange
     wrps. , adv. in English on outer back.   Ger. transl. of entry 367.

371 [Schmucker, Samuel M.] The Life of Col. John Charles Fre-
     mont, and His Narrative of Explorations and Adventures. ...
     The Memoir by Samuel M. Smucker. ... New York and
     Auburn: Miller, Orton & Mulligan, 1856.

     Pf. , t. [1], [2], [3]-4, [5]-72, [71 sic]-493, bl. [494], 4
     ℓ ℓ. adv. Red cloth. Pf. and 8 pls. inserted. Life of
     Fremont, pp. [5]-72; Fremont's narrative, pp. [71]-493.

372 _____. The Life of Col. John Charles Fremont. ... New
     York and Auburn: Miller, Orton & Mulligan, 1856.

     Life of Fremont, pp. [5]-69, bl. [70], narrative 71-493,
     adv. [494], ℓ. adv. Maroon cloth. Pf. and 4 pls. in-
     serted.

373 _____. The Life of Col. John Charles Fremont. ... New
     York and Auburn: Miller, Orton & Mulligan, 1856.

     Life of Fremont, pp. [5]-69, letter of acceptance, 69-72,
     narrative, [73]-493, bl. [494]. Black cloth. Pf. only,
     inserted.

374 Upham, Charles Wentworth. Life, Explorations and Public
     Services of John Charles Fremont. With Illustrations.
     Boston: Ticknor and Fields, M. DCCC. LVI.

     Pf. [i-ii], t. [iii], [iv], [v]-vi, [vii]-viii, 9-355, 356.
     Brown cloth. Pf. and 12 pls. inserted. P. 356 a poem.
     Also noted in maroon cloth with gold backstrip; and blue
     cloth with 12 pp. terminal pub. cat. dated July, 1856.

375 _____. Life ... of John Charles Fremont. ... Thirtieth
     Thousand. Boston: Ticknor and Fields, M. DCCC. LVI.

     As in entry 374, except appendix, pp. 356-365, poem, p.
     366, 2 flyleaves, endpaper, pub. cat. dated July, 1856,
     pp. [1]-[12]. Blue green cloth. Also noted with terminal
     pub. cat. dated August, 1856.

376 _____. Life ... of John Charles Fremont. ... Fortieth
     Thousand. Boston: Ticknor and Fields, M. DCCC. LVI.

     As in entry 375, terminal pub. cat. dated August, 1856.
     Maroon cloth.

377 _____. Life ... of John Charles Fremont. ... Forty-Fifth
     Thousand. Boston: Ticknor and Fields, M. DCCC. LVI.

     As in entry 376.

378 _____. Life ... of John Charles Fremont. ... Fiftieth
     Thousand. Boston: Ticknor and Fields, M. DCCC. LVI.

As in entry 375, but lacking terminal pub. cat.   Maroon cloth.

379   Woodworth, Francis C.   The Young American's Life of Fremont.... New York and Auburn: Miller, Orton & Mulligan, 1856.

Pf. [i-ii], t. [iii], [iv], [v]-vi, [vii]-xii, pl. , [13]-282, 3 ℓ ℓ. adv.   Red cloth.   Pf. and 1 pl. inserted, other illus. in text.

FILLMORE, MILLARD (American [Know-Nothing])

380   The American Text Book for the Campaign of 1856.   Baltimore: Published by Bull & Tuttle, "Clipper Office, " 1856.

Cover title [1], [2], bl. [3], [4], [5]-31, adv. [32].   Buff wrps. , sewn.   Lives of Fillmore and Donelson, pp. [5]-9.

381   Barre, W. L.   The Life and Public Services of Millard Fillmore.   Buffalo: Wanzer, McKim & Co. , 1856.

Pf. , t. [i], [ii], [iii]-vii, bl. [viii], [ix]-x, [11]-408.   Red cloth.   Pf. inserted.

382   [Chamberlain, Ivory.]   Biography of Millard Fillmore.   Buffalo: Thomas & Lathrops, Publishers, 1856.

Pf. , t. [i], [ii], [iii]-iv, [v]-xv, bl. [xvi], [17]-215, bl. [216].   Brown cloth.   Pf. inserted.   Also noted in tan wrps. , adv. on outer back.

383   .   Biography of Millard Fillmore.   Buffalo: Thomas & Lathrops; Auburn and New York: Miller, Orton & Mulligan, 1856.

As in entry 382.   Brown cloth.   Copy also noted in tan wrps. , adv. on outer back.

384   The Star Spangled Banner Life of Millard Fillmore.   [New York: R. M. DeWitt, 1856.]

Caption title.   [1]-32.   Sewn.   Title vignette.   Illus. in text.   At foot of p. [1], "R. M. DeWitt (late DeWitt & Davenport), Publisher, 160 & 162 Nassau St. , N. Y. [one line price information; one line imprints]. "   Lives of Fillmore and Donelson, pp. [1]-32, adv. in single col. , p. 32; pr. in dbl. cols.

385   The True American's Almanac and Politician's Manual, for 1857.   Edited by W. S. Tisdale.   New York: Robert M. DeWitt; W. H. Tinson, Printer and Stereotyper [1856.]

Cover title. [1], 2-3, [4-15], [16], 17-71, adv. [72]. Blue
illus. wrps., adv. on inner front and entire back. Title
vignette. Illus. in text. At head of title, Our God, Our
B ble [sic], The Union and the Constitution; life of Fillmore, pp. 21-22; of Donelson, pp. 26-27; pr. in dbl. cols.

386 [Williams, Edwin.] The Life and Administration of Ex-President Fillmore. (From Walker's Statesman's Manual.) ...
and a Sketch of the Life of Andrew Jackson Donelson, of
Tennessee. New York: Edward Walker, 1856.

Pf., t. [1], [2], [3]-39, adv. [40], prospectus and adv.
[41]-48. Lemon wrps., adv. on inner front, entire back
lacking in copies examined. Title vignette. Pf. inserted.
Life of Fillmore, pp. [9]-18; of Donelson, pp. [38]-39
from Leslie's Illustrated Paper.

CASS, LEWIS (Democratic)

387 Smith, W. L. G. Fifty Years of Public Life. The Life and
Times of Lewis Cass. With a Portrait on Steel. New
York: Derby & Jackson, 1856.

Pf., t. [i], [ii], [iii]-iv, [v]-xii, [13]-781, bl. [782]. Brown
cloth. Pf. inserted.

HOUSTON, SAMUEL (American [Know-Nothing])

388 Life of General Sam Houston. [Washington: Printed by J. T.
Towers, 1856.]

Caption title. [1]-15, bl. [16]. Sewn. At foot of p. 15,
"Printed by J. T. Towers, Washington, D. C."; pr. in
dbl. cols.

389 The Life of Sam Houston. (The Only Authentic Memoir of
Him Ever Published.) Illustrated. New York: J. C.
Derby; Boston: Phillips, Sampson & Co.; Cincinnati: H.
W. Derby, 1855.

Half title [i], bl. [ii], pf. [iii-iv], t. [v], [vi], [vii]-xi, bl.
[xii], [13]-402, 3 ℓℓ. adv. Maroon cloth. Pf. and 10 pls.
inserted.

LAW, GEORGE (American [Know-Nothing])

390 A Sketch of Events in the Life of George Law, Published in
Advance of His Biography. Also, Extracts From the Public
Journals. New York: J. C. Derby, Publisher, 1855.

T. [1], bl. [2], [3-4], [5]-23, [24], [25]-96. Lemon illus. wrps., outer front with 10 lines of pubs. and booksellers and imprint of printer and stereotyper; port. on inner front; adv. on inner back; song on outer back.

SEWARD, WILLIAM HENRY (Republican)

391 Baker, George E. The Life of William H. Seward With Selections From His Works. New York: [J. S.] Redfield, 1855.

Pf., t. [1], [2], [3]-4, [5]-11, bl. [12], [13]-170, div. t. [171], bl. [172], [173]-324, div. t. [325], bl. [326], [327]-400, [401]-404, [405]-410, adv. [1]-4, and [1]-4, [1-2]. Purple cloth. Pf. inserted. Life of Seward, pp. [13]-170; selections from works, pp. [173]-324; speeches, pp. [327]-400; appendix, pp. [401]-404; index, pp. [405]-410. Also noted in brown cloth with adv. pp. [1]-2, [1]-4, 3-4.

1860

GENERAL WORKS

392 [Bartlett, David Vandewater Golden.] Presidential Candidates: Containing Sketches, Biographical, Personal and Political, of Prominent Candidates for the Presidency in 1860. New York: A. B. Burdick, 1859.

T. [i], [ii], iii-iv, [v]-vi, 7-360. Brown cloth. Includes sketches of 21 candidates, but omits Lincoln.

393 The Lives of the Present Candidates for President and Vice President of the United States, Containing a Condensed and Impartial History of the Lives, Public Acts, and Political Views of the Present Candidates, With the Platforms of the Parties They Represent, Their Portraits.... Cincinnati: H. M. Rulison, Queen City Publishing House; Philadelphia: D. Rulison, Quaker City Publishing House; St. Louis: C. Drew & Co.; Geneva: J. Whitley, Jr. [1860?]

T. [i], [ii], 3-139, bl. [140], adv. 1-4. Salmon (buff) illus. wrps., 33 state seals on inner front and entire back. Illus. in text. Lives of Bell and Everett, Lincoln and Hamlin, Douglas and Johnson, and Breckinridge and Lane. Wessen 15 notes copy with imprint, Cincinnati: Mack R. Barnitz, 1860.

394   Portraits and Sketches of the Lives of All the Candidates for
the Presidency and Vice-Presidency, for 1860.   Comprising
Eight Portraits Engraved on Steel, Facts in the Life of
Each.. ..   New York: J. C. Buttre, 1860.

T. [1], bl. [2], port. , [3]-[25], bl. [26], 15 [sic]-32, 2 ℓ ℓ.
advs.   Cream wrps. , adv. on entire back.   8 pls. inserted.   Lives of Lincoln and Hamlin, Bell and Everett,
Douglas and Johnson, and Breckinridge and Lane.   Wessen
16.

395   Wells' Illustrated National Campaign Hand-Book for 1860.   Part
First. Embracing the Lives of All the Candidates for President and Vice-President. . ..   With Portraits of Each. . ..
57 Illustrations.   New York: J. G. Wells; Cincinnati:
Mack R. Barnitz, 1860.

Flyleaf [1-2], half title [3], f. [4], t. [5], [6], [7], bl. [8],
[9], bl. [10], illus. [11], bl. [12], 13-199, bl. [200]; Part
II: bl. [i], f. [ii], t. [iii], bl. [iv], [v-vi], [9]-159, bl.
[160].   Blue cloth.   Illus. in text.   Lives of Bell and
Everett, Lincoln and Hamlin, Douglas and Johnson, Breckinridge and Lane, and Sam Houston.   Wessen 14 notes
black cloth.

LINCOLN, ABRAHAM (Republican)

396   Barrett, Joseph Hartwell.   Barrett's Authentic Edition.   Life
of Abraham Lincoln, (of Illinois.) With a Condensed View
of His Most Important Speeches; Also a Sketch of the Life
of Hannibal Hamlin (of Maine.)   Cincinnati: Moore, Wilstach, Keys & Co. , 1860.

Pf. , t. [i], [ii], [iii], bl. [iv], v-viii, 9-193, 194, port. ,
195-216.   Salmon wrps. , National Republican Platform on
inner front and back, adv. on outer back.   Pf. and 1 pl.
inserted.   Life of Lincoln, pp. 9-193; of Hamlin, pp. 195-
216.   Wessen 10 notes adv. on inner front and entire back
of wrps.   Copy also noted in maroon cloth with first state
of the port. of Lincoln, "lith Cin. O. " clearly evident despite what Wessen notes, p. 18.

397   _____ .   Barrett's Authentic Edition. . ..   Indianapolis: Ash-
er & Company; Cincinnati: Moore, Wilstach, Keys & Co. ,
1860.

As in entry 396.   Brown cloth.   Wessen 10, Variant A.

*398   [Bartlett, David Vandewater Golden.]   The Life and Public Ser-
vices of Hon. Abraham Lincoln.   New York: H. Dayton,
Publisher, 1860.

T. [1], [ii], [iii], bl. [iv], v-vi, [15]-150.   Pale blue, buff,
tan and light brown illus. wrps. noted, adv. on inner front
and entire back.   See Wessen 2 for this and variants.

399 _____ .   Authorized Edition.   The Life and Public Services
of Hon. Abraham Lincoln.   New York: H. Dayton, Publisher, 1860.

T. , copyright notice on verso, [15]-150.   Tan illus. wrps. ,
as in Wessen 2 except inner front bl.   Copies noted with
imprint, New York: Derby & Jackson, Publishers, 1860,
and wrps. as described.   Wessen 2 "Second (Revised) Edition. "

*400 _____ .   The Life and Public Services of Hon. Abraham
Lincoln ... to Which Is Added a Biographical Sketch of
Hon. Hannibal Hamlin.   New York: H. Dayton, Publisher,
1860.

For this and variant, see Wessen 7.

401 _____ .   Authorized Edition.   The Life and Public Services
of Hon. Abraham Lincoln, With a Portrait on Steel.   To
Which Is Added a Biographical Sketch of Hon. Hannibal
Hamlin.   New York: H. Dayton, Publisher, 1860.

Pf. , [i-ii], t. [iii], [iv], [v]-vii, bl. [viii], [15]-354.   Blue
cloth, backstrip reads Life and Speeches of Abraham Lincoln (not recorded by Wessen).   Also noted under imprint
of Derby & Jackson, and in black, green, tan, brown, and
maroon cloths.   Wessen 7 "Second (Revised) Edition. "   For
Variants A-F, all examined, see Wessen, above.   Blue
cloth, not recorded by Wessen, also noted for copies of
Variant F.

*402 Codding, Ichabod.   A Republican Manual for the Campaign.
Facts for the People: The Whole Argument in One Book.
Princeton, Ill. :   Printed at the "Republican" Book and Job
Printing Office, 1860.

See Wessen 5.

*403 Fry, William Henry.   The Republican "Campaign" Text-Book
for 1860.   New York: A. B. Burdick, Publisher, 1860.

108 pp. , wrps.   Sabin 26101.

404 Hanes Bywyd Abraham Lincoln, o Illinois, a Hannibal Hamlin,
o Maine, yr Ymgeiswyr Gwerinol am yr Arlywyddiaeth a'r
Is-Lywyddiaeth; yn Nghyd a'r Araeth a Draddododd Mr.
Lincoln yn Cooper's Institute, N. Y. , ar y 27 o Chwefror,
1860.   Hefyd, yr Esgynlawr Gwerinol, yn Nghyd a Chan
Etholiadol.   Utica: David C. Davies, Argraffydd a Chyhoed-
dydd, 1860.

Cover title [1], song [2], [3]-16.   Sewn.   Title vignette.
Pr. in dbl. cols.   Life of Lincoln in Welsh.   Wessen 20.

405   Hanes Bywyd Abraham Lincoln, o Illinois, a Hannibal Hamlin,
o Maine; yr Ymgeisyddion Gwerinaidd am Arlywydd ac Isly-
wydd yr Unol Dalaethau, Erbyn yr Etholiad yn Tachwedd,
1860; yn Nghyd a Golygiadau ac Egwyddorion y Gwerinwyr,
&c.   Pottsville, Pa. : Argraffwyd gan B. Bannan, swyddfa
y "Miners' Journal, " 1860.

Cover title [1], [2]-16.   Sewn.   Title vignette.   Pr. in dbl.
cols.   Wessen 21.

406   [Hinton, Richard Josiah.]   Wide-Awake Edition.   The Life and
Public Services of Hon. Abraham Lincoln, of Illinois, and
Hon. Hannibal Hamlin, of Maine.   Boston: Thayer &
Eldridge, 1860.

Pf. , t. [1], [2], [3]-5 bl. [6], [7]-12, [13]-102, port. , div.
t. [103], port. [104], [105]-106, [107]-128, div. t. [129],
bl. [130], [131]-308, div. t. [309], bl. [310], [311]-318,
319-320.   Plum cloth.   Pf. and 1 pl. inserted.   Life of
Lincoln, pp. [13]-102; of Hamlin, pp. [107]-128; speeches
of Lincoln, pp. [131]-308; speech of Hamlin, pp. [311]-318;
acceptance letters, pp. 319-320.   Also noted in green,
black, and brown cloths.   Wessen 8.

407   Hon. Abram [sic] Lincoln, of Illinois.   Republican Candidate
for President.   In Harper's Weekly, Vol. IV, No. 178,
May 26, 1860.

Pp. [321]-322, pr. in 4 cols. , port.   Copies noted removed
and matted.   Concludes with sketch of Hamlin; port. of
Hamlin, p. 340, in June 2, 1860, issue.

408   Howard, James Quay.   The Life of Abraham Lincoln: With
Extracts From His Speeches.   Columbus: Follett, Foster
and Company, 1860.

T. [1], [2], [3]-102, bl. ℓ., 4 ℓℓ. adv. Orange wrps. ,
adv. on inner front and back, illus. on outer back.   For
comments on supposed variants, see Wessen 13.

*409 _____ .   Das Leben von Abraham Lincoln, nebst auszugen
aus seinen Reden.   Aus dem englischen von J. Q. Howard,
Uebersezt druch Professor Wilhelm Grauert.   Columbus:
Follett, Foster und Compagnie, 1860.

See Wessen 18.

*410   [Howells, William Dean.]   Lives and Speeches of Abraham Lincoln
and Hannibal Hamlin.   Columbus: Follett, Foster & Co., 1860.

170 pp.   See Wessen 9.

411 _____ . Lives and Speeches of Abraham Lincoln and Hannibal Hamlin. Columbus: Follett, Foster & Co. , 1860.

Half title [1], bl. [2], pf. , t. [3], [4], 5, bl. [6], 7, bl.
[8], div. t. [9], bl. [10] xi-xii, xiii-xv, bl. [xvi], 17-94,
bl. [95], illus. [96], div. t. 97, bl. [98], 99-111, bl.
[112], div. t. 113, bl. [114], 115-304, port. , div. t. 305,
bl. [306], 307-406. Brown cloth. Pf. and 1 pl. inserted.
Life of Lincoln, pp. 17-94; speeches of Lincoln, pp. 115-
304; Hayes's Hamlin, pp. 307-406, incl. speeches. Cloths
noted in black, red, plum, green, blue, maroon, and tan.
For Variants A-G, see Wessen 11; for further reference
see BAL, Vol. 4, 9538.

412 Das Leben von Abraham Lincoln, nebst einer kurzen Skizze
des Lebens von Hannibal Hamlin. Republikanische Candidaten für Präsident und Vice-Präsident der vereinigten
Staaten.... Chicago: Druck von Hoeffgen und Schneider,
1860.

T. [1], bl. [2], [3]-108. Cream illus. wrps. , quote in
German by Lincoln on inner front, adv. on entire back.
Wessen 17.

413 Lewis, Joseph J. Lincoln's Kalamazoo Address Against Extending Slavery. Also His Life by Joseph J. Lewis, Both
Annotated by Thomas I. Starr. Detroit Fine Book Circle,
1941.

Half title [1], bl. [2], t. [3], [4], [5], bl. [6], [7-8], [9]-
31, bl. [32], [33]-46, [47]-49, bl. [50], [51]-63, [64].
Blue cloth. Fac. letter and 2 pls. inserted. Title vignette. Address, pp. [35]-46; life of Lincoln, pp. [51]-63;
colophon, p. [64]. Ltd. to 1000 copies, designed by Paul
McPharlin and printed at the Blue Ox Press. First published life of Lincoln written by Lewis and printed unsigned
in the Chester County Times, at Westchester, Pa. , February 11, 1860. Also noted in blue illus. wrps. , ltd. to
250 copies.

414 The Life and Public Services of Hon. Abraham Lincoln, of
Illinois, and Hon. Hannibal Hamlin, of Maine. Boston:
Thayer & Eldridge, 1860.

Pf. , t. [1], [2], [3]-5, bl. [6], [7]-12, [13]-102, div. t.
[103], port. [104], [105]-106, [107]-128. Green illus.
wrps. , adv. on inner front and entire back. Life of Lincoln, pp. [13]-102; of Hamlin, pp. [107]-128. Wessen 3
("first edition. ").

415 The Life ... of Hon. Abraham Lincoln.... Boston: Thayer
& Eldridge, 1860.

Pf. , t. [1], [2], [3]-4, [5]-8, [9]-101, port. [102], t. [103], bl. [104], [105]-106, [107]-128. Green wrps. , as above. Life of Lincoln, pp. [9]-101; of Hamlin, pp. [107]-128. Wessen 3 ("Second [Emasculated] Edition").

416   The Life, Speeches, and Public Services of Abram [sic] Lincoln, Together With a Sketch of the Life of Hannibal Hamlin. Republican Candidates for the Offices of President and Vice-President of the United States. New York: Rudd & Carleton, M DCCC LX.

Bl. [1], pf. [2], t. [3], [4], [5]-110 div. t. [111], bl. [112], [113]-117, bl. [118], adv. i-ii. Salmon illus. wrps. , adv. on inner front and entire back; front (and t.) noting The "Wigwam Edition. " Life of Lincoln, pp. [5]-110; of Hamlin, pp. [113]-117. For Variants A-E, see Wessen 1. Copies also noted with additional wrps. imprints: Springfield, Mass.: M. Bessey & Co.; and Lancaster, Pa.: Elias Barr & Co. , both unrecorded in Wessen.

417   New-Yorker Demokrat. Flugblatt No. 9. Das Leben Von Abraham Lincoln. [N. p. , n. d. , 1860?]

Caption title. [1]-16. Sewn. Illus. in text.

418   [Scripps, John Locke.] Life of Abraham Lincoln. [Chicago: Chicago Press and Tribune Co. c1860.]

Caption title. [1]-32. Sewn. At lower margin of p. [1], copyright notice set in 2 lines; pr. in dbl. cols. , incl. adv. which takes up lower 2/3 of p. 32. First edition; in second edition, adv. , on p. 32 set in single col. Wessen 12.

418a   . Tribune Tracts. No. 6. Life of Abraham Lincoln. [New York: Horace Greeley & Co. c1860.]

Caption title. [1]-32. Sewn. At lower margin of p. [1], copyright notice set in 2 lines; pr. in dbl. cols.; adv. which takes up lower 2/3 of p. 32 set in single col. Wessen 12, "New York Edition. "

419   Vose, Reuben. Leben, Wirken und Reden des republicanischen Präsidentschafts-Candidaten Abraham Lincoln. Nach den Beften americanischen Quellen: D. W. Bartlett, Reuben Vose u. a. Deutsch Bearbeitet. New York: Bei Freidrich Gerhard, 1860.

T. [1], [2], 3-106. Buff illus. wrps. , numbered [1]-4, but not part of text; inner front and back pr. , adv. on outer back. Wessen 19.

420   . The Life and Speeches of Abraham Lincoln, and Hannibal Hamlin, Edited and Published by Reuben Vose ... New York. New York: Hilton, Gallaher & Co. [c1860.]

Cover title [i], [ii], iii-Li, 42 [sic]-118, 2 ℓℓ. adv. lettered A-D.   Tan wrps. , copyright notice on inner front, adv. on entire back.   Wessen 6.

421   Washburne, E. B.   Abraham Lincoln, His Personal History and Public Record.   Speech of ... Delivered in the U. S. House of Representatives, May 29, 1860.   [N. p.] Published by the Republican Congressional Committee [1860.]

Caption title.   [1]-8.   Sewn.   At foot of p. [1], "Published by the Republican Congressional Committee.   Price 50 Cents per Hundred. "; pr. in dbl. cols.   Wessen 4.

DOUGLAS, STEPHEN A.   (Northern Democratic)

*422   Biographical Sketch of Stephen A. Douglas.   [Washington: Printed by Towers, 1860?]

Caption title.   8 pp.   Sabin 20696 (note).

423   Biographie von Stephan Arnold Douglas.   Präsidentschafts-Candidaten der americanischen Democratie.   Herausgegeben von der National-Executiv-Committee.   New York: Gedruckt in der Office der "New-Yorker Staats-Zeitung" [1860.]

Cover title [1], [2], [3]-32.   Sewn.   Pr. in dbl. cols.

424   [Flint, Henry Martyn.]   Life of Stephen A. Douglas, United States Senator From Illinois.   With His Most Important Speeches and Reports.   By a Member of the Western Bar. New York: Derby & Jackson, Publishers; Chicago: D. B. Cooke & Co. , 1860.

Half title [i], bl. [ii], pf. , t. [iii], [iv], [v], bl. [vi], [vii]-xi, bl. [xii], [13]-270, [4]-187, bl. [188].   Purple gold cloth.   Pf. inserted.   Life of Douglas, pp. [13]-270; speeches, pp. [4]-187.   Also noted in brown cloth.

425   _____ .   Life of Stephen A. Douglas.... New York: Derby & Jackson, Publishers; Chicago: D. B. Cooke & Co. , 1860.

As in entry 424, except [vii]-x, [13]-264, div. t. [1], bl. [2], [3]-187, bl. [188], 2 ℓℓ. adv.   Green cloth.

426   _____ .   Life of Stephen A. Douglas.... New York: Derby & Jackson, Publishers; Chicago: D. B. Cooke & Co. , 1860.

Half title [i], bl. [ii], t. [iii], [iv], [v], bl. [vi], [vii]-x, [13]-264.   Lemon illus. wrps. , adv. for expanded version on inner front, adv. on entire back.

427   . Life of Stephen A. Douglas.... New York: H.
Dayton, Publisher, 1860.

As in entry 425, but lacking 2 ℓℓ. adv. All copies examined rebound.

428   . Life of Stephen A. Douglas to Which Are Added His
Speeches and Reports. By H. M. Flint. Philadelphia: The
Keystone Publishing Company [1860?]

T. [1], [2], 3-4, [v]-viii, 9-222, [3]-218. Brown cloth.
At head of title, Authorized Edition; life of Douglas, pp. 9-
222; speeches, pp. [3]-218.

429   . Life of Stephen A. Douglas, United States Senator
From Illinois. With His Most Important Speeches and Re-
ports. By H. M. Flint. New York: Derby & Jackson,
Publishers, 1860.

T. [i], [ii], [iii], bl. [iv], [v]-viii, [9]-215, bl. [216].
Salmon illus. wrps., adv. on inner front and entire back.
At head of title, Authorized Edition.

430   . Life of Stephen A. Douglas.... New York: Derby
& Jackson, Publishers, 1860.

As in entry 429, but bl. [216], [3]-187, bl. [188]. Purple
gold cloth. Pf. inserted. Speeches, pp. [3]-187.

*431 Life of Stephen A. Douglas, U. S. Senator From Illinois.
Baltimore: John P. Des Forges, 1860.

12 pp. Sabin 20695.

432 Sheahan, James W. The Life of Stephen A. Douglas. New
York: Harper & Brothers, Publishers, 1860.

Bl. [i], pf. [ii], t. [iii], [iv], [v], bl. [vi], [vii]-xi, bl.
[xii], [1]-528, 6 ℓℓ. adv. Brown cloth.

433 Warden, Robert. A Voter's Version of the Life and Character
of Stephen Arnold Douglas. Columbus: Follett, Foster and
Company, 1860.

T. [1], [2], [3]-15, bl. [16], div. t. [17], bl. [18], 19-69,
bl. [70], div. t. [71], bl. [72], 73-112, div. t. [113], bl.
[114], 115-128, 129-131, bl. [132]. Purple cloth. Text,
part I, pp. 19-69; part II, pp. 73-112; part III, pp. 115-
128; index, pp. 129-131. Also noted in brown cloth.

BRECKINRIDGE, JOHN C. (Southern Democratic)

434 Breckinridge and Lane Campaign Document, No. 8.   Biographi-
     cal Sketches of Hon. John C. Breckinridge, Democratic
     Nominee for President, and General Joseph Lane, Demo-
     cratic Nominee for Vice President. Washington: Issued by
     the National Democratic Executive Committee; McGill &
     Witherow, Printers, 1860.

     Cover title [1], bl. [2], [3]-32. Sewn. Illus. (ports.) in
     text.

435 Breckinridge and Lane Campaign Document, No. 8.... Wash-
     ington City: Issued by the National Democratic Executive
     Committee, 1860.

     Cover title, [1], bl. [2], port. [3], bl. [4], 5-32. Sewn.
     Illus. (ports.) in text.

*436 Portraits and Sketches of John C. Breckinridge and Joseph
     Lane, Together With the National Democratic Platform....
     New York: J. C. Buttre, 1860.

     Cover title, 32 pp. Separately issued from entry 394?
     Sabin 64406.

BELL, JOHN (Constitutional Union)

437 John Bell: His "Past History Connected With the Public Ser-
     vice." [Nashville: Printed at the Union and American Of-
     fice, 1860.]

     Caption title. [1]-40. Sewn. At foot of p. 40, "Printed
     at the Union and American Office, Nashville, Tennessee,
     for the Democratic State Central Committee."; pr. in dbl.
     cols. Anti-Bell.

438 The Life, Speeches, and Public Services of John Bell, Together
     With a Sketch of the Life of Edward Everett. Union Can-
     didates for the Offices of President and Vice-President of
     the United States. New York: Rudd & Carleton, M DCCC
     LX.

     Bl. [1], pf. [2], t. [3], [4], [5]-96, [97]-101, 102-118.
     Pink illus. wrps., adv. on inner front, entire back lacking
     on all copies examined. At head of title, The "Union Edi-
     tion."; life of Bell, pp. [5]-96; of Everett, pp. [97]-101.

*439 Who Is John Bell? [N. p., 1860.]

     4 pp. Sabin 4463.

FREMONT, JOHN CHARLES (Republican)

*440 [Schmucker, Samuel.] The Life of Col. John Charles Fre-
         mont.... New York: C. M. Saxton, Barker & Co.; San
         Francisco: H. H. Bancroft & Co., 1860.

         72, 71-493 pp.   Sabin 85161.

SEWARD, WILLIAM HENRY (Republican)

*441 The Life of William H. Seward, Including His Most Famous
         Speeches. By a Jeffersonian Republican. Boston: Thayer
         and Eldridge, 1860.

         144 pp.   Sabin 79598.

1864

GENERAL WORKS

442 Hiatt, J. M. The Political Manual, Comprising Numerous Im-
        portant Documents Connected With the Political History of
        America, Compiled From Official Records, With Biographi-
        cal Sketches and Comments. Indianapolis: Asher & Adams,
        1864.

        Bl. [1], f. [2], [3], [4], 5-238, [239], adv. [240]. Black
        cloth. Illus. in text. Ports. and sketches of candidates,
        pp. 145-164; p. [239] numbered as 237.

LINCOLN, ABRAHAM (Republican)

443 Abott, Abott A. The Life of Abraham Lincoln. New York:
        T. R. Dawley, Publisher for the Million, 1864.

        T., copyright notice on verso, [11]-100, 2 ℓℓ. adv. Yel-
        low illus. wrps., adv. on inner front and entire back.

444 Abraham Africanus I. His Secret Life, as Revealed Under the
        Mesmeric Influence. Mysteries of the White House. New
        York: J. F. Feeks, Publishers [c1864.]

        T. [1], [2], [3], 4-57, adv. [58-60]. Yellow coated illus.
        wrps., adv. on inner front and back, outer back bl. Title
        vignette. Illus. in text. Text in verse and narrative.
        Anti-Lincoln.

*445 Abraham Lincoln and Ulysses S. Grant: Their Character and
      Constitution Scientifically Explained, With Engravings....
      San Francisco, Published by A. F. Röllner, Practical
      Phrenologist, 1864.

      15 pp. A phrenological description of Lincoln. Monaghan
      268; Sabin 41170.

446   Address by the Union League of Philadelphia, to the Citizens
      of Pennsylvania, in Favor of the Re-Election of Abraham
      Lincoln. Philadelphia: King & Baird, Printers, 1864.

      Cover title [1], bl. [2], [3]-28, 29-30, bl. ℓ. Green
      wrps. ?

447   Barrett, Joseph H. Life of Abraham Lincoln, Presenting His
      Early History, Political Career, and Speeches in and Out
      of Congress; Also a General View of His Policy as Presi-
      dent of the United States; With His Messages, Proclama-
      tions, Letters, etc., and a Concise History of the War.
      Cincinnati: Moore, Wilstach & Baldwin, 1864.

      Pf., t. [i], [ii], 3-iv, 5-viii, 9-483, 484-518, 5 ℓℓ. adv.
      All copies examined rebound. Pf. inserted. Preface, pp.
      3-iv, dated May 14, 1864.

448   [Hudson, Charles.] Character of Abraham Lincoln, and the
      Constitutionality of His Emancipation Policy. [N. p., n.
      d., 1863?]

      Caption title. [1]-16. Sewn.

449   _____. Character of Abraham Lincoln, President of the
      United States. [N. p., n. d., 1863.]

      Caption title. [1]-16. Sewn.

450   Old Abe's Jokes. Fresh From Abraham's Bosom Containing
      All Iis [sic] Issues, Excepting the "Greenbacks," to Call
      in Some of Which, This Work Is Issued. New York: T.
      R. Dawley, Publisher [c1864.]

      T. [i], [ii], [21]-135, bl. [136]. Light yellow illus. wrps.,
      adv. on inner front and entire back. Port. between pp.
      38-39, inserted (misplaced pf. ?). Life of Lincoln, pp.
      [21]-27; anecdotes, pp. 27-135.

451   Old Abe's Jokes.... New York: T. R. Dawley, Publisher
      [c1864.]

      As in entry 450, but pf., inserted, and anecdotes, pp. 27-
      140, ℓ. adv.

452 Only Authentic Life of Abraham Lincoln, Alias "Old Abe. " A
     Son of the West. Also of Gen. Geo. B. McClellan, Alias
     "Little Mac. " With an Account of His Numerous Victories,
     From Phillipi to Antietam. The Two Lives in One Volume.
     New York: Published by J. C. Haney [1864.]

     Cover title. [1]-16, [1]-16. Orange coated illus. wrps. ,
     adv. on outer back. Title vignette. Illus. in text. Life
     of Lincoln, pp. [1]-16; of McClellan, pp. [1]-16. Both
     lives reissued separately. Burlesque lives.

453 Only Authentic Life of Abraham Lincoln, Alias "Old Abe. " A
     Son of the West. With an Account of His Birth and Educa-
     tion, His Rail-Splitting and Flat-Boating, His Joke-Cutting
     and Soldiering, With Some Allusions to His Journeys From
     Springfield to Washington and Back Again. [New York?
     J. C. Haney & Co. ? 1864?]

     Cover title. [1]-16. Orange coated illus. wrps. , as
     above. Pr. in larger type size than above. Title vignette.
     Monaghan 336 notes "four cover variants. "

454 [Portrait, Character and Biography of Candidate Abraham Lin-
     coln.] In American Phrenological Journal and Life Illus-
     trated, Vol. 40, Number 4, Whole Number 310, New York,
     October, 1864.

     Pp. [97]-98. Copies noted removed and matted.

455 Raymond, Henry J. History of the Administration of President
     Lincoln: Including His Speeches, Letters, Addresses,
     Proclamations, and Messages. With a Preliminary Sketch
     of His Life. New York: J. C. Derby & N. C. Miller,
     1864.

     Pf. , t. [1], [2], [3]-4, [5]-6, [13]-50, div. t. [51], bl.
     [52], [53]-484, [485]-492, [493]-496, ℓ. adv. Maroon
     cloth. Pf. inserted. Life of Lincoln, pp. [13]-50; history
     of administration, pp. [53]-484; appendix, pp. [485]-492;
     index, pp. [493]-496. Copies also noted in black cloth;
     other copies noted with 4 ℓ ℓ. adv. For variants in termi-
     nal adv. , see Monaghan 347.

456 _____ . The Life of Abraham Lincoln, of Illinois, By ...
     and the Life of Andrew Johnson, of Tennessee. By John
     Savage. New York: Derby and Miller, 1864.

     Adv. [1], [2], t. [3], [4], [5]-83, bl. [84], 85-136, 4 ℓ ℓ.
     adv. Brown green illus. wrps. , inner front and back with
     adv. , port. on outer back. Life of Lincoln, pp. [5]-83; of
     Johnson, pp. 85-136.

457 _____ . The Life of Abraham Lincoln. New York:
     Derby and Miller, 1864.

T., copyright notice on verso, [5]-83, bl. [84], 85-136, 5
ℓ ℓ. adv. Wrps. as above.

458 _____ . The Life of Abraham Lincoln ... and of Andrew
Johnson, by John Savage. New York: National Union Executive Committee [1864].

Cover title. [5]-83, adv. [84], 85-136. Brown illus.
wrps., inner front and back bl. Title vignette. Text as
in entry 456.

459 Thayer, William M. The Character and Public Services of
Abraham Lincoln, President of the United States.... Boston: Walker, Wise, and Company, 1864.

Pf., f., t. [i], [ii], iii, bl. [iv], div. t. [v], bl. [vi],
[vii], bl. [viii], 9-76, bl. [77], adv. [78]. Pink illus.
wrps., adv. on outer back. Pf. and f. inserted.

460 _____ . The Character ... of Abraham Lincoln.... Boston:
Dinsmoor and Company, 1864.

Pf. [1-2], f. [3-4], t. [5], [6], [7], bl. [8], 9-75, adv.
[76], ℓ. adv. Buff illus. wrps., adv. on inner front and
entire back; front notes The "Campaign Document." Copies
also noted in pink wrps. as above.

461 _____ . Life and Character of Abraham Lincoln. Boston:
Walker, Wise, and Company, 1864.

Adv., recto bl., pf., f., t. [i], [ii], iii-[iv], div. t. [v],
bl. [vi], [vii], bl. [viii], 9-310, ℓ. adv. Red cloth. Pf.
and f. inserted. Also noted in pink wrps., adv. on outer
back; front noting The "Campaign Document." and citing
title as Character and Public Services of Abraham Lincoln.
Monaghan 354 also notes imprint, Boston: Dinsmoor and
Company, 1864.

*462 Victor, Orville James. The Private and Public Life of Abra-
ham Lincoln; Comprising a Full Account of His Early
Years, and a Succinct Record of His Career as Statesman
and President. New York: Beadle and Adams, Publishers
[1864.]

96 pp., other copies, 98 pp. See Monaghan 362, 363.

463 [Williamson, David Brainerd.] Life and Public Services of
Abraham Lincoln. Sixteenth President of the United
States.... With a Full History of His Life ... Up to the
Present Time. Philadelphia: T. B. Peterson & Brothers
[c1864.]

T., copyright notice on verso, 17-20, 21-187, adv. [188].
Brown cloth. Copies also noted in brown and maroon

cloths with pf. inserted and pub. cat. 1-17, ℓ. adv. Monaghan 366 also cites copy in wrps.

464   A Workingman's Reasons for the Re-Election of Abraham Lincoln. [N. p., n. d., 1864.]

Caption title. [1]-8. Sewn.

McCLELLAN, GEORGE B. (Democratic)

465   Addey, Markinfield. "Little Mac," and How He Became a Great General: A Life of George Brinton McClellan, for Young Americans. With Illustrations. New York: James G. Gregory, M DCCC LXIV.

F., eng. t., t. [1], [2], [3], bl. [4], [5]-10, 11-352. All copies examined rebound. F., eng. t., and 4 pls. inserted. Preface, p. [3], dated Oct. 1864.

466   A Brief Sketch of the Life and History of General McClellan, With Incidents in His Illustrious Career. [New York? 1864?]

Caption title. 1-10, bl. ℓ. Sewn. Pr. in dbl. cols.

467   Delmar, Alexander. The Life of Geo. B. McClellan, by Alex'r Delmar.... New York: T. R. Dawley, Publisher for the Million [c1864.]

T. [i], [ii], [11]-109, adv. [110], 3 $\ell\ell$. adv. Yellow illus. wrps., adv. on inner front and entire back.

468   Gallatin, James. Address by ... Before the Democratic Union Association, October 18, 1864. George B. McClellan as a Patriot, a Warrior, and a Statesman.... [N. p., n. d., 1864?]

Caption title. [1]-14, [16]. Sewn. Pr. in dbl. cols., pp. [15-16] in single cols.

469   Hillard, G. S. Life and Campaigns of George B. McClellan, Major-General U. S. Army. Philadelphia: J. B. Lippincott & Co., 1864.

Pf., t. [1], [2], 3, bl. [4], 5, bl. [6], 7-8, 9-373, bl. [374], 375-391, bl. [392], 393-396. Brown cloth. Pf. inserted. Appendix, pp. 375-391; index, pp. 393-396; t. in red and black.

470   Hurlbert, William Henry. General McClellan and the Conduct of the War. New York: Sheldon and Company, 1864.

F., t. [i], [ii], [iii]-iv, [v]-vii, bl. [viii], [9]-312.   All
copies examined rebound.   F. (map) and 3 maps (one fld.)
inserted.   Dated Sept. 27, 1864.   Despite disclaimers and
emphasis upon Civil War, this is a campaign biography.

471   The Life and Public Services of Major-General McClellan.
      Which Includes a Complete Summary of His Report.   Writ-
      ten by a Gentleman Who Accompanied Him Through His
      Campaigns.   Philadelphia: Martin & Randall, 1864.

      T. [1], [2], 3-77, 78-84.   Cream illus. wrps., adv. on
      outer back.

472   The Life and Services of Gen. Geo. B. McClellan.   Campaign
      Document, No. 4.   [N. p., n. d., 1864?]

      Cover title [1], 2-63, [64].   Sewn.   Quotes by McClellan,
      p. [64].   Copy in leather also noted with binding noting
      "Devised by Cyrus Mason.   Written by Wm. H. Hurlbut.
      Published by Rand & Avery."

473   The Life ... of Gen. Geo. B. McClellan....

      As in entry 472, but at head of title, Sold at 13 Park Row,
      New York, and at All Democratic Newspaper Offices, at $1
      per 1,000 Pages.

474   The Life, Campaigns, and Public Services of General McClel-
      lan.   George B. McClellan.   The Hero of Western Vir-
      ginia! ... With a Full History ... Up to the Present Time.
      Philadelphia: T. B. Peterson & Brothers [c1864.]

      T., copyright notice on verso, 17-18, 19-194, pub. cat. 1-
      9, adv. [10], ℓ. adv.   Illus. wrps., adv. on inner front
      and entire back.   Also noted in maroon cloth.

475   The Life ... of General McClellan....   Philadelphia: T. B.
      Peterson & Brothers [c1864.]

      Pf., t., copyright notice on verso, 17-18, 19-184, pub.
      cat. 1-19, adv. [20], ℓ. adv.   Maroon cloth.   Pf. in-
      serted.

476   Only Authentic Life of Geo. Brinton McClellan, Alias Little
      Mac.   With an Account of His Numerous Victories, From
      Phillipi to Antietam.   [New York:]   American News Com-
      pany Wholesale Agents [1864.]

      Cover title.   [1]-16.   Oranged coated illus. wrps., adv.
      on outer back.   Title vignette.   Illus. in text.   Burlesque
      life.

477   Richards, G. W.   A Brief History of the Rebellion, and a
      Life of Gen. McClellan; Containing Some Facts Never

Before Published. Philadelphia: Published by J. Magee, 1862.

T. [1], [2], 3-31, bl. [32]. Cream wrps., front and back pr. in red and blue, adv. on outer back; front noting at top, Liberty and Union Forever, at foot, copyright notice.

478 Sights and Notes: By a Looker on in Vienna. Dedicated to the Union Army! Washington: 1864.

Unpaged, 12 ℓℓ., cover title [1], bl. [2], [3-23], bl. [24]. Sewn. Title vignette. Illus. in text. Burlesque life in cartoons, poems, and text.

479 Sights and Notes: ... Seventh (of November) Edition. Copy, Righted and Corrected. Washington: 1864.

Unpaged, 9 ℓℓ., cover title [1], [2], [3-18]. Sewn. Title vignette. Illus. in text. As in entry 478.

480 Swinton, William. McClellan's Military Career Reviewed and Exposed: The Military Policy of the Administration Set Forth and Vindicated. Washington: Printed by Lemuel Towers, 1864.

Cover title [1], [2], [3]-32. Self wrps. Anti-McClellan; a condensation and revision of 12 articles appearing in the Times, February-March, 1864.

481 _____. McClellan's Military Career.... Washington: Published by the Union Congressional Committee; Printed by Lemuel Towers, 1864.

As in entry 480.

482 _____. The "Times" Review of McClellan: His Military Career Reviewed and Exposed. Revised From The N. Y. Times. New York: Published by the N. Y. Times, 1864.

Cover title [1], [2], [3]-32. Yellow wrps.

483 [Victor, Orville James.] The Life of Maj.-Gen. Geo. B. McClellan, General-in-Chief U. S. A. Including Services in Mexico ... by Louis Legrand, M. D. New York [and] London: Beadle and Company [c1862.]

Pf., t. [i], [ii], [iii], [iv], [9]-98. Dark yellow illus. wrps., adv. on inner front and entire back; front notes Beadle's Dime Biographical Library. No. 12. Title vignette.

484 Wilkes, George. McClellan: From Ball's Bluff to Antietam. New York: Sinclair Tousey, Wholesale Agent, 1863.

T. [1], [2], [3]-4, [5]-40. Cream wrps. , adv. on outer
back. Also noted in green wrps. Anti-McClellan.

485 _____ . McClellan: Who He Is and What He Has Done.
New York: Sinclair Tousey, Wholesale Agent, 1862.

T. [1], [2], [3]-12. Cream wrps. Originally appeared
August 4, 1862, in Wilkes' Spirit of the Times.

486 _____ . McClellan: Who He Is.... By George Wilkes,
Editor of "Wilkes' Spirit of the Times".... New York:
Sinclair Tousey, Wholesale Agent, 1863.

T. [1], [2], [3]-4, [5]-39, bl. [40]. Cream wrps.

487 _____ . "McClellan:" Who He Is and What He Has Done,
and Little Mac: "From Ball's Bluff to Antietam. " Both
in One. Revised by the Author. By an Old-Line Democrat.
New York: The American News Company [1864?]

T. [1], bl. [2], [3]-14, bl. ℓ. Pink wrps. , adv. on inner
front and entire back.

FREMONT, JOHN CHARLES (Independent Republican)

488 Denslow, Van Buren. Fremont and McClellan, Their Political
and Military Careers Reviewed.... Yonkers: Printed at
the Office of the Semi-Weekly Clarion, 1862.

T. [1], [2], [3], bl. [4], [5]-31, bl. [32]. Buff wrps. , adv.
on outer back. Pro-Fremont.

489 _____ . Fremont and McClellan.... Second Edition. Yonkers: Printed at the Office of the Semi-Weekly Clarion,
1862.

T. [1], [2], [3]-32. Buff wrps. , adv. on outer back.

BUTLER, BENJAMIN FRANKLIN (Republican)

490 Life and Public Services of Major-General Butler. (Benjamin
F. Butler.) The Hero of New Orleans.... Philadelphia:
T. B. Peterson & Brothers [c1864.]

T. [i], [ii], 17-18, 19-108, ℓ. adv. Illus. wrps. , adv. on
inner front and entire back.

GRANT, ULYSSES SIMPSON (Republican)

491 [Denison, Charles Wheeler.] The Tanner-Boy and How He Became Lieutenant-General. By Major Penniman. Fifth

<u>Thousand</u>. Boston: Roberts Brothers, Publishers, 1864.

F., t. [i], [ii], [iii], bl. [iv], v-vi, vii-viii, 9-316. Green cloth. F. and 3 pls. inserted. Also noted in blue cloth.

492 _____. The Tanner-Boy.... <u>Tenth Thousand</u>. Boston: Roberts Brothers, Publishers [1864.]

As in entry 491, but text, pp. 9-336. Terra-cotta cloth. Also noted in green cloth.

493 Headley, P. C. <u>The Hero Boy; Or, the Life and Deeds of Lieut. -Gen. Grant</u>. New York: William H. Appleton, 1864.

T. [i], [ii], [i], [ii], [iii]-iv, [v]-ix, bl. [x], 1-336, [337]-340. All copies examined rebound. F. and 8 pls. inserted (copies examined lack f. and pl. before t.).

494 Larke, Julian K. <u>General Grant and His Campaigns</u>. Illustrated With a Portrait on Steel.... New York: J. C. Derby & N. C. Miller, 1864.

Pf., t. [1], [2], [3]-4, [5]-12, [13]-469, bl. [470], div. t. [1], bl. [2], [3]-40, 3 ℓℓ. adv. Green cloth. Pf. and 4 pls. inserted. Appendices, pp. [3]-40.

495 _____. <u>General Grant</u>.... New York: J. C. Derby & N. C. Miller, 1864.

As in entry 494, but text [13]-473, bl. [474], appendices, pp. [3]-40, 2 ℓℓ. adv. Brown cloth.

496 <u>The Life and Services as a Soldier of Major-General Grant, the Hero of Fort Donelson!</u>... Philadelphia: T. B. Peterson & Brothers [c1864.]

T. [i], [ii], 19-66, pub. cat. 1-[14]. Illus. wrps., adv. on inner front and entire back.

497 Stansfield, F. W. H. <u>The Life of Gen'l. U. S. Grant, the General in Chief of the United States Army</u>. New York: T. R. Dawley, Publishlr [sic] [c1864.]

T. [i], [ii], [iii], bl. [iv], [17]-104, 2 ℓℓ. adv. Light yellow illus. wrps., adv. on inner front and entire back. Copies also noted with different adv. matter on terminal 2 ℓℓ.

1868

GENERAL WORKS

498   Brockett, Linus P.   Men of Our Day; Or, Biographical Sketches
of Patriots, Orators ... Including Those Who in Military,
Political, Business and Social Life Are the Prominent Leaders of the Time in This Country.... Elegantly Illustrated
With Forty-Two Portraits. Philadelphia, Cincinnati, Chicago [and] St. Louis: Published by Zeigler, McCurdy &
Co., 1868.

F., t. [i], [ii], iii-v, bl. [vi], vii, bl. [viii], ix-xxiv, 17-
653, bl. [654]. Black cloth. F. and 5 pls. inserted.
Preface, pp. iii-v, dated March, 1868. Includes 42 biog.
sketches, many of which deal with potential 1868 Presidential candidates.

499   McPhetres, S. A.   A Political Manual for the Campaign of
1868, for Use in the New England States, Containing ...
Party Platforms, and Other Valuable Information. Boston:
A. Williams and Company; Lowell: Press of Stone & Huse,
1868.

T. [i], [ii], [7]-8, [9]-[90], adv. 91-96. Brown wrps.,
adv. on outer back. Intro., pp. [7]-8, dated July, 1868;
includes brief biog. sketches of the Democratic and Republican candidates.

GRANT, ULYSSES SIMPSON (Republican)

500   Abbott, John S. C.   The Life of General Ulysses S. Grant.
Containing a Brief But Faithful Narrative of Those Military
and Diplomatic Achievements Which Have Entitled Him to
the Confidence and Gratitude of His Countrymen.... Illustrated. Boston: B. B. Russell, Publisher; Cincinnati:
White, Corbin, Bouvé, & Co.; San Francisco: H. H. Bancroft & Co., 1868.

Pf., t. [1], [2], 3-4, [5]-9, bl. [10], 11-309, bl. [310].
Maroon cloth. Pf. and 10 pls. inserted.

501   [Adams, William Taylor.]   Our Standard-Bearer; Or, the Life
of General Ulysses S. Grant: His Youth, His Manhood,
His Campaigns ... As Seen and Related by Captain Bernard
Galligasken, Cosmopolitan, and Written Out by Oliver Optic.
Illustrated by Thomas Nast. Boston: Lee and Shepard,
1868.

F. , t. [1], [2], [3], bl. [4], [5]-8, 9-14, 15-348, adv. [1]-
4. Green cloth. F. and 5 pls. inserted. Preface, pp.
[5]-8, dated July 11, 1868. Also noted in red cloth.

502 Brisbin, James S. The Campaign Lives of Ulysses S. Grant,
and Schuyler Colfax. Cincinnati: C. F. Vent & Co. , Publishers; Chicago: J. S. Goodman & Co. , 1868.

Pf. , t. [v], [vi], vii-x, 11-20, div. t. [21], bl. [22], 23-
352, port. , div. t. [353], bl. [354], 355-411, adv. [412-
416]. Blue cloth. Pf. and pl. inserted, other illus. in
text. Life of Grant, pp. 23-352; of Colfax, pp. 355-411.

*503 Brockett, Linus P. Grant and Colfax: Their Lives and Ser-
vices. New York: Richardson and Company [1868.]

vi, [7], 136 pp. , f. , ports. , maps, plans. Reissued separately from entry 498? Sabin 8155.

504 Coppée, Henry. Grant and His Campaigns: A Military Biography. New York: Charles B. Richardson; Cincinnati:
C. F. Vent & Co. ; Springfield: W. J. Holland, 1866.

Pf. , t. [1], [2], [3]-4, [5]-12, [13]-472, [473]-512, [513]-
521, bl. [522], 2 ℓ ℓ. adv. Purple cloth. Pf. , 7 pls. , 4
ℓ ℓ. maps (3 pr. on rectos only) inserted, other illus. in
text. Pub. prospectus dated, 1865, also noted.

505 _____ . Life and Services of Gen. U. S. Grant. New
York: Richardson and Company, 1868.

Preliminary ℓ. of letters, pf. , t. [1], [2], [3]-4, [5]-12,
[13]-455, bl. [456], [457]-465, bl. [466]. Brown cloth.
Pf. and 3 maps (one fld.) inserted, other illus. in text.
Basically a reprint of entry 504.

506 _____ . Life and Services of Gen. U. S. Grant. New
York: Richardson and Company, 1868.

Half title, letter on verso, pf. , t. [1], [2], [3]-4, [5]-12,
[13]-455, bl. [456], port. , [557 sic]-566. Brown cloth with
cream endpapers. Pf. , pl. and 4 maps (one fld.) inserted,
other illus. in text. Preface, pp. [3]-4, concludes with
preface to rev. ed. , June, 1868; life of Grant, pp. [13]-
455; of Colfax, pp. [557]-566. Also noted with orange endpapers.

507 Cortambert, L. , and Tranaltos, F. de. Le Général Grant
Esquisse Biographique.... New York: H. de Mareil, Edi-
teur, en Face de la Poste, 1868.

Cover title [i], bl. [ii], [1]-34. Sewn. At foot of p. 34,
"Messager Franco-Américain, Printing Office, 51, Liberty

Street, New-York. "; at head of title, Bibliothèque du Messager Franco-Américain.

508 Crafts, William A. Life of Ulysses S. Grant: His Boyhood, Campaigns, and Services, Military and Civil. With a Fine Portrait on Steel. Boston: Samuel Walker and Company, 1868.

Illus. half title [i], bl. [ii], pf., t. [iii], [iv], v-vi, vii-viii, 1-172. Purple cloth. Pf. inserted. Also noted in brown illus. wrps., adv. on outer back.

509 Dana, Charles A. The Life of Ulysses S. Grant, General of the Armies of the United States. By ... Late Assistant Secretary of War; and J. H. Wilson, Brevet Major-General U. S. A. Springfield: Published by Gurdon Bill & Company; Cincinnati: H. C. Johnson; Chicago, Charles Bill, 1868.

Pf., t. [i], [ii], [iii]-iv, [v]-xvi, [17]-424, 2 ℓ ℓ. adv. 3/4 black cloth, leather backstrip. Pf. and 4 maps inserted. Also noted in calf, brown cloth, and blue coated paper bds.

510 Deming, Henry C. The Life of Ulysses S. Grant, General United States Army. Hartford: S. S. Scranton and Company; Cincinnati: National Publishing Company; Philadelphia: Parmelee Brothers; Chicago: O. F. Gibbs, 1868.

Pf., eng. t., t. [1], [2], [3-4], 5-6, 7-17, bl. [18], 19-533, bl. [534]. Bluish green cloth. Pf. and eng. t. inserted.

511 Dye, John Smith. Life and Public Services of Gen. U. S. Grant, the Nation's Choice for President in 1868. By Deacon Dye. Philadelphia: Samuel Loag, Printer, 1868.

Two blue ℓ ℓ. adv., pr. in black, t. [1], [2], 3-48, 2 blue ℓ ℓ. as before. Salmon illus. wrps., adv. on inner front and entire back; outer front notes at head, 4th Edition, 20,000 Copies. Price 25 Cents and at foot, Deacon Dye, Author and Publisher, Office, 607 Chestnut St., Bulletin Building, Philadelphia.

*512 _____ . Life and Public Services of Gen. U. S. Grant. Philadelphia: The Author, 1868.

82 pp. Sabin 21578.

*513 _____ . Life and Public Services of Gen. U. S. Grant. Philadelphia: S. Loag, Printer, 1868.

93, [3] pp., adv. 92-[96]. On cover: Fifteenth Edition. Lives and Eminent Public Services of Grant and Colfax ...

With Proceedings and Platforms of Republican and Democratic Conventions of 1868.

514 1868. Text Book for the Republican Campaign ... for President, Gen. Ulysses S. Grant, of Illinois, for Vice-President, Hon. Schuyler Colfax, of Indiana. New York: American Literary Publishing Association, 1868.

Adv. [i-ii], t. [iii], [iv], [v]-vi, [vii], [8]-184, adv. 185-
192. Buff illus. wrps. Adv., p. 183; sketches of Grant
and Colfax, pp. 36-41.

515 Headley, Joel Tyler. The Life of Ulysses S. Grant, General-
in-Chief U. S. A.... Illustrated. Sold by Subscription.
New York: E. B. Treat & Co., Publishers; Chicago: C.
W. Lilley; Pittsburg: A. L. Talcott; Philadelphia: A.
H. Hubbard; San Francisco: A. Roman & Co., 1868.

Pf., t. [i], [ii], [iii]-v, [vi], [vii]-xv, map [xvi], [17]-417,
bl. [418], [427 sic]-458, 3 ℓℓ. adv. Maroon cloth. Pf.
and 3 pls. inserted, map in text.

516 _____ . The Life of Ulysses S. Grant.... New York: E.
B. Treat & Co.; Chicago: C. W. Lilley; Pittsburg: A. L.
Talcott; San Francisco: E. E. Shear; Philadelphia: A. H.
Hubbard, 1868.

As in entry 515. Green cloth.

517 Headley, P. C. The Life and Campaigns of Lieut.-Gen. U. S.
Grant, From His Boyhood to the Surrender of Lee....
With Portraits on Steel of Stanton, Grant, and His Generals,
and Other Illustrations.... New York: The Derby and
Miller Publishing Co., 1866.

Half title [1], bl. [2], pf., t. [3], [4], [5]-6, port., [7]-14,
[15], bl. [16], pl., fac. letter, [17]-720. All copies examined rebound. Pf., 18 pls. and 2 fac. letters inserted.

518 Howland, Edward. Grant as a Soldier and Statesman: Being
a Succinct History of His Military and Civil Career. Hartford: J. B. Burr & Company, 1868.

Pf., t., copyright notice, [i], [ii], [iii]-iv, [vii]-xi, [xii],
11-466, 467-631, bl. [632], ℓ. adv. Green cloth. Pf.
and 8 pls. inserted. Appendix, pp. 467-631.

519 Illustrated Life, Campaigns and Public Services of Lieut. General Grant. The Hero of Fort Donelson!... With a Portrait of General Grant, and Other Illustrative Engravings....
Philadelphia: T. B. Peterson & Brothers [c1865.]

Pf., 2 pls., t. [i], [ii], 15-21, bl. [22], 23-271, adv. 1-
15, ℓ. adv. Dark brown cloth. Pf. and 4 pls. inserted.
Also noted in purple cloth.

520 [Larke, Julian K.] The Life Campaigns and Battles of General
Ulysses S. Grant Comprising a Full and Authentic Account
of the Famous Soldier.... With an Introduction by Benson
J. Lossing.... Illustrated... New York: Published by
Ledyard Bill; Chicago: Charles Bill, 1868.

Cld. f., t. [i], [ii], [i]-iv, 5-12, [13]-499, [500]-502.
Maroon cloth. Cld. f. and 4 pls. inserted. Chronology,
pp. [500]-502; t. pr. in red and black.

521   . The Life ... of General Ulysses S. Grant.... New
York: Published by Ledyard Bill; Chicago: Charles Bill,
1868.

As in entry 520, but t. pr. in black only and lacking men-
tion of Benson J. Lossing.

522 Life and Services of General U. S. Grant, Conqueror of the
Rebellion, and Eighteenth President of the United States....
Washington: Philp & Solomons, 1868.

T. [1], [2], [3]-160. Pink wrps., list of committees on
inner front, adv. on entire back. "Published under the authority of the Republican National and Congressional Committees." Also noted in blue and light green wrps., as
above.

523 The Lively Life U. S. G., H. U. G. and U. H. G. the Poli-
tical Triplets, and Somewhat Known to Fame as the Dummy
Candidate! Together With a Series of Vigorous Illustrations
and a Useful Hint as to How His Friends Ought to Go to
Work to Elect Him. New York: Published at No. 41 Ann
Street, 1868.

T. [1], illus. [2], [3]-24, illus. [25], bl. [26], bl. ℓ.
Yellow wrps., adv. on inner front and entire back. Cartoon illus. in text. Burlesque life, anti-Grant.

524 The Lives and Public Services of General U. S. Grant, U. S.
A. and of Hon. Schuyler Colfax, Speaker of the House of
Representatives. Philadelphia: 1868.

Cover title [1], [2], [3]-24. Sewn. Title vignette. At
head of title, No. 182. "Let Us Have Peace."; life of
Grant, pp. [3]-20; of Colfax, pp. [21]-24.

525 The Lives of General U. S. Grant, and Schuyler Colfax.
This Work Is a Complete History of the Lives.... With
Portraits of General U. S. Grant, Hon. Schuyler Colfax,
and Other Illustrative Engravings. Philadelphia: T. B.
Peterson & Brothers [c1868.]

Flyleaf [1-2], 2 pf. [3-6], 2 illus. [7-10], t. [11], [12],
13-22, 23-334, 335-362, pub. cat. 1-[16]. Brown cloth.

2 pf. and 4 pls. inserted. At head of title, "Grant and Colfax. " Campaign Edition; life of Grant, pp. 23-334; of Colfax, pp. 335-362. Also noted in green cloth.

526 Lives of Ulysses S. Grant, and Schuyler Colfax, Candidates of the National Republican Party for President and Vice President of the United States. Illustrated With Portraits. Containing Also, a Correct Genealogical Summary of the Grant Family, Now First Published. Cincinnati: Padrick & Co. , 1868.

Pf. , t. [i], [ii], xiii-xiv, 15-77, port. [78], 79-103, 104. Salmon illus. wrps. , adv. on outer back. Pf. and port. in text. At head of title, People's Edition for the Campaign; life of Grant, pp. 15-77; of Colfax, pp. 79-103.

527 Mansfield, Edward D. A Popular and Authentic Life of Ulysses S. Grant. Cincinnati: R. W. Carroll & Co. , Publishers, 1868.

Pf. , eng. t. , t. [1], [2], [3], bl. [4], [5]-9, bl. [10], [11]-14, div. t. [15], bl. [16], 17-377, bl. [378]. Purple cloth. Pf. and eng. t. inserted, maps in text.

528 _____ . Popular and Authentic Lives of Ulysses S. Grant and Schuyler Colfax. Cincinnati: R. W. Carroll & Co. , Publishers, 1868.

Pf. , eng. t. , t. [1], [2], [3], bl. [4], [5]-[10], [11]-14, div. t. [15], bl. [16], 17-377, bl. [378], bl. ℓ. [379-380], port. , div. t. [381], bl. [382], [383]-425, bl. [426], 3 ℓ ℓ. adv. Purple cloth. Pf. , eng. t. , and pl. inserted, maps in text. Dedication, p. [3], dated May 13, 1868; life of Colfax, pp. [383]-425.

529 Phelps, Charles A. Life and Public Services of General Ulysses S. Grant, From His Boyhood to the Present Time. And a Biographical Sketch of Hon. Schuyler Colfax.... Embellished With Two Steel Portraits, and Four Illustrations From Designs by Hammatt Billings. Boston: Lee and Shepard, 1868.

2 pf. , t. [i], [ii], ℓ. , iii-iv, v-xvi, illus. , 1-341, 342-344. Green cloth. 2 pf. , 4 pls. , and ℓ. (6 quotes by Grant on recto) inserted. At head of title, People's Edition.; life of Grant, pp. 1-321; of Colfax, pp. 322-341; appendix, pp. 342-344. Also noted in terra cotta and purple cloths.

530 Richardson, Albert D. A Personal History of Ulysses S. Grant, Illustrated by Twenty-Six Engravings; Eight Fac-Similes ... and Six Maps. With a Portrait and Sketch of Schuyler Colfax.... Hartford: American Publishing Com-

pany; Newark: Bliss and Company; Chicago: G. & C. W.
Sherwood, 1868.

Pf. , eng. t. , t. [i], [ii], [iii], bl. [iv], [v]-viii, [ix]-xiv,
[xv], bl. [xvi], [17]-552, port. , 553-560, 2 ℓℓ. adv. Purple cloth. Pf. , eng. t. , and 25 pls. inserted, other illus.
in text. Life of Grant, pp. [17]-552; of Colfax, pp. 553-
560. Copies also noted lacking terminal adv.

531 _____ . A Personal History of Ulysses S. Grant.... Hart-
ford: American Publishing Company; Newark: Bliss and
Company; Chicago: G. & C. W. Sherwood; San Francisco:
R. J. Trumbull & Co. , 1868.

As in entry 530. Purple cloth.

532 Sketches of the Lives and Services of Ulysses S. Grant and
Schuyler Colfax, National Republican Candidates for Presi-
dent and Vice President of the United States. [Washington:
Chronicle Print. , 1868.]

Caption title. [1]-8. Sewn. Illus. in text. At foot of p.
8, "Chronicle Print. , Washington, D. C. "; pr. in dbl.
cols.

533 Sloane, James. Speech of ... Delivered in the Wigwam of the
Seventeenth Ward, Cincinnati, August 28, 1868. An Analy-
sis and Estimate of the Character of General Grant, With
Respect to His Fitness for the Presidency.... Cincinnati:
Robert Clarke & Co. , Printers, 1868.

Cover title [1], bl. [2], [3]-31, bl. [32]. Sewn.

534 [Stowe, Harriet Beecher.] For President, Ulysses S. Grant,
of Illinois for Vice President, William A. Buckingham, of
Connecticut. Norwich: Bulletin Office, 1868.

T. [i], bl. [ii], [iii], bl. [iv], [1]-5, [6]-14, [15]-16. Pink
wrps. 2 pls. inserted. Letter in favor of Buckingham for
Vice President, pp. [1]-5. Issued by the Connecticut Republican Party prior to the National Convention. "From
Mrs. Harriet Beecher Stowe's forthcoming work 'Men of
Our Times, ' we condense the following relating to General
Grant--a portion of our sketch of Gov. Buckingham being
also derived from the same source. " Unrecorded Stowe
first edition.

535 _____ . For President, Ulysses S. Grant.... Norwich:
Bulletin Office, 1868.

T. [i], bl. [ii], [1]-16, [17], bl. [18]. Pink wrps. P.
[17], press notices.

536 Willett, Edward. The Life of Ulysses Sydney [sic] Grant,
     Lieutenant-General, U. S. A.... New York: Beadle and
     Company, Publishers [c1865.]

     T. [i], [ii], [iii], [iv], [9]-100. Orange illus. wrps., adv.
     on inner front and entire back; front also notes Beadle's
     Dime Biographical Library, No. 15.

537 Wilson, James Grant. The Life and Campaigns of Ulysses
     Simpson Grant, General-in-Chief of the United States Army.
     Comprising A A [sic] Full and Authentic Account of the
     Illustrious Soldier From His Earliest Boyhood to the Present
     Time.... New York: Robert M. DeWitt, Publisher [c1868.]

     T. [i], [ii], 7 [sic], [8], [9]-10, [11]-88, 89-98, 99-100.
     Buff yellow illus. wrps., adv. on inner front and entire
     back. Life of Grant, pp. [11]-88; appendix, pp. 89-98;
     Republican platform, pp. 99-100; pr. in dbl. cols.

SEYMOUR, HORATIO (Democratic)

538 Croly, David G. Seymour and Blair, Their Lives and Services
     With an Appendix Containing a History of Reconstruction.
     New York: Richardson and Company, 1868.

     Pf., t. [1], [2], [3]-4, [5]-6, [7]-218, port., [219]-253,
     bl. [254], fac., [255]-275, bl. [276]. Purple cloth. Pf.,
     pl. and fac. inserted. Life of Seymour, pp. [7]-218; of
     Blair, pp. [219]-253; appendix, pp. [255]-275. Also noted
     in green cloth, spine citing Authorised Edition, and fac.
     inserted after p. [276].

539 _____. Seymour and Blair.... New York: Richardson and
     Company, 1868.

     Pf., t. [1], [2], [3]-4, [5]-6, [7]-228, port., [229]-263, bl.
     [264], fac., [265]-285, bl. [286]. Brown cloth. Pf., pl.
     and fac. inserted. Also noted in maroon and green cloths,
     the latter again citing Authorised Edition.

540 Lives of Horatio Seymour and Frank P. Blair, Jr.... From
     Their Birth Up to the Present Time. Philadelphia: T. B.
     Peterson & Brothers [c1868.]

     T. [i], [ii], 19, bl. [20], 21-95, adv. [96] being p. 1 of
     pub. cat. 1-[17]. Cream illus. wrps., adv. on inner front
     and entire back. At head of title, Seymour and Blair.
     Campaign Edition.; life of Seymour, pp. 21-70; of Blair,
     pp. 71-95. Also noted as being available in cloth.

541 [Locke, David Ross.] The Impendin Crisis uv the Dimocracy
     ... Incloodin the Most Prominent Reesons Why Evry Dimo-

krat Who Loves His Party Shood Vote for Seemore and
Blare, and Agin Grant and Colfax.   By Petroleum V. Nasby....   Toledo: Miller, Locke & Co. , 1868.

Cover title [1], [2], [3]-23, adv. [24]. Self wrps.   Title
vignette.   Sketches of Seymour and Blair, pp. 11-15; of
Grant and Colfax, pp. 15-17.

542   McCabe, James D. Jr.   The Life and Public Services of Horatio Seymour: Together With a Complete and Authentic Life
of Francis P. Blair, Jr.   New York: United States Publishing Company; Cincinnati, Chicago, St. Louis, Atlanta:
Jones Brothers & Co. ; San Francisco: H. H. Bancroft &
Co. , 1868.

2 pf. , t. [i], [ii], [iii], bl. [iv], [v]-viii, [ix]-xiv, div. t.
[xv], bl. [xvi], [17]-292, div. t. [293], bl. [294], [295]-
297, bl. [298], [299]-503, bl. [504].   Purple cloth.   2 pf.
inserted.   Life of Seymour, pp. [17]-292; of Blair, pp.
[299]-503.

543   _____ .   The Life ... of Horatio Seymour....   New York:
United States Publishing Company [etc.] 1868.

As in entry 542, but bl. [504], appendix, pp. [505]-511, bl.
[512].   Purple cloth.

JOHNSON, ANDREW (Republican)

544   Foster, Lillian.   Andrew Johnson, President of the United
States; His Life and Speeches....   New York: Richardson
& Co. , 1866.

T. [1], [2], [3]-4, [5]-7, bl. [8], [9]-32, [33]-316.   Green
cloth.   Pf. present, but not in all copies examined.   Life
of Johnson, pp. [9]-32; speeches, pp. [33]-316.

545   Life and Times of Andrew Johnson, Seventeenth President of
the United States.   Written From a National Stand-Point.
By a National Man....   New York: D. Appleton and Company, 1866.

Pf. , t. [i], [ii], [iii]-vi, [vii]-xii, 1-363, bl. [364], adv.
[i-ii], [1]-6.   Green cloth.   Pf. inserted.   Author, Kenneth
Raynor?   Also noted in purple cloth.

546   [Locke, David Ross.]   Andy's Trip to the West, Together With
a Life of Its Hero.   By Petroleum V. Nasby....   [New
York: J. C. Haney & Co. , c1866.]

Cover title.   [1-12], div. t. [13], bl. [14], [15]-38, 3 ℓℓ.
adv. Illus. wrps. , adv. on inner front and outer back.

Title vignette.   Illus. in text.   Text of trip in cartoons, pp. [1-12]; of life, pp. [15]-38.

547 Savage, John. The Life and Public Services of Andrew Johnson, Seventeenth President of the United States.... With an Accurate Portrait on Steel By Ritchie and Other Illustrations. New York: Derby & Miller, Publishers, 1866.

Pf. , t. [1], [2], 3-5, bl. [6], 9-[12], pl. , [13]-408, 1-130, 1-19, bl. [20], ℓ. adv. All copies examined rebound. Pf. and 4 pls. inserted. Appendix, pp. 1-130; index, pp. [1]-19.

PENDLETON, GEORGE HUNT (Democratic)

548 Bloss, G. M. D. Life and Speeches of George H. Pendleton.... Cincinnati: Miami Printing and Publishing Company, 1868.

Pf. [i-ii], t. [iii], [iv], [5]-108. Buff illus. wrps. , adv. on outer back.

1872

GENERAL WORKS

549 Chamberlin, Everett. The Struggle of '72. The Issues and Candidates of the Present Political Campaign: Containing Biographical Sketches of All the Candidates for President and Vice-President.... Embellished With Many Portraits and Humorous Illustrations. Chicago [and] Philadelphia: Union Publishing Company; San Francisco: A. L. Bancroft & Co. , 1872.

F. [1-2], t. [3], [4], 5-6, [7], 10-17, bl. [18], 19-547, bl. [548], 549-570. Brown cloth. F. and 19 pls. inserted. Also noted in calf.

550 Champion, Frank. Campaign Handbook and Citizen's Manual.... With Biographical Sketches of the Presidents and Presidential Candidates.... Hartford: F. C. Bliss & Company, 1872.

F. , t. [i], [ii], [iii]-iv, [v]-viii, [ix], x-xiii, bl. [xiv], 15-232. All copies examined rebound. F. and 5 pls. inserted, other illus. in text. Includes brief sketches of Greeley and Brown, Grant and Wilson.

GRANT, ULYSSES SIMPSON (Republican)

551 The Comic Life of General Grant....   New York: 1872.

    Cover title [1], [2], [3]-16. Self wrps. Title vignette.
    Illus. in text. Burlesque life.

552 Conkling, Roscoe. Issues of the Day. Speech of ... Deli-
    vered at Cooper Institute, New York, July 23, 1872. [N.
    p. , n. d. , 1872.]

   '   Caption title. [1]-20. Sewn. Pr. in dbl. cols.

553 _____ . Die Präsidentschafts Campagne von 1872. Grant
    und sein Berläumder; Thaten gegen Worte. Auszug aus der
    Rede Hon. Roscoe Conkling, im Cooper Institut, New York,
    Dienstag, 23. Juli, 1872. [New York: Oestlichen Post,
    1872.]

    Caption title. [1]-16. Sewn. At foot of p. 16, "Druck
    der 'Oestlichen Post, ' No. 12 North William Str. , New-
    York. "

554 _____ . The Presidential Battle of 1872. Grant and His
    Defamers: Deeds Against Words. Speech of ... at Cooper
    Institute, New York, July 23, 1872. [Buffalo: Commercial
    Advertiser, 1872.]

    Caption title. [1]-31, bl. [32]. Sewn. At head of title,
    Buffalo Commercial Advertiser Campaign Document No. 1. ;
    pr. in dbl. cols.

555 _____ . The Presidential Battle of 1872....   New York,
    Tuesday, July 23, 1872. [Utica: Roberts, Book and Job
    Printer, 1872.]

    Caption title. [1]-48. Sewn. At foot of p. 48, "Roberts,
    Book and Job Printer, 60 Genesee St. , Utica, N. Y. "

556 Corckell, William. The Eventful History of Grant and His
    Wonderful Donkey....   Illustrated. Algonquin: Peoples'
    Publishing Company, MDCCCLXXII.

    T. [1], [2], [3-4], [5]-14, [15], [16]. Green illus. wrps. ,
    adv. on inner front and back, outer back pr. G. A. H. (A.).
    Burlesque poem dealing with Grant's life from age 10.

557 Cross, Nelson. Life of General Grant, His Political Record,
    etc. New York: J. S. Redfield, Publisher [1872.]

    Pf. , t. [i], bl. [ii], 11-182. Green cloth with pr. paper
    label on backstrip. Pf. inserted. Also issued under the
    following title.

558 _____ . The Modern Ulysses LL. D.   His Political Record.
New York: J. S. Redfield, Publisher, 1872.

Bl. [1], f. [2], t. [3], [4], [5], bl. [6], 7-9, bl. [10], 11-
182, ℓ. adv. Grey wrps. Anti-Grant.

*559 Headley, Joel Tyler.   The Life of Ulysses S. Grant.   New
York: E. B. Treat & Co. , 1872.

xv, 18-458 pp. , pf. , illus. (including pls. and chart).   New
and enlg. ed.

560 The Lives of "Grant and Wilson. "   The Lives of General U. S.
Grant, and Henry Wilson.   This Work Is a Complete History ... Up to the Present Time.   With Portraits of General U. S. Grant, Hon. Henry Wilson, and Other Illustrative
Engravings.   Philadelphia: T. B. Peterson & Brothers
[c1872.]

2 pf. [1-4], 2 pls. [5-8], t. [9], [10], 11-21, bl. [22], 23-
373, bl. [374].   All copies examined rebound.   2 pf. and
4 pls. inserted.   Life of Grant, pp. 23-346; of Wilson, pp.
347-373.

561 Phelps, Charles A.   Life and Public Services of Ulysses S.
Grant, From His Birth to the Present Time, and a Bio-
graphical Sketch of Hon. Henry Wilson.   Embellished With
a Steel Portrait, and Four Illustrations From Designs by
Hammatt Billings.   Boston: Lee and Shepard, Publishers;
New York: Lee, Shepard and Dillingham, 1872.

Pf. , t. [i], [ii], [iii], [iv], v-[xvi], illus. , 1-371, bl.
[372], [1]-2.   Blue cloth.   Pf. and 4 pls. inserted.   At
head of title, People's Edition. ; preface to new ed. , p.
[iii]; life of Grant, pp. 1-349; of Wilson, pp. 350-371;
press notices of 1868 ed. , pp. [1]-2.   Also noted in terra
cotta cloth; and salmon illus. wrps. , adv. on outer back,
front noting Campaign Edition, and pr. in red and black,
spine in black only.

*562 Sinclair, Robert.   Life of Ulysses S. Grant, President of the
U. S. and Commander-In-Chief of the United States Army.
New York: Norman L. Munro, 1872.

108 pp.   Sabin 81407.

GREELEY, HORACE (Democratic)

563 The Comic Life of Horace Greeley....   New York: Published
at "Wild Oats" Office [c1872.]

Cover title [1], [2], [3]-31, illus. [32].   Sewn.   Title vignette.   Illus. in text.   Pr. in dbl. cols.   Anti-Greeley.

564   Cornell, William M.   The Life and Public Career of Hon.
      Horace Greeley.   Boston: Published by Lee and Shepard;
      New York: Lee, Shepard, & Dillingham; Philadelphia: H.
      C. Johnson, 1872.

      Pf., t. [1], [2], [3], bl. [4], 5-6, 7-8, 9-12, 13-306,
      port., 307-312.   Terra cotta cloth.   Pf. and pl. inserted.
      Life of Greeley, pp. 13-306; of Brown, pp. 307-312.

565   Democratic and Liberal Ticket....   For President, Horace
      Greeley, the Woodchopper of Chappaqua.   For Vice Presi-
      dent, B. Gratz Brown.   [N. p., n. d., 1872.]

      Cover title [1], [2], [3]-29, 30-32.   Sewn.   Title vignette.
      Illus. in text.   Poems, pp. 30-32.   Anti-Greeley.

566   Fun From Under the Old White Hat.   Written by Old-Time
      Editors and Reporters of the Tribune.   New York: Pub-
      lished by Fay & Cox, 1872.

      T. [1], [2], [3]-48.   Buff wrps.   Title vignette.   Illus. in
      text.   Anti-Greeley.   Also noted in light green wrps.

*567 Greeley, Horace.   Autobiography; Or, Recollections of a Busy
      Life.   To Which Are Added Miscellaneous Essays and Pa-
      pers.   New York: E. B. Treat, 1872.

      624 pp., illus., ports. [c1868].

568   The Life and Public Services of Hon. Horace Greeley, Liberal
      Republican Candidate for President of the United States, and
      of Hon. B. Gratz Brown, Candidate for Vice President....
      Illustrated.   Chicago, Cincinnati, St. Louis, New Orleans,
      [and] New York: Published by Goodspeed's Empire Publish-
      ing House, 1872.

      T., [1], [2], pf., [3]-56, port. [57], bl. [58], [59]-61, 61-
      71, 72-[75], illus. [76], [77-79], illus. [80].   Lemon
      wrps., adv. on inner front and entire back.   Life of
      Greeley, pp. [3]-56; of Brown, pp. [59]-61; poems, pp.
      72-[75].

569   Parton, James.   The Life of Horace Greeley, Editor of "The
      New-York Tribune," From His Birth to the Present Time.
      With Portrait and Illustrations.   Boston: James R. Osgood
      and Company (late Ticknor & Fields, and Fields, Osgood,
      & Co.), 1872.

      Pf., t. [i], [ii], iii-xi, [xii], illus., 1-548.   Purple cloth.
      Pf. and 8 pls. inserted.

570   _____ .   The Life of Horace Greeley....   Boston: James
      R. Osgood and Company; Cincinnati, Memphis [and] Atlanta:

National Publishing Company; Chicago: Jones Brothers & Co. , 1872.

As in entry 569.

571 _____ . Das Leben Horace Greeley's.   Nach dem englischen des James Parton von Adolph Rahmer. Boston: James R. Osgood u. Comp. , 1872.

Pf. , t. [i], [ii], [iii], [iv], [1]-126.   Grey green illus. wrps. , adv. on inner front and entire back.   Pf. inserted, other illus. in text.   Foreword, p. [iii], dated Sept. 1872; pr. in dbl. cols.

572 Reavis, L. U.   A Representative Life of Horace Greeley, With an Introduction by Cassius M. Clay....   New York: G. W. Carleton & Co. , Publishers; London: S. Low, Son & Co. , M. DCCC. LXXII.

Pf. , t. [i], [ii], [i], bl. [ii], [iii], bl. [iv], [v], bl. [vi], [vii]-viii, [ix]-xi, bl. [xii], [15]-16, [17]-571, bl. [572], [573]-579, bl. [580], pub. cat. [1]-[8].   Purple cloth.   Pf. inserted.

*573 Rosewood, J. B.   Life of Greeley ... A Series of Wonderful Facts and Startling Revelations....   New York: Fisher & Denison [1872.]

112 pp. , illus.   Sabin 73285.

*574 _____ . Life of Greeley ... Written in $9\frac{1}{2}$ Minutes by the Great Trance Medium.   New York: American News Co. [1872].

30, [2] pp.   Sabin 73284.

TRAIN, GEORGE (Women's Rights)

575 The Man of Destiny.   Presidential Campaign, 1872....   The People's Candidate for President, 1872, Geo. Francis Train....   [N. p. , n. d. , 1872.]

Cover title [1], [2], [3]-94.   Lemon illus. wrps. , adv. on outer back.   Title vignette.   Pr. in dbl. cols.   Compiled by John Wesley Nichols, "Presidential photographer to the next President of America. "

1876

GENERAL WORKS

576 Townsend, George Alfred. Events at the National Capital and
the Campaign of 1876. . . . Full Biographies of Hayes,
Wheeler, Tilden, and Hendricks, Besides Various Political
Statistics. Hartford: Jas. Betts & Co.; Chicago: S. M.
Betts & Co.; St. Louis: J. H. Chambers & Co.; San Francisco: A. L. Bancroft & Co.; Minneapolis: Haber Bros.,
1876.

F. , t. [i], [ii], [iii]-iv, [v]-xiii, bl. [xiv], [15]-18, [19]-
456. Terra cotta cloth. F. and 18 pls. inserted, other
illus. in text.

HAYES, RUTHERFORD B. (Republican)

577 Conwell, Russell H. Life and Public Services of Gov. Rutherford B. Hayes. Boston: Published by B. B. Russell; Philadelphia: Quaker City Publishing House; San Francisco:
A. L. Bancroft & Co.; Detroit: R. D. S. Tyler & Co.;
Portland: John Russell [c1876.]

Pf. , t. [1], [2], [3], bl. [4], 5-9, bl. [10], 11-16, 17-20,
21-308, port. , div. t. [309], bl. [310], 311-328, ℓ. adv.
Terra cotta cloth. Pf. and pl. inserted, other illus. in
text. Life of Hayes, pp. 21-308; of Wheeler, pp. 311-328.

578 Howard, James Q. The Life, Public Services and Select
Speeches of Rutherford B. Hayes. Cincinnati: Robert
Clarke & Co. , 1876.

Pf. , t. [i], [ii], iii-v, bl. [vi], 9-165, bl. [166], 167-260.
Rose cloth. Pf. inserted. Speeches, pp. 167-260. Also
noted in blue and green cloths.

579 Howells, William Dean. Sketch of the Life and Character of
Rutherford B. Hayes. Also a Biographical Sketch of Wil-
liam A. Wheeler. With Portraits of Both Candidates. New
York: Published by Hurd and Houghton; Boston: H. O.
Houghton and Company; Cambridge: The Riverside Press,
1876.

Pf. , t. [i], [ii], [iii]-iv, [v]-vi, 1-195, bl. [196], div. t.
[1], bl. [2], port. , [3]-31, bl. [32], 2 ℓℓ. adv. Terra
cotta cloth. Pf. and pl. inserted. Preface, pp. [iii]-iv,

dated Sept. 7, 1876; life of Hayes, pp. [1]-195; of Wheeler, pp. [3]-31. Copies also noted in green cloth. For cloth variants, see BAL, Vol. 4, 9572.

580 Johnston, Judge. Speech of ... on the Life and Character of R. B. Hayes. Delivered at Avondale, Ohio, July 21, 1876. Cincinnati: Robert Clarke & Co., 1876.

Cover title [1], bl. [2], [3]-14, bls. [15-16]. Light green wrps.

581 Two Pictures 1876. [N. p., n. d., 1876.]

Cover title [1], bl. [2], [3]-16. Self wrps. Caption title, Hayes Or Tilden; pr. in dbl. cols. Pro-Hayes.

TILDEN, SAMUEL J. (Democratic)

582 Buckman, Benjamin E. Samuel J. Tilden Unmasked! New York: Published for the Author, 1876.

Pf., t. [i], [ii], [iii]-iv, [v]-ix, bl. [x], [1]-104, illus., [105]-109, bl. [110], illus., [111]-120, illus., [121], bl. [122]. Light blue grey illus. wrps. Pf. (of author) and 10 pls. inserted, other illus. in text. Intro., pp. [v]-ix, and summary, pp. [105]-109, pr. in red. Anti-Tilden.

583 Cook, Theodore P. The Life and Public Services of Hon. Samuel J. Tilden, Democratic Nominee for President of the United States. To Which Is Added a Sketch of the Life of Hon. Thomas A. Hendricks, Democratic Nominee for Vice-President. With Portraits on Steel. New York: D. Appleton and Company, 1876.

Pf., t. [i], [ii], [iii]-iv, [v]-vi, 1-360, div. t. [361], bl. [362], port., [363]-443, bl. [444], adv. [i]-ii. 3/4 marbled paper bds., brown cloth backstrip. Pf. and pl. inserted. Life of Tilden, pp. 1-360; of Hendricks, [363]-443. Also noted in terra cotta cloth.

584 _____. The Life ... of Hon. Samuel J. Tilden.... New York: D. Appleton and Company, 1876.

Pf., t. [i], [ii], [iii]-iv, 1-350, div. t. [351], bl. [352], port., [353]-434, adv. [i]-ii. Marbled paper bds. as above.

585 Cornell, William Mason. The Life of Hon. Samuel Jones Tilden, Governor of the State of New York; With a Sketch of the Life of Hon. Thomas Andrews Hendricks, Governor of the State of Indiana. Boston: Lee & Shepard, 1876.

Pf. , t. [1], [2], [3], bl. [4], 5-6, 7-12, 13-14, 15-180,
port. , div. t. [181], bl. [182], 183-336.   Green cloth.   Pf.
and pl. inserted.   Life of Tilden, pp. 15-180; of Hendricks,
pp. 183-336.

586   Lester, C. Edward.   Lives and Public Services of Samuel J.
Tilden and Thomas A. Hendricks.   1776.   1876.   A Revo-
lution for Independence.   A Revolution for Reform....   New
York: Frank Leslie's Publishing House, 1876.

Pf. , t. [i], [ii], [iii]-vi, illus. , [7]-190, [191]-192.   3/4
marbled paper bds. , leather backstrip.   Pf. and 6 pls. inserted.   Also noted in green cloth.

COOPER, PETER (Greenback [Independent])

587   Zachos, J. C.   A Sketch of the Life and Opinions of Mr. Peter
Cooper.   Compiled From Original Sources.   New York:
Murray Hill Publishing Company, John P. Jewett, Manager,
1876.

Pf. , t. [1], [2], [3]-9, bl. [10], [11]-96.   Green wrps. ,
adv. on inner front and entire back.   Pf. inserted.

CHANDLER, ZACHARIAH (Republican)

588   The Republican Presidential Candidate.   "Nominate the Right
Man. "   [N. p. , n. d. , 1876.]

Caption title.   Broadside, 14 x 8 $\frac{1}{4}$, pr. in 3 cols.   Sketch
taken from the Washington Chronicle, May 18, 1875 ("a
year ago").   "He is not an aspirant for the office, but this
is only another evidence of his modesty and good sense.
The office should seek the man, not the man the office. "

MORTON, OLIVER P. (Republican)

589   Oliver P. Morton, of Indiana.   Sketch of His Life and Public
Services.   Prepared by Direction of the Indiana Republican
State Central Committee.   Indianapolis: Journal Company,
Printers, 1876.

T. [i], bl. [ii], [iii], bl. [iv], [1]-77, bl. [78], [79]-88.
Grey wrps.   Pp. [79]-88, "A Leaf from History, " pr. on
white rag paper as opposed to preceding which is cream
coated.   Favorite son candidate, see p. [iii].

1880

GENERAL WORKS

590 Lives of the Presidential Candidates, Garfield & Hancock.
[Philadelphia: Pennsylvania Mutual Life Insurance Co.,
1880.]

Cover title. [1]-12. Peach illus. wrps., adv. on inner
front and back. Title vignette. At foot of p. 12, "Geddes
Sons, Prs., 724 Chestnut St., Phila."; life of Garfield,
pp. [1]-4; of Hancock, pp. [8]-12.

591 Our Presidential Candidates and Political Compendium. Also
Containing Lives of the Candidates for Vice-President....
Illustrated. Newark: F. C. Bliss & Company, 1880.

Div. t., verso bl., f., t. [1], [2], 3-4, 5-6, pl., [7]-222,
div. t., verso bl., t. [i], [ii], [iii]-iv, [v]-viii, [ix], x-
xiii, bl. [xiv], 15-198. Orange cloth. 12 pls. inserted,
other illus. in text. Political Compendium, Part II, pp.
15-198. Also noted in tan cloth.

GARFIELD, JAMES A. (Republican)

592 Brisbin, James S. The Early Life and Public Career of
James A. Garfield, Maj. Gen'l U. S. A. The Spicy Record of a Wonderful Career.... Including Also a Sketch of
the Life of Hon. Chester A. Arthur.... Philadelphia:
Published by H. W. Kelley [c1880.]

Pf., t. [i], [ii], [iii], [iv], [v-vii], bl. [viii], ix-xii, [xiii],
[xiv], div. t. [xv], [xvi], pl., 21-533, bl. [534], div. t.
[535], [536], port., 537-558, div. t. [559], [560], 561-585,
bl. [586]. Terra-cotta cloth. Pf., and 20 pls. inserted.
Life of Garfield, pp. 21-533; of Arthur, pp. 537-558; appendix, pp. 561-585. Pub. prospectus also noted, at head
of title of both, From the Tow-Path to the White House.

593 _____ . The Early Life and Public Career of James A.
Garfield, Maj. Gen'l U. S. A. The Record of a Wonderful
Career.... Philadelphia, Cincinnati, Chicago, and St.
Louis: Published by J. C. McCurdy & Co. [c1880.]

As in entry 592. At head of title, From the Tow-Path to
the White House.

594 _____ . The Early Life ... of James A. Garfield. ... Philadelphia, Springfield, Chicago, Cincinnati [and] Atlanta:
Published by Hubbard Bros.; St. Louis: C. H. Lillingston
& Co.; Emporia: T. Prothero; San Francisco: A. L. Bancroft & Co. [c1880.]

As in entry 592.

595 Bundy, J. M. The Life of Gen. James A. Garfield. Illustrated. New York: A. S. Barnes & Co. , 1880.

Pf. , t. [i], [ii], [iii]-iv, [1]-232, [233]-239, bl. [240].
Light blue wrps. , adv. on outer back, pr. in dark blue.
Pf. inserted, other illus. in text. Also noted in green
cloth with terminal adv. , 1-8; brown cloth with terminal
adv. , 4 ℓℓ. ; and brown cloth with 4 ℓℓ. terminal adv. and
opening adv. , [1]-4 noting 5th ed. of Life now ready.

596 Coffin, Charles Carleton. The Life of James A. Garfield. ...
With a Sketch of the Life of Chester A. Arthur. Illustrated. Boston: James H. Earle, Publisher, 1880.

Half title [1], bl. [2], pf. , t. [3], [4], 5-9, bl. [10], 11-
12, 13-364, port. , 365-376, 377-379, bl. [380], ℓ. adv.
verso blank. Reddish brown cloth. Pf. and pl. inserted,
other illus. in text. Preface, pp. 5-9, dated July 26,
1880; life of Garfield, pp. 13-364; of Arthur, pp. 365-376;
index, pp. 377-379. Copy also noted lacking index; others
in green cloth.

597 Conwell, Russell H. The Life, Speeches and Public Services
of Gen. James A. Garfield of Ohio. ... With Introduction
by Rev. Mark Hopkins, D. D. ... Indianapolis: Fred L.
Horton & Co. , 1880.

Pf. , t. [1], [2], [3], bl. [4], [5-6], [7]-10, [11]-15, bl.
[16], [17], bl. [18], [25]-336, port. , 337-356. Green cloth.
Pf. and 7 pls. inserted, 3 illus. in text. Life of Garfield,
pp. [25]-336; of Arthur, pp. 337-356.

598 _____ . The Life ... of Gen. James A. Garfield of Ohio. ...
Boston: Published by B. B. Russell & Co.; Philadelphia:
Quaker City Publishing House; New York: Charles Drew;
Portland: John Russell; Chicago: J. Fairbanks & Co.;
Indianapolis: Fred L. Horton & Co. , 1880.

As in entry 597, but life of Arthur, pp. 332-354. All
copies examined rebound.

599 [Dement, Richmond S.] Field-Gar-A-Jim. Not By H. W. L.
Chicago: 1880. Orders Supplied by the Western News
Co.

F., t., [1], [2], [3]-4, 5, bl. [6], 7-49, bl. [50], 51-64.
Brown cloth. F. (cartoon) inserted. Burlesque life in
verse, pp. 7-49; Garfield's "scandals," pp. 51-64, in
prose. Anti-Garfield.

600 [Gilmore, James Robert.] James A. Garfield. New York:
Published by Harper & Brothers, Franklin Square Library,
Number 132 [c1880.]

Cover title [1], [2], [3]-64. Sewn. Title vignette. Illus.
in text. Caption title, p. [3], The Life of James A. Garfield, Republican Candidate for the Presidency. With Extracts From His Speeches. By Edmund Kirke.... Preface, p. [2], dated July 4, 1880; 3/4 p. adv. in single
col., p. 64; pr. in triple cols.

601 _____. Leben James A. Garfields, des republikanischen
Candidaten für die Präsidentschaft. Von Edmund Kirke....
New York: Harper Brothers, 1880.

Cover title [1], [2], [3]-48. Sewn. Title vignette. Illus.
in text. Preface, p. [2], as above; $\frac{1}{2}$ p. adv. in single
col., p. 48; pr. in triple cols. German translation of
entry 600.

602 Haven, E. O., ed. The Republican Manual of American Pro-
gress.... Including the Life and Times of General James
A. Garfield, By Rev. Gideon Draper, D.D. to Which Is
Added the Life of Chester A. Arthur. Illustrated. New
York: E. B. Treat; Chicago: R. C. Treat, 1880.

Pf. [1], bl. [2], cld. pl., t. [3], [4], [5], [6], [7]-9, bl.
[10], 11-544, 2 ℓℓ. adv. Reddish brown cloth. Cld. pl.
inserted, other illus. in text.

603 Hinsdale, Burke A. The Life and Character of James A. Garfield. [N. p., n. d., 1880.]

Caption title. [1]-4. Fld. Note concluding p. 4, col. 2,
"The Republican Text Book for the Campaign of 1880 gives
a full survey of the public life and character of Gen. Garfield. It is a 216 page volume, beautifully printed, and
sells for fifty cents. Address D. Appleton & Co., 1, 3,
and 5 Bond Street, New York."; pr. in dbl. cols.

604 _____. The Republican Text-Book for the Campaign of 1880. A Full History of General James A. Garfield's Public Life, With Other Political Information. New
York: D. Appleton and Company, 1880.

T. [i], [ii], [1], bl. [2], [3]-4, [5]-6, [7]-216, adv. [1]-
[6]. Buff illus. wrps. Sketches of Garfield and Arthur,
pp. [7]-88; pr. in dbl. cols.

605 McCabe, James D. From the Farm to the Presidential Chair,
     Being an Accurate and Comprehensive Account of the Life
     and Public Services of Gen. James A. Garfield ... to Which
     Is Added the Life of Gen. Chester A. Arthur.... Philadel-
     phia, Chicago, St. Louis, and Atlanta: The National Pub-
     lishing Co. [c1880.]

     2 pf., t. [1], [2], illus., [3-4], illus., 5-10, illus., [17]-
     540, 2 ℓℓ. adv. All copies examined rebound. 2 pf. and
     15 pls. inserted. Preface, pp. [3-4], dated Aug. 10, 1880;
     life of Garfield, pp. [17]-520; of Arthur, pp. [521]-540.

606 McClure, J. B., ed. Stories and Sketches of Gen. Garfield,
     Including His Early History ... and All the Interesting
     Facts of His Great Career From the Farm Boy to His Can-
     didacy for President. Chicago: Rhodes & McClure, Pub-
     lishers, 1880.

     Bl. [i], pf. [ii], illus. [iii-vi], t. [vii], [viii], [ix], x-[xiv],
     [xv], [xvi], 17-148, bl. [149], 150-158, ℓ. adv. Red cloth.
     Title vignette. Illus. in text. Life of Garfield, pp. 17-
     148; of Arthur, pp. 150-158.

607 _____. Stories and Sketches.... Chicago: Rhodes & Mc-
     Clure, 1880.

     As in entry 606, but life of Garfield, pp. 17-141, and
     Arthur, pp. 142-144.

608 Nevin, David Jenkins. Biographical Sketches of Gen'l James
     A. Garfield and Gen'l Chester A. Arthur, Republican Nomi-
     nees for the Presidency and Vice-Presidency of the United
     States. Philadelphia: Pres. Printing and Publishing Co.,
     1880.

     T. [1], [2], [3]-86, div. t. [87], bl. [88], [89]-111, [112]-
     116, [117]-118, [119]-120. Pink illus. wrps. Life of Gar-
     field, pp. [3]-86; of Arthur, pp. [89]-111; platform, pp.
     [112]-116; song, pp. [119]-120.

609 _____. Biographical Sketches.... Philadelphia: Pres.
     Printing and Publishing Co., 1880.

     As in entry 608, but song, pp. [119]-120; Garfield's ac-
     ceptance of nomination, pp. [121]-125; Arthur's, pp. [126]-
     128. Green illus. wrps.

610 Pierrepont, Edwards. Speech ... Delivered Before the Repub-
     lican Meeting, at the Hall of Cooper Institute, October 6th,
     1880. New York: Cornwell Press, Book and Job Printers,
     and Lithographers, 1880.

     T. [1], bl. [2], [3]-19, bl. [20]. Grey wrps. Pro-Gar-
     field.

611   The Republican Leaders. Biographical Sketches of James A.
      Garfield, Republican Candidate for President, and Chester
      A. Arthur, Republican Candidate for Vice-President. New
      York: Published by the National Republican Committee,
      1880.

      Cover title. [1]-32. Blue wrps. , adv. outer back. Life
      of Garfield, by E. V. Smalley, pp. [1]-21; of Arthur, by
      Edgar L. Murlin, pp. [22]-32.

612   The Republican Leaders.... Letters of Acceptance, and the
      Republican Platform. [N. p. , n. d. , 1880.]

      Cover title. [1]-64. Blue wrps.

613   Riddle, A. G. The Life, Character and Public Services of
      Jas. A. Garfield. Philadelphia: Wm. Flint; New York:
      F. S. Bogue; Chicago: Tyler & Co.; Detroit: R. D. S.
      Tyler & Co.; San Francisco: A. L. Bancroft & Co.; Hart-
      ford: Columbian Book Company; Washington: James J.
      Chapman [c1880.]

      Pf. , t. [i], [ii], [iii], bl. [iv], [1-2], [3-14], div. t. [15],
      bl. [16], 17-405, bl. [406], div. t. [407], bl. [408], port. ,
      409-427, [428]. Charcoal grey cloth. Pf. and pl. in-
      serted, other illus. in text. Life of Garfield, pp. 17-405;
      of Arthur, pp. 409-427. Also noted in green cloth.

614   Smalley, E. V. The Republican Manual.... With Biographi-
      cal Sketches of James A. Garfield and Chester A. Arthur.
      New York: American Book Exchange, 1880.

      Pf. , t. [1], [2], [3], [4], [5]-333, bl. [334], div. t. [335],
      bl. [336], 337-341, bl. [342]. Brown cloth. Pf. and pl.
      inserted. Sketches of Garfield and Arthur, pp. 153-333.
      Also noted in blue cloth.

HANCOCK, WINFIELD SCOTT (Democratic)

615   Armstrong, W. W. A Record of the Statesmanship and Poli-
      tical Achievements of Gen. W. S. Hancock. Compiled
      From the Records, and Written in Blank Verse.... [N. p.]
      1880.

      Cover title. 2 bl. ℓℓ. Cream wrps. Political joke.

616   _____ . A Record of the Statesmanship and Political
      Achievements of Gen. Winfield Scott Hancock, Regular
      Democratic Nominee for President of the United States.
      Compiled From the Records. By a Citizen. [N. p.] 1880.

      As in entry 615, but outer back wrp. pr. Finis. Title
      vignette.

617   A Biographical Review of the Military and Civil Services of
      Major Gen'l W. S. Hancock. [N. p. , n. d. , 1880.]

      Cover title [1], [2]-8. Self wrps.

618   Bright Record of the Patriot Hancock.   Black Record of the
      Politician Garfield.   Washington: The Globe Printing and
      Publishing House, 1880.

      Cover title.   [1]-8. Illus. wrps. , inner front and entire
      back with illus. Title vignette. Pr. in dbl. cols.

619   Brisbin, James S.   A Soldier's Story of a Soldier's Life.
      Winfield Scott Hancock. . . .   His Life, Related in Soldier-
      Fashion. . . .   With a Brief Sketch of William H. English.
      [Philadelphia?] Copyrighted by L. Lum Smith, 1880.

      T. [1], bl. [2], 3, 4, 5, bl. [6], 7-112. Green illus.
      wrps. Illus. in text.

620   The Campaign Text Book.   Why the People Want a Change. . . .
      New York: Issued by the National Democratic Committee,
      1880.

      T. [1], [2], [3]-557, bl. [558], i-ii, iii-xvi. All copies
      examined rebound. Sketches of Hancock and English, pp.
      9-50; list of contents, pp. i-ii; index, pp. iii-xvi.

621   Cole, J. R.   The Life and Public Services of Winfield Scott
      Hancock, Major-General U. S. A. . . .   Also, the Life and
      Services of Hon. William H. English, the Experienced
      Statesman and Man of Business. . . .   Illustrated With Fine
      Full-Page Steel Portraits and Other Engravings.   Cincinnati:
      Douglass Brothers, Publishers, 1880.

      Pf. , t. [1], [2], [3]-8, [9]-15, 16, [17]-221, bl. [222],
      port. , [223]-306, 307-424. Dark maroon cloth. Pf. and
      pl. inserted, other illus. in text. Life of Hancock, pp.
      [17]-221; of English, pp. [223]-306.

622   The Comic Biography of Winfield S. Hancock, Prepared From
      Carefully Selected Stock and Warranted Perfectly Fresh.
      By the Detroit Free-Press Man.   Profusely Illustrated.
      New York: Copyrighted and Published by the Chic Publish-
      ing Company [1880.]

      T. [1], adv. [2], [3]-29, bls. [30-31], adv. [32].   Bluish
      grey illus. wrps. , adv. on inner front and entire back.
      Illus. in text. Anti-Hancock.

623   Denison, C. W.   Hancock "The Superb. "   The Early Life and
      Public Career of Winfield S. Hancock, Major-General
      U. S. A.   The Imposing Record of a Progressive and Bril-

liant Career.... Including Also a Sketch of the Life of Hon. William H. English. Richly Embellished With Many Fine Illustrations.... Detroit: Published by R. D. S. Tyler & Co.; Chicago: Tyler & Co., 1880.

Pf., t. [i], [ii], iii-iv, v-x, 11-431, adv. [432]. Maroon cloth. Pf. and 7 pls. inserted. Life of English, pp. 417-431. Copies also noted with p. [432] bl.

624 _____ . Hancock "The Superb. "... Philadelphia: Published by H. W. Kelley [c1880.]

As in entry 623, adv. p. [432]. Purple cloth. Also noted in red cloth, p. [432] bl.

625 _____ . Hancock "The Superb. "... Philadelphia: Published by William Flint, 1880.

As in entry 623, adv. p. [432]. Maroon cloth.

626 _____ . Hancock "The Superb. "... Cleveland: Published by W. W. Williams, 1880.

As in entry 623, adv. p. [432]. Red cloth.

*627 Eickhoff, U. Leben, Thaten und Grundsätze von Winfield Scott Hancock. [N. p.] 1880.

Cover title.

628 Forney, John W. Life and Military Career of Winfield Scott Hancock. This Work Comprises His Early Life, Education and Remarkable Military Career.... It Also Contains a Succinct Biographical Sketch of Hon. Wm. H. English.... Illustrated. Philadelphia, Chicago, Cincinnati, Springfield [and] Atlanta: Published by Hubbard Bros.; St. Louis: Lillingston & Co.; San Francisco: A. L. Bancroft & Co.; Emporia: T. Prothero [c1880.]

Flyleaf [1-2], pf. [3-4], t. [5], [6], 7-8, unp. ℓ., 9, bl. [10], 11-15, bl. [16], 17-502. Blue cloth, blue endpapers. Pf. and 17 pls. inserted. Sig. 29 (pp. 483-498) bound before sig. 28 (pp. 465-479). Also noted in blue cloth with brown coated endpapers.

629 _____ . Life ... of Winfield Scott Hancock.... Philadelphia, Cincinnati, Chicago and St. Louis: Published by J. C. McCurdy & Co. [c1880.]

As in entry 628. Blue cloth.

630 _____ . Life ... of Winfield Scott Hancock.... Boston: Published by W. H. Thompson [c1880.]

Endpaper [1-2], flyleaf [3-4], pf. [5-6], t. [7], [8], [9], bl. [10], 11-12, 13, bl. [14], 15-16, 17-500. Blue cloth. Pf. and 17 pls. inserted. Copies also noted with this imprint and collation as in entry 628.

631 _____ . Life ... of Winfield Scott Hancock.... Chicago: Published by H. N. Hinckley & Co. [c1880.]

Pf. [1-2], t. [3], [4], [5], bl. [6], 7-8, 9, bl. [10], 11-15, bl. [16], 17-504. Blue cloth. Pf. and 18 pls. inserted.

632 _____ . Life ... of Winfield Scott Hancock.:... Boston and Concord: Published by D. L. Guernsey [c1880.]

As in entry 631, but text pp. 17-502. Blue cloth. Pf. and 17 pls. inserted.

633 _____ . Life ... of Winfield Scott Hancock.... By John W. Forney, Forty Years a Journalist, and the Life-Long Intimate Friend of "The Superb Soldier." Illustrated. Cleveland: Published by C. C. Wick & Co. [c1880.]

As in entry 630. Blue cloth, brown coated endpapers. Pf. and 18 pls. inserted.

634 Freed, A. T. Hancock. The Life and Public Services of Winfield Scott Hancock, Major-General United States Army; Democratic Nominee for President in 1880. Chicago: Henry A. Sumner & Company, Publishers, 1880.

Half title [1], bl. [2], pf. [3-4], t. [5], [6], [7]-74, ℓ. adv. Brown wrps., adv. on inner front and entire back; at head of front, Sumner's Popular Biographical Series. Pf. inserted. Also noted in grey wrps., lacking half title.

635 Gardiner, O. C. Sketch of the Life and Public Services of Winfield S. Hancock.... New York: John Polhemus, Publisher [1880.]

Cover title [1], bl. [2], [3]-31, bl. [32]. Sewn. Title vignette.

636 Gen. Winfield S. Hancock. Democratic Candidate for President of the United States. New York: Published by Currier and Ives [1880.]

Caption title. Cld. lithograph port., $17\frac{1}{4}$ x $13\frac{1}{2}$, with 10 line capsule biography below caption.

637 Goodrich, Frederick E. The Life and Public Services of Winfield Scott Hancock, Major-General, U.S.A. With an Introduction by Hon. Frederick O. Prince.... Boston: Published by Lee & Shepard; Philadelphia: Quaker City Pub-

lishing House; New York: Charles Drew; Indianapolis:
Fred L. Horton & Co. ; Chicago: J. Fairbanks & Co. ,
1880.

Pf. , t. [1], [2], [3], bl. [4], div. t. [5], bl. [6], [7]-8, 9-
12, [13]-20, div. t. [21], bl. [22], [23]-325, bl. [326],
port. , div. t. [327], bl. [328], [329]-367, 368-375, bl.
[376]. Brown cloth. Pf. and 7 pls. inserted. Preface, pp.
[7]-8, dated July 15, 1880; life of Hancock, pp. [23]-325;
of English, pp. [329]-367; appendix, pp. 368-375.

638   . The Life ... of Winfield Scott Hancock.... Boston
        [etc.] 1880.

As in entry 637, but appendix, pp. 368-384. Maroon cloth.

639   . The Life ... of Winfield Scott Hancock.... Indi-
        anapolis: Fred. L. Horton & Co. , 1880.

As in entry 637, but p. [2], copyright, printed upside down.
Brown cloth.

*640 Hancock and English Democratic Campaign Song Book With Por-
      traits and Biographical Sketches.... [Cincinnati:] W. R.
      Swan & Co. [c1880.]

27 pp. , incl. pf. Listed in the Library of Congress but
unexamined.

641 Hutchins, Stilson. Political Manual for 1880. [Washington?]
     Washington Post Publishing Company [1880?]

Cover title. [i]-ii, [1]-252. Grey wrps. , back lacking in
all copies examined. Lives of Hancock and English, pp.
220-228; pr. in dbl. cols.

642 Junkin, D. X. The Life of Winfield Scott Hancock: Personal,
     Military, and Political. By ... and Frank H. Norton....
     Illustrated on Wood With Battle-Scenes by A. R. Waud, and
     Steel Portrait by Hall, From Sarony. New York: D. Ap-
     pleton and Company, 1880.

Pf. , t. [i], [ii], [iii]-iv, [v]-xiii, bl. [xiv], [xv], bl. [xvi],
[1]-398, 3 ℓ ℓ. adv. Blue cloth. Pf. and 12 pls. inserted.

643 The Life, Brilliant Military Career, Public Services of General
     Winfield Scott Hancock. An Extremely Interesting Biography
     and a Useful Text Book.... Philadelphia: Published by
     Barclay & Co. [c1880.]

T. [i], [ii], 19-64. Blue illus. wrps. Also noted in green
wrps.

644 McClure, J. B. , ed. Life of Gen. Hancock Including His Early History, War Record, Public Life, Nomination, and All
the Interesting Facts of His Great Career. ...   Chicago:
Rhodes & McClure, Publishers, 1880.

Rlyleaf [1-2], pf. [3-4], illus. [5-6], t. [7], [8], [9], [10-
14], [15], illus. [16], 17-110, bl. [111], port. 112, 113-
124. Red cloth. Title vignette. Illus. in text. Life of
Hancock, pp. 17-110; of English, pp. 113-124. Also noted
with terminal ℓ. adv.

645 _____ . Life of Gen. Hancock. ...   Chicago: Rhodes & Mc-
Clure, Publishers, 1880.

2 flyleaves [1-4], bl. [5], pf. [6], t. [7] ... 17-64, ornament [65], illus. [66], 67-88, 89-107, port. [108], 109-
114, ℓ. adv. Grey green illus. wrps. , adv. on outer back.
Title vignette. Illus. in text. Life of Hancock, pp. 17-
64; the Nomination, pp. 67-88; misc. , 89-107; English, pp.
109-114.

646 Norton, Frank H. Life and Public Services of Winfield Scott
Hancock. New York: D. Appleton & Company, 1880.

Cover title. [1]-31, adv. [32]. Cream illus. wrps. , inner
front and entire back with illus. Title vignette. Pr. in
dbl. cols.

647 Southworth, Alvan S. Life of Gen. Winfield S. Hancock. ...
With an Introduction by Hon. Thomas F. Bayard. ...   Authorized Edition. New York: The American News Company, 1880.

T. [1], [2], [3], bl. [4], 5-6, 7-14, 15-256. Grey illus.
wrps. , quote on outer back. Preface, p. [3], dated July
20, 1880; introduction, pp. 7-14.

BUTLER, BENJAMIN F. (Greenback)

648 Gen. Benjamin F. Butler's True Record. [Boston? 1879?]

Cover title [1], adv. [2], [3]-32. Sewn. At foot of p. 32,
"Published by Order of Committee. John I. Baker, Secretary. October, 1879. "

649 Bland, T. A. Life of Benjamin F. Butler. Boston: Lee and
Shepard, Publishers; New York: Charles T. Dillingham,
1879.

Pf. , t. [i], [ii], [iii], bl. [iv], [1]-4, [5]-6, 7-202, adv.
1-[8]. Greenish blue cloth. Pf. inserted.

GRANT, ULYSSES SIMPSON (Republican)

650 The Grant Reception Monograph. Comprising a Comprehensive
     Record of the Memorable Events of "Reception Week" in
     Chicago; Biographical Sketch of the Great Hero. ...   Chi-
     cago: L. E. Adams, Publisher, 1879.

     Pf. , t. [3], [4], [5], [6], 7-118, 119-121, bl. [122]. All
     copies examined rebound.

651 The Great American Empire; Or, Gen. Ulysses S. Grant, Em-
     peror of North America. By an American Citizen.   St.
     Louis: W. S. Bryan, Publisher, 1879.

     F. , t. [1], [2], [3]-4, [5]-6, [7]-172. Tan cloth. F. (car-
     toon) inserted, other illus. in text.   Anti-Grant 3rd term.

652 Headley, Joel Tyler.   The Life and Travels of General
     Grant. ... Philadelphia: Hubbard Bros. ; Boston: W. H.
     Thompson & Co. , 1879.

     Flyleaf [i-ii], pf. [iii-iv], t. [v], [vi], vii-viii, ix-xvii,
     xviii-xxii, 23-251, bl. [252], div. t. [1], bl. [2], 3-599,
     bl. [600]. Terra cotta cloth. Pf. inserted, other illus.
     in text.   Life of Grant, pp. 23-251.

653 [Hicks, W. H.] General Grant's Tour Around the World; With
     a Sketch of His Life. Illustrated. Chicago: Rand, Mc-
     Nally & Co. , 1879.

     Pf. , t. [1], [2], [3], bl. [4], 5-6, map [7], bl. [8], 9-288.
     Brown illus. wrps. Illus. in text.

654 Larke, Julian K.   General U. S. Grant: His Early Life and
     Military Career, With a Brief Account of His Presidential
     Administration and Tour Around the World.   New York:
     W. J. Johnston, Publisher, 1879.

     T. [1], bl. [2], [3]-4, [5]-12, [13]-509, [510]-512. Terra
     cotta cloth. Chronology, pp. [510]-512. Also noted in
     green cloth.

655 McCabe, James D.   A Tour Around the World by General
     Grant. ... Philadelphia, Chicago, St. Louis, and Atlanta:
     The National Publishing Co. [c1879.]

     F. , t. [i], [ii], pl. , 21-23, bl. [24], pl. , 25-31, bl. [32],
     33-810, 3 ℓℓ. adv. All copies examined rebound. F. and
     8 pls. inserted, other illus. in text.   Preface, pp. 21-23,
     dated Nov. 12, 1879.

656 McClure, J. B. , ed.   Stories, Sketches and Speeches of Gen-
     eral Grant at Home and Abroad, in Peace and in War.

Including His Trip ... and Important Events of His Life.
Illustrated. Chicago: Rhodes & McClure, Publishers, 1880.

Flyleaf [1-2], pf. [3-4], t. [5], [6], [7], 8-12, [13], 14-15,
illus. [16], 17-216, pub. cat. [i-ii], [1]-[6], ℓ. adv. Red
cloth. Illus. in text. Preface, p. [7], dated Nov. 10,
1879. Also noted in green cloth.

657 Packard, J. F. Grant's Tour Around the World.... Care-
fully Edited and Arranged From the Correspondence of the
New York Herald.... Philadelphia: Published by William
Flint; St. Louis: W. S. Bryan; Detroit: R. D. S. Tyler
& Co., 1880.

T. [i], [ii], iii-iv, v-xi, xii-xvi, 17-802. All copies examined rebound. Pf. (lacking) and 37 pls. inserted, other
illus. in text. Life of Grant, Chapter I.

658 [Palmer, Loomis T.] General U. S. Grant's Reise um die
Welt. Enthaltend Seine Reden, Sowie Eine Beschreibung
Seiner Reisen und der Ihm zu Ehren Veranstalteten Emp-
fangsfeier Lichkeiten, Nebft Biographischen Skizze Seines
Lebens.... Cincinnnati [sic]: Forshee & McMakin, 1880.

Pf., t. [1], [2], [3]-8, [9]-436. Green cloth with L. T.
Remlap cited on front cover. Pf. and 17 pls. (incl. one
fld.) inserted. German ed. of following.

659 _____. General U. S. Grant's Tour Around the World.
Embracing His Speeches, Receptions, and Description of
His Travels. With a Biographical Sketch of His Life.
Edited By L. T. Remlap. Seventh Thousand. Chicago:
J. Fairbanks & Co.; New York: F. O. Evans & Co.;
Fond Du Lac: G. L. Benjamin; Cleveland: C. C. Wick &
Co. [c1879.]

Pf., t. [1], [2], [3]-8, [9]-350. Maroon cloth. Pf. and 7
pls. inserted.

660 _____. General U. S. Grant's Tour.... Fifteenth Thousand. Chicago: J. Fairbanks & Co.; New York: F. O.
Evans & Co.; Hartford: James, Betts & Co.; Topeka:
M. A. Runner & Co.; Cleveland: C. C. Wick & Co.; Detroit: F. B. Drake & Co.; San Francisco: J. B. Hill; Indianapolis: Fred. L. Horton & Co., 1880.

Pf., t. [1], [2], [3]-8, map, [9]-483, 484-487, pub. cat.
[488-496]. All copies examined rebound. Pf. and 21 pls.
inserted. Chronology, pp. 484-487.

661 A Reprint of Certain Articles in Illustration of the Life and
Services of Gen'l U. S. Grant, Both as Soldier & Statesman, and in His Defence Against the Assaults of His En-
emies. [N. p.] 1880.

T. [1], [2], [3]-28.   Grey green wrps.

662   Swift, John L.   About Grant.   Boston: Lee and Shepard, Pub-
      lishers; New York: Charles T. Dillingham, 1880.

      T. [1], [2], 3-4, 5-6, div. t. [7], [8], 9-206, l. adv.
      Red cloth with pr. paper label on backstrip.

SHERMAN, JOHN (Republican)

663   Bronson, S. A.   John Sherman; What He Has Said and Done,
      Being a History of the Life and Public Services of the Hon.
      John Sherman, Secretary of the Treasury of the United
      States.   Columbus: H. W. Derby & Co., Publishers, 1880.

      Pf., t. [i], [ii], iii, bl. [iv], v-xiv, 15-272.   Green cloth.
      Pf. inserted.

664   Poore, Benjamin Perley.   The Life and Public Services of
      John Sherman.   Cincinnati: Published by the Sherman Club,
      1880.

      Cover title.   [1]-43, bl. [44].   Grey wrps., Club informa-
      tion on outer back.   An attempt to persuade the National
      Republican Convention to nominate Sherman for President.

1884

GENERAL WORKS

665   Babcock, Benjamin F.   The Presidential Favorites a Political
      Handbook, Containing the Portraits of Over Twenty Ameri-
      can Statesmen, Together With Their Biographies....   Chi-
      cago: Published by Babcock, Fort & Co., 1884.

      T. [1], [2], [3], illus. [4], [5], [6], port. [7], bl. [8], 9-
      144.   Green wrps., adv. on inner front and back; front
      notes The Presidential Favorites 1884.   Illus. in text.

666   Boyd, James P.   Building and Ruling the Republic....   Phila-
      delphia [and] Brantford, Ont.:   Published by Bradley, Gar-
      retson & Co.; Columbus, Chicago, Nashville, St. Louis
      [and] San Francisco: William Garretson & Co., 1884.

      F., t. [1], [2], 3-4, 5-10, (Parts I-III) 11-712, 713-718,
      div. t. 719, illus. [720], pl., (Part IV) 721-784, pl., div.

t. [1], (Part V) 2-67, bl. [68].   Brown cloth.   F. and 12
pls., dbl. pp. map, inserted.

667   The Lives of the Four Candidates.   Including the Biography of
Each, From His Ancestry to the Present, Together With a
History of His Public Services, National Doings, etc.,
etc....   Chicago: Elder Publishing Company, 1884.

Pf. [1-2], t. [3], bl. [4], 5-115, bl. [116].   Brown wrps.,
adv. on inner front and entire back.   Illus. in text.

668   Our Next President: Sketches and Portraits of the Candidates.
Providence: J. A. & R. A. Reid, Publishers, 1884.

Caption title.   Adv. and illus. [1], 2-4.   Folio.   Title vignette.   Illus. in text.   Below caption, Vol. 1.   No. 1.
Westerly, R. I., Presidential Year, 1884; brief sketches
of Cleveland and Hendricks, Blaine and Logan, Butler, and
John St. John, pp. 2-4, adv. interspersed.

669   Our Next President: Sketches and Portraits of the Prospective
Candidates for President.   Presented With Compliments of
Comstock Bros. Clothiers....   Providence: J. A. & R. A.
Reid, 1884.

Cover title [1], 2-15, adv. [16].   Sewn.   Title vignette.
Illus. in text.   Adv. brochure with brief sketches of Cleve-
land, Blaine, Tilden, Sherman, Bayard, Arthur, Edmunds,
Randall, Payne, Logan, Lincoln, Sherman, McDonald, and
"The Dark Horse," pp. 2-15, each p. also being 1/3 adv.

670   Portraits of Republican and Democratic Candidates With the
Nominating Speeches, and Sketches of the Lives of the Candidates....   Compliments of the Ebbitt House, Washington,
D. C.   Chicago: Vandercook & Co., Engraving and Publishing [1884.]

Cover title.   Adv. [1], port. [2], map [3], adv. 4, 5-9,
adv. 10, port. [11], adv. 12, 13-17, adv. 18, port. [19],
adv. 20, 21-23, adv. 24, ℓ. adv. in green added, port.
[25], adv. [26], 27, adv. 28-32.   Green illus. wrps., adv.
on inner front and entire back.   Illus. in text.   Adv. brochure with sketches of Blaine, pp. 5-9; Logan, pp. 13-17;
Cleveland, pp. 21-23; and Hendricks, p. 27, adv. interspersed.

CLEVELAND, GROVER (Democratic)

671   Barnum, Augustine.   The Lives of Grover Cleveland and
Thomas A. Hendricks, Democratic Presidential Candidates
of 1884.   An Authorized, Authentic and Complete History
of Their Public Career and Private Life....   Superbly

Illustrated With Magnificent Portraits and Full-Page Engravings By T. W. Williams.   Hartford: Published by The
Hartford Publishing Co. , 1884.

Pf. , t. [i], [ii], [iii-iv], [v]-vi, [vii]-viii, [ix]-xxiii, bl.
[xxiv], [25]-502.   Reddish brown cloth blindstamped all
over, backstrip also stamped in gold.   Pf. , port. , and 10
pls. inserted.   Copies noted with pf. and port. present,
but lacking the 10 additional pls. called for.   Also noted in
reddish brown cloth, but front stamped in gold and backstrip in brown.

672 _____.   The Lives of Grover Cleveland ... By Augustine
Barnum, of the Editorial Staff of the New York Mail and
Express.   Superbly Illustrated. ...   Boston: Geo. M. Smith
& Co. , 1884.

As in entry 671.

673 Black, Chauncey F. , ed.   The Lives of Grover Cleveland and
Thomas A. Hendricks, Together With a Complete History of
the Democratic Party. ...   Profusely Illustrated.   Philadelphia: Standard Publishing Co. , 1884.

Pf. , t. [1], [2], 3, 4, 5-6, 7, bl. [8], 9-12, 13-480.
Brown green cloth.   Pf. and 24 pls. inserted.   At head of
title, Two Great Careers.

674 _____.   The Lives of Grover Cleveland. ...   Philadelphia:
John E. Potter and Company [c1884.]

As in entry 673.   Green cloth, front noting Lives of the
Democratic Candidates.

675 Dorsheimer, William.   Life and Public Services of Hon. Grov-
er Cleveland, the Model Citizen. ...   Also, the Life and
Public Services of the Renowned Statesman and Nominee
for the Vice-Presidency, Hon. Thomas A. Hendricks by
W. U. Hensel. ...   Profusely Illustrated.   Philadelphia,
New York, Boston, Cincinnati, Chicago, St. Louis [and]
Kansas City: Hubbard Brothers, Publishers; San Francisco:
A. L. Bancroft & Co. [c1884.]

Pf. [1-2], t. [3], [4], 5-6, 7, bl. [8], 9-14, 15-16, div.
t. [17], bl. [18], [19], bl. [20], 21-172, div. t. [173],
[174], port. [175-176], 177-299, bl. [300], div. t. [301],
bl. [302], 303-578.   Blue cloth.   Pf. and 25 pls. inserted,
that of Arthur, pp. [507-508], being incorrectly placed between pp. 532 and [533].   Life of Cleveland, pp. 21-172;
of Hendricks, pp. 177-299.

676 _____.   Life and Public Services of Hon. Grover Cleveland. ...   New York, Atlanta, Cincinnati, Detroit, Little

Rock [and] Kansas City: Standard Publishing House; Chicago: Empire Publishing House; San Francisco: Eagle
Publishing House [c1884.]

As in entry 675.   Pls. with error present.

677   .   Life and Public Services of Hon. Grover Cleveland. . . .   Springfield: James D. Gill, Publisher [c1884.]

As in entry 675.   Pls. with error present.

678   .   Life and Public Services of Hon. Grover Cleveland. . . .   Boston: Russell & Henderson, Publishers [c1884.]

As in entry 675.   Pls. with error present.

679   Goodrich, Frederick E.   The Life and Public Services of
Grover Cleveland, With Incidents of His Early Life and
an Account of His Rise to Eminence in His Profession. . . .
Illustrated.   Wilkes Barre: James A. Crogan, Publisher,
1884.

Pf. , t. [1], [2], [3], bl. [4], [5-6], [7]-13, bl. [14], [15]-
23, [24], [25]-427, bl. [428], port. , div. t. [429], bl.
[430], [431], bl. [432], [433]-504.   Green cloth.   Pf. , pl.
inserted, other illus. in text.   Life of Cleveland, pp. [25]-
427; of Hendricks, pp. [433]-504; pref. dated July, 1884.

680   .   The Life ... of Grover Cleveland. . . .   Boston:
B. B. Russell [c1884.]

As in entry 679.   Brown cloth.

681   .   The Life ... of Grover Cleveland. . . .   With an Introduction by Hon. Frederick O. Prince, Ex-Mayor of the
City of Boston, and Secretary of the Democratic National
Committee.   Illustrated.   Portland: H. Hallett & Co.
[c1884.]

As in entry 679.   Brown cloth.

682   Grover Cleveland.   The Open Record of an Honest Man.   [New
York: Clarke & Co. , 1884.]

Cover title [1], [2], [3-4], [5]-40.   Self wrps.   Title vignette.   At head of title, [Document No. 1.]   "Public Office,
a Public Trust. "; life of Cleveland, pp. [3-4]; his record,
pp. [5]-40; pr. in dbl. cols.

683   Grover Cleveland.   The Open Record of an Honest Man.   [N.
p. , n. d. , 1884.]

Cover title [1], [2]-3, [4]-35, 35-36.   Stapled.   Title vignette.   At head of title, "Public Office, a Public Trust. ";

life, pp. [2]-3; record, pp. [4]-35; Democratic platform, pp. 35-36; pr. in dbl. cols.

684 Grover Cleveland. Leben und Wirken Eines Ehrenmannes. [N. p. , n. d. , 1884.]

Cover title [1], [2], [3-4], [5]-40. Self wrps. Title vignette. At head of title, Oeffentliche Uemter Beruhen auf Öffentlichem Vertrauen. (above that at upper left, [Document B.]. German translation of entry 682.

685 Handford, Thomas W. Early Life and Public Services of Hon. Grover Cleveland, the Fearless and Independent Governor of the Empire State.... Also, the Life of Hon. Thomas A. Hendricks.... Illustrated With Portraits of the Candidates.... Mansfield, Ohio: The Home Publishing Co. , 1884.

Pf. , [1], [2], 3-4, 5, bl. [6], 7-12, pl. , 13-230, port. , 231-297, bl. [298], 299-510. Green cloth. Pf. , 19 pls. , fac. inserted. Life of Cleveland, pp. 13-230; of Hendricks, pp. 231-297. Sketch of Cleveland by Eugene Tyler Chamberlain?

686 _____ . Early Life ... of Hon. Grover Cleveland.... Chicago and New York: Caxton Publishing Company, 1884.

As in entry 685.

687 King, Pendleton. Life and Public Services of Grover Cleveland. New York and London: G. P. Putnam's Sons, The Knickerbocker Press, 1884.

Pf. , t. [i], [ii], [iii]-v, bl. [vi], [vii], [viii], [1]-220, [221]-224. Pink wrps. , adv. on inner front and entire back, front noting Grover Cleveland pr. in red. Pf. and 2 pls. inserted. Preface, pp. [iii]-v, dated July 31, 1884. Also noted in brown cloth.

688 La Fevre, Benjamin. Biographies of S. Grover Cleveland, the Democratic Candidate for President, and Thomas A. Hendricks, the Democratic Candidate for Vice-President.... Chicago and New York: Baird & Dillon, 1884.

Pf. [i-ii], pf. [iii-iv], t. [v], [vi], vii-ix, bl. [x], div. t. [xi], bl. [xii], [1]-96, div. t. [1], bl. [2], 3-318, div. t. [1], bl. [2], 3-101, bl. [102]. Brown cloth. 2 pf. inserted. Biographies, pp. [1]-96; political parties, pp. 3-318; platforms, pp. 3-101. At head of title, Campaign of '84. ; pr. in dbl. cols.

689 _____ . Biographies of S. Grover Cleveland.... San Francisco: J. Dewing & Co. , 1884.

As in entry 688.

690 _____. Biographies of S. Grover Cleveland. ...   Burlington, Iowa: L. F. Segner, 1884.

As in entry 688.

691 _____. Biographies of S. Grover Cleveland. ...   Philadelphia: Fireside Publishing Company, 1884.

As in entry 688, but biographies, pp. [1]-95, political parties, pp. 3-313, and platforms, pp. 3-94. All copies examined rebound.

692 Life of Grover Cleveland. A Record of Incompetency, Dema-
goguery and Mediocrity. ...   Philadelphia: John D. Avil &
Co. , Printers & Publishers [1884.]

Cover title [1], [2], [3]-32. Stapled. Text pr. in dbl.
cols. At head of title, Campaign of 1884. Anti-Cleveland.

693 The Political Reformation of 1884. A Democratic Campaign
Book. New York: By Authority of the National Democratic
Committee, 1884.

T. [1], bl. [2], [3]-293, 294-297, bl. [298], 299-302.
Brown cloth. Lives of Cleveland and Hendricks, pp. 18-
89; appendix, pp. 294-297; contents, pp. 299-302. Also
noted in dark green cloth and grey wrps.

694 Triplett, Frank. The Authorized Pictorial Lives of Stephen
Grover Cleveland and Thomas Andrews Hendricks. ...   New
Steel Plate Portraits and Fine Engravings From Original
Photographs, etc. New York and St. Louis: N. D. Thomp-
son & Co. , Publishers, 1884.

Pf. , [i-ii], t. [iii], [iv], v-xi, illus. xii, xiii-xxxii, 33-
568. Purple cloth. Pf. , pl. inserted, other illus. in text.
At head of title, The Standard Bearers. [dash] Official Edition. ; life of Cleveland, pp. 33-192; of Hendricks, pp. 195-
350.

695 _____. ... Lives of Stephen Grover Cleveland. ...   Chicago: J. S. Goodman & Co. , Publishers, 1884.

As in entry 694.

696 Welch, Deshler. Stephen Grover Cleveland, a Sketch of His
Life to Which Is Appended a Short Account of the Life of
Thomas Andrews Hendricks. New York: John W. Lovell
Company [c1884.]

Pf. , t. [i], [ii], [iii]-iv, fac. letter [v], bl. [vi], [vii]-
viii, bl. [ix], illus. [x], [1]-193, bl. [194], [195]-222.

Red and green wrps., pr. in black, adv. on inner front
and entire back, front also noting Lovell's Library, No.
427. 25 Cents Vol. 8, No. 427 Sept 2, 1884. Fac. letter,
fld., inserted. Preface, pp. [iii]-iv, dated July 21, 1884.

697 _____. Stephen Grover Cleveland.... New York: R.
Worthington, 1884.

As in entry 696. Blue cloth with green coated endpapers.

BLAINE, JAMES G. (Republican)

698 Balch, William Ralston. An American Career and Its Triumph.
The Life and Public Services of James G. Blaine, With the
Story of John A. Logan's Career.... Profusely Illustrated.
Philadelphia: John E. Potter and Company [c1884.]

Pf., t. [1], [2], [3], bl. [4], 5-7, bl. [8], 9-11, 12, 13-
546. Green cloth noting on front Lives of the Republican
Candidates, purple coated floral endpapers. Pf. and 25 pls.
inserted, 1 map in text.

699 _____. An American Career.... St. Louis: John Burns
Publishing Co., 1884.

As in entry 698. Blue cloth noting on front An American
Career and Its Triumph 1884 in the Life of James G.
Blaine, green coated floral endpapers. Also noted with
aqua endpapers as above.

700 _____. An American Career.... Philadelphia: Thayer,
Merriam & Co., Limited, 1884.

As in entry 698. All copies examined rebound.

701 Balestier, Charles Wolcott. James G. Blaine a Sketch of His
Life With a Brief Record of the Life of John A. Logan.
New York: John W. Lovell Company [c1884.]

Pf., t. [i], [ii], fac. letter, [iii]-v, bl. [vi], [vii]-viii, [3]-
244, bl. [245], port. [246], div. t. [247], bl. [248], [249]-
261, bl. [262], [263]-296, 6 ℓℓ. adv. Green wrps., pr. in
red and black, adv. on inner front and entire back, front
also noting Lovell's Library (Vol. 8, No. 405, July 12,
1884). Pf., pl., and fac. letter inserted. Life of Blaine, pp.
[3]-244; of Logan, pp. [249]-261; appendices, pp. [263]-296.

702 _____. James G. Blaine.... New York: R. Worthington,
1884.

As in entry 701, but life of Blaine, pp. [1]-244, port., div.
t. [245], bl. [246], Logan, pp. [247]-261, bl. [262], appendices, pp. [263]-296. Brown cloth.

703 Biographies of Blaine and Logan, With the Proceedings of the
National Convention and an Account of the Issues of the
Campaign of '84. [N. p. , n. d. , 1884.]

Cover title. 2 pf. , [1]-70, 71-79, 80-95, 96. Brown
wrps. , entire back lacking on all copies examined. 2 pf.
inserted. Life of Blaine, pp. [1]-48; of Logan, pp. 49-70.

*704 Blaine & Logan Campaign Songster With Sketches of the Can-
didates. Canal Dover, O. : Arnold Brothers, 1884.

16 pp. , illus.

705 Boutwell, George S. Why I Am a Republican ... With Biographical Sketches of the Republican Candidates. Hartford:
Wm. J. Betts & Co. , 1884.

T. [1], [2], [3]-4, 5, [6], 7-195, bl. [196], i-lii. Blue
cloth. 2 pls. inserted. Lives of Blaine and Logan, pp.
165-195.

706 _____ . Why I Am a Republican. ... Springfield: Bay State
Publishing Co. , 1884.

As in entry 705. Greenish blue cloth.

707 _____ . Why I Am a Republican. ... Tecumseh, Mich. :
A. W. Mills, 1884.

As in entry 705. Blue cloth.

708 Buel, J. W. Authorized Pictorial Lives of James Gillespie
Blaine and John Alexander Logan. ... New Steel Plate Portraits and Fine Engravings From Original Photographs, etc.
New York and St. Louis: N. D. Thompson & Co. , Publishers, 1884.

Pf. [i-ii], t. [iii], [iv], [v]-vii, viii-xv, xvi, [17]-300, port.
[301], bl. [302], 303-502. Blue cloth. Pf. , pl. inserted,
other illus. in text. Life of Blaine, pp. [17]-300; of Logan,
pp. 303-502. At head of title, The Standard Bearers.
[dash] Official Edition. Also noted with the following imprints, all unexamined: Brandon, Vt. : Sidney M. South-
ard, 1884. (537 pp.) Chicago: J. S. Goodman & Co. , 1884.
(538 pp.) New York: Treat, 1884. (502 pp.) Philadelphia:
A. Gorton & Co. , 1884. (502 pp.) Philadelphia: W. H.
Thompson, 1884. (538 pp.) St. Louis: Historical Publishing
Co. , 1884. (538 pp.) San Francisco: A. L. Bancroft &
Co. , 1884. (538 pp.)

709 Conwell, Russell H. The Life and Public Services of James
G. Blaine, With Incidents, Anecdotes, and Romantic Events
Connected With His Early Life. ... With an Introduction

by His Excellency, Frederick Robie, Governor of Maine. <u>Illustrated.</u> Augusta, Maine: E. C. Allen & Co. [c1884.]

Pf., t. [1], [2], [3], bl. [4], [5], bl. [6], [7], bl. [8], [9], bl. [10], [11]-14, [15]-22, [23], bl. [24], [25]-440, illus. [441], bl. [442], port., div. t. [443], bl. [444], [445]-446, [447]-504. Brown cloth. Pf., pl. inserted, other illus. in text. Life of Blaine, pp. [25]-440; of Logan, pp. [447]-504. Also noted in green cloth.

710   . <u>The Life ... of James G. Blaine....</u> Hartford: S. S. Scranton & Co. [c1884.]

As in entry 709. Green cloth.

711   . <u>The Life ... of James G. Blaine....</u> Cincinnati: Forshee & McMakin [c1884.]

As in entry 709. Green cloth.

712   . <u>The Life ... of James G. Blaine....</u> Springfield: Enterprise Publishing Co. [c1884.]

As in entry 709. All copies examined rebound.

713 Cooke, Vincent. <u>The Life and Public Services of Our Greatest Living Statesman. Hon. James G. Blaine, "The Plumed Knight."... To Which Is Added the Life of Gen'l John A. Logan.... Embellished With Fine Steel Portraits of Blaine and Logan and Numerous Illustrations on Wood.</u> Rochester: H. B. Graves [c1884.]

2 pf., iii, bl. [iv], t. [i], [ii], v-vi, 8 $\ell\ell$. illus., 17-123, 124-172, 17-396, A 1-92, B 1-54, C 1-[18], D 1-14, E-G 1-20, H 1-4, I 1-[26], J-L 1-42. Green cloth. 2 pf. inserted, other illus. in text. Life of Blaine, pp. 17-123; of Logan, pp. 124-172; political compendia, pp. 17-396; appendices separately paged; preface, pp. v-vi, July 18, 1884.

714 Cooper, Thomas V. <u>Biographies of James G. Blaine, the Republican Candidate for President, and John A. Logan, the Republican Candidate for Vice-President....</u> Chicago, New York: Baird & Dillon [c1884.]

Pf. [i-iv], t. [v], [vi], vii-ix, bl. [x], div. t. [xi], bl. [xii], Part I [1]-96, div. t. [1], bl. [2], Part II 3-313, bl. [314], div. t. [1], bl. [2], Part III 3-94. Brown cloth. 2 pf. inserted. At head of title, <u>Campaign of '84.</u>; sketches of candidates in Part I; text, excluding charts, pr. in dbl. cols.

715   . <u>Biographies of James G. Blaine....</u> Philadelphia: Fireside Publishing Company, 1884.

As in entry 714. All copies examined rebound. Also noted with the following imprints, both unexamined: Burlington, Iowa: I. F. Segner [c1884.] San Francisco: J. Downing, 1884.

*716 Craig, Hugh. The Biography and Public Services of Hon. James G. Blaine.... New York and Chicago: H. S. Goodspeed & Co., 1884.

360, x, 361-712 pp., incl. front., pls., ports. Also contains A Biography of Gen. John A. Logan by Byron Andrews.

717 Cressey, E. K. Pine to Potomac Life of James G. Blaine His Boyhood, Youth, Manhood, and Public Services. With a Sketch of the Life of Gen. John A. Logan. Boston: James H. Earle, Publisher, 1884.

Pf., t. [i], [ii], [1], bl. [2], [3]-6, [9 sic]-16, pl., 21-408, port., [409]-421, bl. [422]. Green cloth, backstrip noting White House Series. Pf. and 4 pls. inserted. At head of title, "Log Cabin to White House" Series.; life of Blaine, pp. 21-408; of Logan, pp. [409]-421. Also noted in blue cloth.

718 Didier, Eugene L. The Political Adventures of James G. Blaine. Baltimore: The People's Publishing Company [c1884.]

T. [1], [2], [3]-12. Greyish brown wrps., back lacking in all copies examined. Anti-Blaine.

719 Haven, E. O. The National Hand-Book of American Progress.... Including the Life and Times of Hon. James G. Blaine. By J. Sanderson, D. D. Illustrated. Canton, Ohio: Memento Publishing Co. [1884.]

Pf., cld. half title [1], bl. [2], t. [3], bl. [4], [5], [6], [7]-9, bl. [10], 11-502, 503-550. Reddish brown cloth. Pf., cld. half title, t. added, other illus. in text. Sketches of Blaine and Logan, pp. 503-550; at head of title, [Blaine and Logan Edition.]

720 Houghton, Walter R. Early Life and Public Career of Hon. James G. Blaine, Patriot, Statesman and Historian.... Including a Biography of Gen'l John A. Logan.... Fully Illustrated With Portraits and Other Engravings.... Des Moines: W. D. Condit & Company, 1884.

Pf., t. [1], [2], 3-4, 5-14, pl., 15-576. Orange cloth. Pf. and 13 pls. inserted.

721 _____. Early Life ... of Hon. James G. Blaine.... Mansfield, Ohio: The Home Publishing Co., 1884.

As in entry 720.   Calf with black leather label on backstrip.   Also noted in orange cloth.

722 _____ . Early Life ... of Hon. James G. Blaine.... Chicago, Kansas City, Minneapolis, Columbus, Lexington, San
Francisco [and] Buffalo: Union Publishing House, 1884.

As in entry 720.   Orange cloth.

723 How Shall I Vote? Candidates and Parties Face to Face a
Startling Contrast of Lives and Records by a Citizen.   New
York: Funk & Wagnalls, 1884.

Cover title [1], adv. [2], [3], bl. [4], [5]-37, 38, adv.
[39-40]. Sewn. At head of title, Price, 10 Cents. ; electoral votes, p. 38; pr. generally in dbl. cols.

724 How Shall I Vote?... New York: Funk & Wagnalls, 1884.

Cover title [1], adv. [2], [3], 4, [5]-37, [38], adv. [39],
[40]. Sewn. At head of title, Price, 10 Cents. ; electoral
votes, p. 4; synopses of Republican candidates, p. [38];
"Compliments of Republican State Committee, " p. [40]; pr.
generally in dbl. cols.

725 J. G. Blaine. [Columbus: The Blaine Club of Columbus,
1884.]

Cover title [1], bl. [2], [3]-6, sm. sheet, [7]-8. Sewn.
Title vignette. Below title, This Pamphlet Is Sent to You
With the Compliments of the Blaine Club of Columbus. ;
"Pen Portrait of James G. Blaine" by H. J. Ramsdell, pp.
[3]-6; Robert Ingersoll's speech on Blaine, pp. [7]-8, the
last p. concluding with a note. Sm. sheet tipped in contains Blaine's position on the currency question.

726 Knox, Thomas W. The Lives of James G. Blaine and John A.
Logan Republican Presidential Candidates of 1884.   An Au-
thorized, Authentic, and Complete History of Their Public
Careers and Private Life.... Superbly Illustrated With
Magnificent Portraits and Full-Page Engravings By T. W.
Williams. Hartford: Published by The Hartford Publishing
Co., 1884.

Pf., t. [i], [ii], [iii], bl. [iv], [v]-vi, [vii]-viii, [ix]-xxiii,
bl. [xxiv], 25-502. Maroon cloth. Pf. and 13 pls. inserted. Preface, pp. [v]-vi, dated June, 1884. ; life of
Blaine, pp. 52-241; of Logan, pp. 242-369. Pub. prospectus also noted.

727 _____ . The Lives of James G. Blaine.... Chicago: Ex-
celsior Publishing Company, 1884.

As in entry 726.

728   Landis, John H.   The Life of James Gillespie Blaine.   By ...
       and Israel Smith Clare.   Lancaster, Pa.:   The New Era
       Printing House, 1884.

       Pf., t. [i], [ii], iii-iv, [5]-220.   Green cloth, front stamped
       James G. Blaine.   Pf. inserted.

729   Ramsdell, H. J.   Life and Public Services of Hon. James G.
       Blaine the Brilliant Orator and Sagacious Statesman. . . .
       Also the Life of the Courageous Soldier, Distinguished
       Senator and Nominee for the Vice-Presidency, Gen. John
       A. Logan, By Ben. Perley Poore. . . .   Profusely Illus-
       trated.   Philadelphia, New York, Boston, Cincinnati, Chi-
       cago, St. Louis [and] Kansas City: Hubbard Brothers,
       Publishers; San Francisco: A. L. Bancroft & Co. [c1884.]

       Pf. [1-2], t. [3], [4], 5-6, 7-14, 15-16, div. t. [17], bl.
       [18], 19-678.   Purple cloth.   Pf. and 33 pls. inserted.
       Copies also noted in red cloth; pub. prospectus noted.

730   _____.   Life ... of Hon. James G. Blaine. . . .   Indianapolis:
       F. B. Ainsworth & Company, Publishers [c1884.]

       As in entry 729.   Purple cloth.

731   _____.   Life ... of Hon. James G. Blaine. . . .   Boston,
       New York, Philadelphia, Chicago, Cincinnati, Cleveland,
       Baltimore [and] Hartford: Gately & Co., Publishers [c1884.]

       As in entry 729.   Purple cloth.

732   _____.   Life ... of Hon. James G. Blaine. . . .   New York:
       John S. Willey Publishing Company [c1884.]

       As in entry 729.   Purple cloth with green coated floral end-
       papers in contrast to brown coated floral endpapers found in
       entries 729-731.

733   _____.   Life ... of Hon. James G. Blaine. . . .   East Winn,
       Me.:   L. L. Johnson, Publisher [c1884.]

       As in entry 732.

734   Republican National Committee Campaign 1884.   Document No.
       One.   Republican Platform. . . .   Portraits and Sketches of
       the Lives of Jas. G. Blaine & John A. Logan. . . .   Phila-
       delphia: Avil & Co., Printers [1884.]

       Caption title.   [1]-46, bl. [47], adv. [48].   Stapled.   Illus.
       in text.   Brief sketches of Blaine, pp. 8-9, and Logan,
       pp. 10-11.

735   Ridpath, John Clark.   Life and Public Services of James G.
       Blaine, Embracing a Sketch of His Childhood and Youth;

His Education; the Beginning of His Public Career.... Together With a Sketch of the Life of Gen. John A. Logan. ...
With an Introduction by Wm. H. Blaine. Illustrated. Cincinnati, Chicago, St. Louis: Jones Brothers & Company
[c1884.]

Pf., t. [1], [2], 3-8 [9]-16, pl., 17-30, bl. [31], illus.
[32], 33-560. Brown cloth. Pf. and 9 pls. inserted, other
illus. in text.

736 _____. Life ... of James G. Blaine.... Detroit: J. C.
Chilton & Co. [c1884.]

As in entry 735. Also noted with the following imprints,
both unexamined: New York: Byron, Taylor & Co. [c1884.]
San Francisco: Occidental Publishing Co. [c1884.]

737 Vail, Walter S., ed. The Words of James G. Blaine on the
Issues of the Day.... With a Biographical Sketch. To-
gether With the Life and Public Service of John A. Logan.
Boston: D. L. Guernsey, 1884.

T. [i], [ii], fac. letter, verso bl. [iii-iv], [v], bl. [vi],
[vii]-viii, div. t. [ix], bl. [x], [1]-303, [304], fac. letter
[305-306], adv. [307], bl. [308]. Orange illus. wrps.

738 [Williams, C. R.] Lives of Blaine and Logan. The People's
Edition---Book of Reference.... Philadelphia: E. T.
Haines & Co., Publishers, 1884.

T. [1], illus. [2], 3-60, 61-64. Orange illus. wrps. Title
vignette. Illus. in text. Life of Blaine, pp. 3-52; of
Logan, pp. 53-60; platform, pp. 61-64.

739 [Wyatt, H. F.] The Head and Tail of That Dreadful Ticket.
[New York: Published by H. F. Wyatt, 1884.]

Unpaged, 30 ℓℓ. T. [i], bl. [ii], bl. [iii], cartoon [iv],
[1-55], bl. [56], 2 bl. ℓℓ. Orange illus. wrps., adv. on
outer back, front noting the following: Designed & Written
By H. F. Wyatt; Drawn By C. M. Connolly, Jr.; Published
By H. F. Wyatt--12 Bible House N Y C; Copyrighted Sept.
1884, By H. F. Wyatt.; Price 25 Cents. Cartoon illus. in
text. Anti-Blaine burlesque life alternating between cartoon
and text.

LOGAN, JOHN ALEXANDER (Republican)

740 A Review of the Presidential Battle-Field With Gen. John A.
Logan as the Republican Standard-Bearer in 1884. Washington: 1884.

Cover title [1], pf. [2], [3]-18.   Sewn.   Pre-convention
publication.

1888

GENERAL WORKS

741 [Brown, W. E. ?] The Presidential Candidates.   Sketches and
     Portraits of the Nominees of All Parties. [Providence:
     Published by J. A. & R. A. Reid; trade supplied by Amer-
     ican News Co., New York, c1888.]

     Cover title [1], 2-16. Newspaper format, sewn. Title
     vignette. Illus. in text. Pr. in triple cols., adv. inter-
     spersed. This copy with port. of Benjamin Harrison on
     cover, others noted with port. of Grover Cleveland.

742 Contest of 1888.   Lives of the Candidates, Election Statistics
     and Party Platforms.... Detroit: F. B. Dickerson & Co.,
     1888.

     T. [1], [2], [3], bl. [4], 5-124, 125-128. Illus. wrps.,
     pr. in red and blue. Illus. in text. Sketches of Harrison
     and Morton and Cleveland and Thurman.

743 Fallows, Samuel.   The American Manual and Patriot's Hand-
     book.... Chicago: The Century Book and Paper Co.,
     1889.

     Bl. [1], pf. (author), [2], t. [3], [4], 5-14, bl. [15], illus.
     [16], 17-423, bl. [424]. Blue cloth. Illus. in text. Lives
     of all candidates, pp. 399-420; work copyrighted in 1888;
     pub. before election?

744 Herringshaw, Thomas W.   The Biographical Review of Promi-
     nent Men and Women of the Day. With Biographical
     Sketches and Reminiscences. Lives & Services of All the
     Presidential Candidates for 1888....   Illustrated With 350
     Portraits. Chicago: The Lewis Publishing Co., 1888.

     T., copyright notice of verso, added, [i]-iv, [i]-xii, [19]-
     500, 501-576. Blue cloth. Illus. in text. Campaign sec-
     tion, pp. 501-576, includes brief biographies of candidates
     of all parties.

745 _____ .   The Biographical Review....   With Biographical
     Sketches and Reminiscences. To Which Is Added a Birds-

eye View of the History of Our Republic, and Much Other
Valuable Information.... Illustrated With 350 Portraits.
Chicago: Donohue & Henneberry, Publishers [c1888.]

As in entry 744. Yellow cloth. Illus. in text. Campaign
section captioned "A Birdseye View of Our Republic. "

746 National Contest, Containing Portraits and Biographies of Our
National Favorites.... Detroit: Darling Bros. & Co. ,
1888.

F. , t. [1], [2], [3], bl. [4], 5-128. Silvery grey cloth.
Illus. in text. Includes sketches of Harrison and Morton
and Cleveland and Thurman.

747 Our Presidents From Washington to Cleveland ... and Portraits and Sketches of the Lives of the Present Candidates.
New York: Nicoll & Roy, Publishers, 1888.

Unpaged, 49 ℓℓ. Text 43 ℓℓ. [86 pp.], 2 ℓℓ. opening and
4 terminal, adv. Light green wrps. , adv. on inner front
and entire back, front pr. in aqua and silver. Illus. in
text. Text begins with biographies of Harrison and Morton
and Cleveland and Thurman.

748 The Presidential Favorites 1888. Compliments of Ward &
Jones Clothiers.... Norwalk, Ohio: Laning Ptg. Co. ,
1888.

Cover title. Unpaged, 16 ℓℓ. Light yellow wrps. , "To
Our Patrons" on inner front, adv. on inner back, and 1888
calendar outer back. Illus. in text. Includes ports. and
brief sketches of Cleveland, Blaine, Edmunds, Carlisle,
Randall, Foraker, Hawley, Morrison, Sheridan, Henry
George (Labor), DePew, Ingalls, Hoadly, Hill, Hewitt,
Evarts, Cox, Sherman, Holman, Gresham, and McDonald,
all but one being Republican or Democratic possibilities.

HARRISON, BENJAMIN (Republican)

749 Harney, Gilbert. The Lives of Benjamin Harrison and Levi
P. Morton. With a History of the Republican Party, and a
Statement of Its Position on the Great Issues ... By Edwin
C. Pierce. Illustrated. Providence: J. A. & R. A. Reid,
Publishers, 1888.

Pf. , t. [i], [ii], [1]-2, [3]-14, [15], port. [16], [17]-237,
cut [238], div. t. [239], port. [240], [241]-335, cut [336],
div. t. [337], illus. [338], [339]-486. Red cloth. Title
vignette. Pf. inserted, other illus. in text. Life of Harrison, pp. [17]-237; of Morton, pp. [241]-335; Republican
Party, pp. [339]-486. Also noted in tan cloth.

750 _____ . The Lives of Benjamin Harrison.... Providence:
J. A. & R. A. Reid, Publishers, 1888.

As in entry 749 except Republican Party, pp. [339]-[480].
Buff wrps. Also noted in green cloth.

*751 Harrison and Morton Campaign Songster, Including Biographical
Sketches and Constitution for Campaign Clubs.

48 pp. , illus.

752 [Hopkins, Alphonso Alva?] Short Review of the Public and
Private Life of Gen'l Benj. Harrison. What the Working
Men Say of Him. His Record as a Soldier, and How He
Appears at Home. [N. p. , n. d. , 1888.]

Cover title [1], [2]-30, bl. [31], [32]. Sewn. Title vignette. Harrison's opinions in 1878, p. [32].

753 Long, John D. The Republican Party: Its History, Principles,
and Policies.... New York: The M. W. Hazen Co. , 1888.

Pf. (Lincoln) [1-2], t. [3], [4], [5]-6, [7]-10, [11]-427, bl.
[428]. All copies examined rebound. Pf. and 11 pls. inserted. Life of Harrison, pp. 359-405; of Morton, pp.
406-419.

754 _____ . The Republican Party.... Boston: William E.
Smythe Company, 1888.

As in entry 753, but t. a cancel. Rust brown cloth.

755 Northrop, Henry Davenport. The Life and Public Services of
Gen. Benj. Harrison, the Great American Statesman....
To Which Is Added the Life and Public Services of Hon.
Levi P. Morton.... Embellished With a Fine Steel Por-
trait of General Harrison and Numerous Illustrations on
Wood. Providence: Buker Publishing Co. [c1888.]

Pf. , ℓ. , verso bl. , t. [i], [ii], iii-vi, 17-340, 17-110, A
1-10, B 1-[26], C 1-[18], D-F 1-[24], G 1-[26], [1-68].
Blue cloth. 2 pf. and a 16 pp. sig. pls. inserted, other
illus. in text. The Presidents, 2nd pp. 17-110; appendices
separately paged; Republican Party, pp. [1-68]; at head of
title, Only Authorized and Official Edition. , followed by 3
lines.

756 _____ . The Life ... of Harrison.... Cincinnati: Forshee
& McMakin [c1888.]

As in entry 755. Subscription library binding.

757 _____ . The Life ... of Harrison.... Philadelphia: Gar-
retson & Co. [c1888.]

As in entry 755. All copies examined rebound.

758 _____ . The Life ... of Harrison.... [N. p. , n. d. ,
    c1888.]

As in entry 755. Subscription library binding. Also noted
with the following imprints, all unexamined: Augusta, Me. :
True & Co. [c1888.] Philadelphia: International Publishing
Company, 1888. Portland, Me. : G. Stinson & Co. [c1888.]
Worcester, Mass. : Lyman Drury [c1888.]

759 Wallace, Lew. Life of Gen. Ben Harrison. Illustrated. Phi-
    ladelphia, Chicago, Kansas City: Hubbard Brothers, Pub-
    lishers; San Francisco: A. L. Bancroft [c1888.]

Pf. , t. [i], [ii], [iii]-iv, 5-6, 7-9, bl. [10], 13, bl. [14],
div. t. 15, bl. [16], 17-348. Blue cloth. Pf. and 7 pls.
inserted.

760 _____ . Life of Gen. Ben Harrison. Also, Life of Hon.
    Levi P. Morton. By George Alfred Townsend. (Gath.)
    Fully Illustrated. Philadelphia, Chicago, Kansas City:
    Hubbard Brothers, Publishers; Boston: Guernsey Publish-
    ing Co. ; Cincinnati: Jas. Morris & Co. ; Denver: Perry
    Publishing Co. ; San Francisco: A. L. Bancroft [c1888.]

Pf. [1-2], t. [3], [4], 5-6, 7-12, 13-14, div. t. 15, bl.
[16], 17-348, pl. , div. t. 349, bl. [350], port. , 351-438,
pl. , 439-578. 3/4 marbled bds. , leather backstrip. Pf.
and 25 pls. inserted. Life of Harrison, pp. 17-348; of
Morton, pp. 351-438. Also noted in grey cloth.

761 _____ . Life of Gen. Ben Harrison.... Springfield: Winter
    & Co. , Publishers, 1888.

As in entry 760, t. added. Grey cloth.

762 _____ . Life of Gen. Ben Harrison.... Cleveland: N. G.
    Hamilton & Co. , Publishers [c1888.]

As in entry 760, t. added. Grey cloth.

763 _____ . Life of Gen. Ben Harrison.... Hartford: S. S.
    Scranton & Co. [c1888.]

As in entry 760, t. added. Grey cloth.

764 _____ . Life of Gen. Ben Harrison. Also, Life of Hon.
    Levi P. Morton, Sketches of Former Presidents, Citizen's
    Handbook, etc. Fully Illustrated. Hillsdale, Mich. : W.
    E. Allen & Co. [c1888.]

As in entry 760. Light blue cloth. Life of Morton by
George Alfred Townsend.

765 _____ . Life of Gen. Ben Harrison.... Springfield: Winter
     & Co. [c1888.]

As in entry 764.

CLEVELAND, GROVER (Democratic)

766 Boyd, James P. Biographies of Pres. Grover Cleveland and
     Hon. Allen G. Thurman.... Philadelphia: Franklin News
     Co., Number 14, July, 1888.

     Cover title. Pf., 1-64, port., 1-16. Light blue stiff
     wrps. pr. in brown, adv. on inner front and entire back.
     Pf., pl. inserted. At head of title, price information and
     The Franklin Library; life of Cleveland, pp. 1-64; of Thur-
     man, pp. 1-16.

767 The Campaign Text Book of the Democratic Party of the United
     States, for the Presidential Election of 1888.... Prepared
     by Direction of the National Democratic Committee. New
     York, Chicago, Washington: Published by Brentanos
     [c1888.]

     T. [i], [ii], [iii]-v, bl. [vi], [vii]-viii, ix-xvi, [3]-648, div.
     t. [649], bl. [650], [651]-656. Purple wrps. Lives of
     Cleveland and Thurman, pp. 20-26.

768 Dieck, Herman. The Life and Public Services of Our Great
     Reform President, Grover Cleveland ... to Which Is Added
     the Life and Public Services of Allen G. Thurman the Grand
     Old Democratic Statesman.... Embellished With a Fine
     Steel Portrait of Cleveland and Numerous Illustrations on
     Wood. Philadelphia: John C. Winston & Co. [c1888.]

     2 pf., dedication, verso bl., t. added [i], [ii], iii-vi, 17-
     264, 265-320, 17-110, A 1-10, B 1-26, C 1-[18], D-F 1-
     [24], G 1-[26], H 1-40, J 1-18. Subscription library bind-
     ing. 2 pf and a 16 pp. sig. pls. inserted, other illus. in
     text. At head of title, Only Authorized and Official Edition.
     followed by 3 lines; life of Cleveland, pp. 17-264; of Thur-
     man, pp. 265-320; the Presidents, pp. 17-110; appendices,
     paged separately.

769 _____ . The Life ... Grover Cleveland.... Indianapolis:
     Union Publishing Co. [c1888.]

     As in entry 768.

770 _____ . The Life ... Grover Cleveland.... Philadelphia:
     S. I. Bell & Co. [c1888.]

     As in entry 768, but life of Thurman, pp. 265-306.

771   Goodrich, Frederick E.   The Life and Public Services of
      Grover Cleveland, With Incidents of His Boyhood and an
      Account of His Rise to Eminence....   With an Introduction
      by Hon. Frederick O. Prince....   Illustrated.   Boston:
      Lindsay & Co., 1888.

      Pf. [1-2], t. [3], [4], [5], bl. [6], [7-8], [9]-13, bl. [14],
      [15]-23, [24], [25]-514, port., div. t. [515], bl. [516],
      [517], bl. [518], [519]-549, bl. [550].   Brown cloth.   Pf.,
      pl. inserted, other illus. in text.   Preface, pp. [7-8],
      dated June 1888; life of Cleveland, pp. [25]-514; of Thur-
      man, pp. [519]-549.   Imprint added with rubber stamp.

772   _____.   The Life ... of Grover Cleveland....   Springfield:
      Winter & Co., Publishers, 1888.

      As in entry 771, imprint rubber stamped.   Brown cloth.

773   _____.   The Life ... of Grover Cleveland....   Portland,
      Me.:   H. Hallett & Co. [c1888.]

      As in entry 771, imprint rubber stamped.   Brown cloth.

774   Hensel, W. U.   Life and Official Services of President Cleve-
      land the Unanimous Nominee of the Democratic Party....
      Also, of the Renowned Statesman ... Hon. Allen G. Thur-
      man....   Profusely Illustrated.   Cleveland: N. G. Hamil-
      ton & Co. [c1888.]

      Pf., t. [i], [ii], iii-iv, vii [sic]-xii, ℓ. lacking, illus. xv-
      xvi, div. t. [19], bl. [20], 21-299, bl. [300], div. t. [301],
      [302], port. [303], bl. [304], 305-448, [449]-588.   Blue
      cloth.   Pf. and 26 pls. inserted.   Life of Cleveland, pp.
      21-299; of Thurman, pp. 305-448; ℓ. pp. xiii-[xiv] lacking.
      Pub. prospectus also noted.

775   _____.   Life ... of President Cleveland....   Philadelphia,
      Chicago, Kansas City: Hubbard Brothers, Publishers; Bos-
      ton: Guernsey Publishing Co.; Cincinnati: Jas. Morris &
      Co.; Denver: Perry Publishing Co.; San Francisco: A. L.
      Bancroft & Co. [c1888.]

      As in entry 774, but vii-xiii, bl. [xiv] ... bl. [302].
      Copies also noted lacking xiii-[xiv] and with quotes on p.
      [302] as in entry 774.

776   _____.   Life ... of President Cleveland....   New York:
      W. A. Houghton [c1888.]

      As in entry 775, t. added.

777   Norton, C. B.   The President and His Cabinet Indicating the
      Progress of the Government of the United States Under the

Administration of Grover Cleveland.... Illustrated With
Portraits and Views.   Boston: Cupples and Hurd, Publishers, 1888.

Pf., t. [1], [2], [3], bl. [4], [5], bl. [6], [7], [8], 9-15,
bl. [16], 17-249, bl. [250], 3 ℓℓ. adv. Green illus. stiff
wrps., adv. on outer back.   Pf. and 13 pls. inserted.

778 Stoddard, William O.   The Lives of the Presidents.   Grover
Cleveland....   New York: Frederick A. Stokes & Brother,
1888.

Pf., t. [i], [ii], [iii]-vi, [1]-263, bl. [264], p. adv., bl.
Red cloth.   Pf. and 3 pls. inserted.   Vol. [X], "The Lives
of the Presidents" series.

FISK, CLINTON B. (Prohibition)

779 Foster, John O.   Life Sketches and Speeches of Gen. Clinton
B. Fisk ... With an Introduction by Miss Frances E. Wil-
lard, Pres. N. W. C. T. U.   Chicago: Woman's Temp-
erance Publication Association, 1888.

Pf., t. [1], [2], [3], [4], 5-6, [7]-108, 3 pp. adv., bl.
Blue illus. wrps., pr. in blue.   Pf. inserted, other illus.
in text.   At head of title, Our Standard Bearer.

780 Hopkins, Alphonso A.   The Life of Clinton Bowen Fisk.   With
a Brief Sketch of John A. Brooks.   New York: Funk &
Wagnalls, 1888.

Pf., t., copyright on verso, [i], bl. [ii], [iii], bl. [iv],
[v]-vi, [vii]-x, [1]-266, port., div. t. [267], bl. [268],
[269]-295, bl. [296].   Blue cloth.   Pf. and 2 pls. inserted.
Life of Fisk, [1]-266; of Brooks, pp. [269]-295.

SHERMAN, JOHN (Republican)

781 Bronson, S. A.   John Sherman.   What He Has Said and Done.
Being a History of the Life and Public Services of the Hon.
John Sherman.   Cincinnati: Robert Clarke & Co., 1888.

Pf., t. [i], [ii], iii, bl. [iv], v-xiv, 15-272, 273-277, bl.
278.   Green cloth.   Pf. inserted.   T. ℓ. a cancel; addendum, pp. 273-277, dated "Mansfield, 1888."

782 Lawrence, William.   Brief Sketch of the Life and Public Services of John Sherman With Some Considerations in Favor
of His Nomination in 1888 as the Republican Candidate for
the Presidency.   Cincinnati: Published by The Sherman
League, of Cincinnati and Hamilton County, 1888.

T. [1], bl. [2], [3]-80. Brown wrps., all copies examined
lacking entire back. At foot of p. [3], "This pamphlet is
in part an enlargement of an article which appeared in the
North American Review for November, 1887, in favor of
Mr. Sherman's nomination ... and is in other respects a
compilation."; text dated January 6, 1888. Copies also
noted with sm. pr. label reading Bellefontaine, Ohio affixed
to t. immediately following author's name.

1892

GENERAL WORKS

783 Boyd, James P. Men and Issues of '92. A Grand National
     Portrait Gallery Containing Photographs of Leading Men of
     All Parties.... Also the Lives of Republican and Demo-
     cratic Candidates for President.... [N. p.] Publishers
     Union, 1892.

     F. [1-2], t. [3], [4], 5-8, 9-14, 15-16, 17-656. Grey
     cloth with green coated dec. endpapers. Illus. in text.
     Copies also noted in grey cloth with orange coated dec.
     endpapers. 2 pub. prospectuses noted, one with imprint,
     Philadelphia, Chicago: S. I. Bell & Co. [c1892.]

784 Facts and Figures Relating to the Presidential Campaign
     of 1892.... Presented by the National Fire Insurance
     Co. Hartford: The National Fire Insurance Co.
     [1892.]

     Cover title. Unpaged, 10 ℓℓ. Brown coated wrps., adv.
     on inner front and entire back. Brief sketches of Demo-
     cratic and Republican candidates.

CLEVELAND, GROVER (Democratic)

785 Campbell-Copeland, Thomas. Cleveland and Stevenson. Their
     Lives and Record.... The Democratic Campaign Book for
     1892.... Over Sixty Illustrations and Maps.... Three
     Volumes in One. New York: Charles L. Webster & Com-
     pany, 1892.

     Fld. map, t. [1], [2], 3-4, 5-[6], [7], bl. [8], port., Part
     I 9-44, div. t., verso bl., Part II 1-42, div. t., verso
     bl., pl., Part III 1-318, pl., 319-422, 423-432, div. t.
     [433], bl. [434], 435-438. Brown cloth. Fld. map and 24

pls. inserted, maps in text. Sketches of the candidates, pp. 9-44. Also noted in blue cloth.

786 Fulton, Chandos. The History of the Democratic Party.... Lives of Cleveland and Stevenson. Profusely Illustrated With Elegant Wood Engravings. New York: P. F. Collier, Publisher, 1892.

T. [1], bl. [2], port. [3], bl. [4], port. [5], bl. [6], 7-8, 9-14, [15]-20, 21-24, 25-608. All copies examined rebound. 2 pls. inserted, other illus. in text.

787 Grady, John Randolph. The Life and Public Services of the Great Reform President, Grover Cleveland.... To Which Is Added the Life and Public Services of Adlai E. Stevenson.... Embellished With Fine Portraits and Numerous Other Attractive Engravings. Philadelphia: National Publishing Company [c1892.]

2 f., [i], bl. [ii], pl., t. [i], [ii], iii-vi, pl., 17-312, 17-112, A 1-[26], B 1-10, C 1-16, D 1-15, E [1-3], F 1-[26], H 1-40, J 1-19, bl. [20]. Bluish grey cloth. 2 f. and 13 pls. inserted, other illus. in text. At head of title, Only Authorized and Official Edition., followed by 3 lines; the Presidents, pp. 17-112; appendices paged separately.

788 Hensel, W. U. Life and Public Services of Grover Cleveland.... With a Sketch of the Life and Public Services of Adlai E. Stevenson.... Profusely Illustrated. [N. p.] Edgewood Publishing Company, 1892.

Pf., t. [i], [ii], [iii-iv], illus. [v-vi], 21-345, bl. [346], div. t. [347], bl. [348], port. [349], bl. [350], 351-382, pl., [383]-556. Brown cloth. Pf. and 20 pls., inserted, other illus. in text. Life of Cleveland, pp. 21-345; of Stevenson, pp. 351-382. Pp. [159-160] lacking.

789 _____ . Life and Public Services of Grover Cleveland.... An Introductory Sketch by the Late Hon. William Dorsheimer, Enlarged and Continued.... Also, a Sketch of the Life and Services of Hon. Adlai E. Stevenson.... By Professor Charles Morris, Illustrated. [N. p.] Edgewood Publishing Company [c1892.]

As in entry 788, but port. [347], bl. [348], div. t. [349], bl. [350].

790 Life of Hon. Grover Cleveland, Ex-President, U. S. A. ... With a Sketch of the Life and Public Services of Hon. Adlai E. Stevenson.... [N. p.] Political Publishing Co. [c1892.]

Pf., t. [1], [2], [3]-7, bl. [8], port. [9-10], [11]-385, bl. [386], pl., [387-388], [389-391], bl. [392], [1]-53, bl.

[54], [425 sic]-454, pl., [1]-40, ℓ. adv.   Blue cloth.   Pf.
and 5 pls. inserted, other illus. in text.   Free Trade, pp.
[1]-53; Free Coinage, etc., pp. [425]-454; convention, pp.
[1]-40.   Also noted in red leather; pf. and 6 pls. noted in
other copies.

791   Parker, George F.   A Life of Grover Cleveland With a Sketch
      of Adlai E. Stevenson.   New York: Cassell Publishing
      Company [c1892.]

      T. [i], [ii], iii-ix, bl. [x], xi, bl. [xii], [1]-323, bl. [324],
      325-333, bl. [334], 3 ℓℓ. adv.   Wrps., adv. on entire
      back, front noting Cassell's Sunshine Series, Issued Semi-
      Monthly, Number 129, Sept. 5, 1892.   Preface, pp. iii-ix,
      dated September 10, 1892.

792   _____.   The Writings and Speeches of Grover Cleveland
      Selected and Edited With an Introduction....   Authorized
      Edition.   New York: Cassell Publishing Company [c1892.]

      Half title, verso bl., pf., t. [i], [ii], iii-v, bl. [vi], vii-
      xxvi, xxvii, bl. [xxviii], [1]-550, 551-571, bl. [572].
      Green cloth.   Pf. inserted.   Intro., pp. vii-xxvi, primarily
      biog.; index, pp. 551-571.   Also noted in blue cloth.

HARRISON, BENJAMIN (Republican)

793   Campbell-Copeland, Thomas.   Harrison and Reid.   Their
      Lives and Record....   The Republican Campaign Book for
      1892....   Over Sixty Illustrations and Maps....   Three
      Volumes in One.   New York: Charles L. Webster & Com-
      pany, 1892.

      Fld. cld. map, t. [1], [2], 3-4, 5, bl. [6], 7-8, port.,
      Part I 9-31, bl. [32], div. t., verso bl., Part II 1-42, div.
      t., verso bl., pl., Part III 1-318, 319-422, 423-432, div.
      t. [433], bl. [434], 435-438.   Blue cloth.   Fld. map and
      22 pls. inserted, maps in text.   Sketches, pp. 9-31; ap-
      pendix, pp. 319-422; addenda, pp. 423-432; index, pp. 435-
      438.

*794 Harrison and Reid Campaign Songster; Sketch of the Candidates'
      Lives and Full Text of the Republican Platform.   [Philadel-
      phia: c1892 by W. F. Shaw.]

      64 pp., illus.

795   Knox, Thomas W.   The Republican Party and Its Leaders....
      Lives of Harrison and Reid....   Profusely Illustrated With
      Elegant Wood Engravings.   New York: P. F. Collier,
      Publisher, 1892.

T. [1], bl. [2], pl. [3], bl. [4], pl. [5], bl. [6], 7-8, 9-
16, 17-26, 27-30, div. t. [31], bl. [32], 33-608. Brown
cloth. 2 pls. inserted, other illus. in text.

796 [Messaros, Waldo?] Life of Gen. Benjamin Harrison. ... With
a Sketch of the Life and Public Services of Whitelaw
Reid. ... Sold by Subscription Only. [N. p.] Political
Publishing Co. [c1892.]

Cld. f., t. [1], [2], [3]-7, [8], port. [9-10], [11]-511, adv.
[512-513], bl. [514]. Blue cloth. F. and 8 pls. inserted,
other illus. in text. Also noted in maroon cld. leather.
Pub. prospectus noted.

797 Northrop, Henry Davenport. The Life and Public Services of
Benjamin Harrison, the Great American Statesman. ... To
Which Is Added the Life and Public Services of Hon. Whitelaw Reid. ... Embellished With Numerous Fine Engravings
and Portraits. Cincinnati: Forshee & McMakin [c1892.]

Pub. prospectus. At head of title, Only Authorized and
Official Edition., followed by 3 lines.

798 _____. The Life ... of Benjamin Harrison. ... Chicago:
Mercantile Publishing & Advertising Co. [c1892.]

2 pf., dedication, verso bl., t. [i], [ii], iii-vi, port., 17-
368, 17-112, 1-70, A 1-[26], B 1-10, C 1-16, D 1-15, E
[1-3], F 1-[26]. Light blue cloth. 2 pf. and 13 pls. inserted, other illus. in text. Sketches, pp. 17-368; the
Presidents, pp. 17-112; Republican Party, pp. 1-70; appendices paged separately; t. added.

799 _____. The Life ... of Benjamin Harrison. ... Cleveland:
N. G. Hamilton & Co. [c1892.]

2 pf., dedication, verso bl., port., t. [i] as in entry 798.
Light blue cloth. T. added. Also noted with the following
imprints, all unexamined: Chicago: Monarch [c1892.]
New York: W. J. Holland [c1892.] Philadelphia: Royal
Publishing House [c1892.] Springfield, Ill.: Home Educa-
tional Publishing Co. [c1892.]

800 The Republican Campaign Text-Book for 1892. ... New York:
Issued by the Republican National Committee, 1892.

Cover title. 1-263, bl. [264]. Orange wrps., quote by
Harrison on outer back, front noting Voters' Library, Vol.
III, No. 1. September 19th, 1892 ... Published Tri-
Weekly, by Franklin Publishing Co., New York. Sketches
of Harrison and Reid, pp. 1-7. Also noted in grey green
wrps. pr. in blue and lacking above reference to Voters'
Library and the Franklin Publishing Co.

801 Wallace, Lew. Life and Public Services of Hon. Benjamin
       Harrison.... With a Concise Biographical Sketch of Hon.
       Whitelaw Reid Ex-Minister to France. By ... and Hon.
       Murat Halstead.... Richly Illustrated. [N. p.] Edgewood
       Publishing Co. [c1892.]

       Pf. [i-ii], t. [iii], [iv], v-vii, bl. [viii], 7-[10], [11], bl.
       [12], div. t. [15], bl. [16], [17], bl. [18], 17-530. Green
       cloth. Pf. and 16 pls. inserted, other illus. in text.
       Pub. prospectus in chocolate brown cloth also noted with
       publication date cited in imprint. Another pub. prospectus
       noted with imprint, Cleveland: N. G. Hamilton & Co.
       [c1892.]

WEAVER, JAMES B. (People's Party)

802 Allen, E. A. The Life and Public Services of James Baird
       Weaver.... To Which Is Added the Life and Public Ser-
       vices of James G. Field.... Cincinnati: Forshee & Mc-
       Makin [c1892.]

       Pf., bl. ℓ., t. [1], [2], 3-4, 5-12, [13-14], div. t. [15],
       ornament [16], Part I 17-142, bl. ℓ., port., Part II 17-
       546. Light green cloth. Pf. and pl. inserted (additional
       pls. ?); all copies examined in various states of disrepair.
       At head of title, Only Authorized and Official Edition. , fol-
       lowed by 2 lines. Pub. prospectus also noted.

BLAINE, JAMES G. (Republican)

803 Johnson, Willis Fletcher. An American Statesman. The
       Works and Words of James G. Blaine.... Philadelphia:
       A. R. Keller & Co. , 1892.

       Pf. [i-ii], t. [iii], [iv], [v-vii], bl. [viii], [ix-xiii], bl.
       [xiv], [xv-xvi], 17-535, bl. [536]. All copies examined re-
       bound. Pf. and 30 pls. inserted.

804 McClure, J. B. , ed. Life and Speeches of the Hon. James
       G. Blaine.... Chicago: Rhodes & McClure Publishing
       Co. , 1890.

       Pf. [1], bl. [2], t. [3], illus. [4], [5], 6-11, illus. [12],
       13-287, adv. [288]. All copies examined rebound. Illus.
       in text.

1896

GENERAL WORKS

805 Babcock, Benjamin F. The Presidential Favorites. A Political Hand-Book, Containing the Portraits of Thirty American
Statesmen, Together With Their Biographies....   Washington: Published by Campaign Publishing Company, 1896.

T. [1], [2], [3], 4, illus. [5], 6, [7]-192. All copies examined rebound. Illus. in text.

806 Boyd, James P. Parties Problems and Leaders of 1896....
Also Lives of the Candidates for President and Vice-President.... [N. p.] Publishers' Union, 1896.

F. [1], bl. [2], t. [3], [4], 5-9, bl. [10], 11-18, pl. [19-
20], 21-22, 23-615, bl. [616]. Grey cloth. F. and 31
pls. inserted. Pub. prospectus also noted with imprint,
Baltimore: R. H. Woodward Company [c1896.]

807 Clark, James Hyde. The Presidential Battle of 1896 Embracing ... Lives of Men Who Are the Standard-Bearers of the
Republican, Democratic and Prohibition Parties....   Profusely Illustrated....   Philadelphia: Published by Globe
Bible Publishing Co. [c1896.]

F [1-2], t. [3], [4], 5-9, bl. [10], 11-18, pl. [19-20], 21-
22, 23-594, pl. [595-596]. All copies examined rebound.
F. and 29 pls. inserted.

808 [Cummings, Amos Jay.] The Political Handbook. Political
Information for Present Use and Future Reference. New
York: The Political Handbook Publishing Company [1896.]

T. , verso bl. , [5], bl. [6], [7], bl. [8], [9]-228, [229-
232]. Green wrps. , adv. on inner front and back. Illus.
in text. Includes brief sketches of all candidates.

809 Great Leaders and National Issues of 1896. Containing the
Lives of the Republican and Democratic Candidates for
President and Vice-President....   Over 100 Portraits and
Illustrations. [N. p.] Non-Partisan Bureau of Political In-
formation [c1896.]

F. , t. [1], [2], 3, bl. [4], 5-13, 14-16, 17-644. Grey
cloth. F. and 63 pls. inserted, other illus. in text.

810   Oldroyd, Osborn H.   Lincoln's Campaign or the Political Revolution of 1860.... Profusely Illustrated With Fourteen Portraits and Biographies of Presidential Possibilities for 1896. Chicago: Laird & Lee, Publishers [c1896.]

Half title [i], [ii], f., t. [iii], [iv], [v], illus. [vi], [1]-241, bl. [242].   Blue green cloth.   F. and 3 pls. inserted, other illus. in text.   Includes sketches of McKinley, Reed, Morton, Allison, Cullom, Manderson, Quay, Cleveland, Carlisle, Whitney, Hill, Morrison, Russell and Bland.

811   The Parties and the Men Or Political Issues of 1896.... The Lives of the Candidates for President and Vice-President of the United States....   [N. p., c1896.]

F. [i], bl. [ii], t. [iii], [iv], [v]-vii, bl. [viii], [ix-x], 9-14, [17]-[548], [i]-xxii.   Green cloth.   F. and 48 pls. inserted.   Addenda, pp. [i]-xxii.

812   Prescott, Lawrence F.   1896 the Great Campaign Or Political Struggles of Parties, Leaders and Issues.... Biographies of All the Presidential Candidates.... Cincinnati: A. Nielen [c1896.]

3 pf., t. [i], [ii], iii-iv, v-vi, 17-[512].   Blue cloth.   3 pf. and 25 pls. inserted.   Includes the Prohibition Party.

813   _____.   1896 the Great Campaign....   [N. p.] Loyal Publishing Co. Publishers [c1896.]

T. [i], [ii], iii-iv, v-vi, pls., 17-592.   Illus. paper bds., blue cloth backstrip.   16 pp. sig. pls., included in pagination.

814   The Presidential Candidates and Platforms, Biographies and Nominating Speeches.   Brooklyn: Brooklyn Eagle Library, 1896.

T. [1], [2], [3], [4], [5]-40.   Salmon wrps., adv. on outer back.   Illus. in text.   At head of title, Brooklyn Eagle Library.   Vol. XI. August, 1896.   No. 4; includes Republican, Democratic, and Populist candidates; pr. generally in dbl. cols.

McKINLEY, WILLIAM (Republican)

815   Andrews, Byron.   One of the People.   Life and Speeches of William McKinley....   To Which Is Added a Brief Sketch of Garret A. Hobart, Candidate for Vice-President.   Chicago, New York: F. Tennyson Neely, Publisher, 1896.

Pf., t. [i], [ii], [iii], bl. [iv], [v]-vi, [vii]-viii, [ix]-xv, [xvi], [1]-362, [363]-[367], bl. [368].   Blue cloth.   Pf. and

7 pls. inserted, other illus. in text. Pp. [363]-364 a cancel. Copies also noted lacking f. , and pp. 365-[367], but with inserted pls. between pp. 16-17, 48-49, 80-81, and 112-113. Other copies noted in yellow coated illus. wrps. pr. in red and brown, adv. on inner front and entire back with the following differences: (a) adv. on inner back for "Owl Short Stories"; also, pf. , recto bl. , adv. p. [368], 16 ℓ ℓ. adv. (b) adv. on inner back for "N. Amer. Review"; also 2 pf.

816   Halstead, Murat.   Life and Distinguished Services of Hon. Wm. McKinley and the Great Issues of 1896.   Containing Also a Sketch of the Life of Garret A. Hobart....   With an Introduction by Chauncey M. Depew, Esq.   Profusely Illustrated.   [N. p.] Edgewood Publishing Company, 1896.

Pf. , t. [i], [ii], iii-v, bl. [vi], [vii-viii], [ix-xii], vii [sic]-xiii, bl. [xiv], pl. [xv-xvi], 17-501, bl. [502]. Orange cloth.   Pf. and 15 pls. inserted, other illus. in text.   Also noted in yellow green cloth.

817   Official Proceedings of the Eleventh Republican National Convention....   Reported by James Francis Burke of Pittsburg, Pa. , Official Stenographer.   [N. p.] 1896.

T. [1], [2], [3], port. [4], [5], port. [6], [7], [8], [9], [10-12], [13]-16d, [17]-23, bl. [24], [25]-165, bl. [166], [167]-170, adv. [171], bl. [172].   All copies examined rebound.   Illus. in text.   Sketch of McKinley, p. [5]; of Hobart, p. [7].

818   Ogilvie, J. S. , ed.   Life and Speeches of William McKinley. Containing a Sketch of His Eventful Life ... Sketch of the Candidate for Vice-President....   With Introduction by Hon. Stewart L. Woodford.   New York: J. S. Ogilvie Publishing Company, 1896.

Pf. , t. [i], bl. [ii], [iii]-iv, 5, bl. [6], 7, bl. [8], [11]-337, bl. [338].   Purple cloth.   Pf. inserted, other illus. in text.   Copies also noted in brown cloth with p. 338 a song, 5 pp. adv. , bl. p.

819   Oldroyd, Osborn H.   The March to Victory ... With Platform, Portraits, Biographies and Sketches of McKinley & Hobart. Profusely Illustrated.   Chicago: Laird & Lee Publishers [c1896.]

F. , t. [i], [ii], [iii], bl. [iv], [I]-XLIV, bl. , illus. on verso, [1]-207, bl. [208], 2 ℓ ℓ. adv. Green illus. wrps. pr. in red and black, adv. on outer back, front noting The Pastime Series ... No. 43, Aug. , 1896.   F. inserted, other illus. in text.   Campaign of 1896, pp. [I]-XLIV; of 1860, pp. [1]-207.

820   Paget, R. L.   McKinley's Masterpieces.   Selections From the
      Public Addresses in and Out of Congress of William Mc-
      Kinley.   Boston: Joseph Knight Company,   1896.

      Half title [i], bl. [ii], pf. [iii], bl. [iv], t. [v], [vi], vii-
      viii, [ix]-x, xi-xx, 21-207, bl. [208].   Light blue green
      cloth, front noting Famous Men Series.   Pf. inserted.
      Sketch of McKinley, pp. xi-xx.   Also noted in cream cloth.

821   Porter, Robert P.   Life of William McKinley Soldier, Lawyer,
      Statesman.   Cleveland: The N. G. Hamilton Publishing
      Co. ,   1896.

      2 pf. , t. [i], [ii], [iii]-iv, [v]-xii, [xiii]-xiv, [1]-13, bl.
      [14], 15-439, bl. [440].   3/4 maroon cloth, leather back-
      strip.   2 pf. and 15 pls. inserted, other illus. in text.

822   _____ .   Life of William McKinley, Soldier, Lawyer, States-
      man.   With Biographical Sketch of Hon. G. A. Hobart.
      Fourth Edition.   Cleveland: The N. G. Hamilton Publish-
      ing Company,   1896.

      2 pf. , t. [1], [2], [3]-4, [5]-12, [13]-14, [15]-27, bl. [28],
      29-505, bl. [506].   Blue cloth.   2 pf. and 15 pls. inserted,
      other illus. in text.   Also noted in green cloth.

823   _____ .   Life of William McKinley.... Fourteenth Edition.
      Cleveland: The N. G. Hamilton Publishing Company,   1896.

      2 pf. , t. [1], [2], [3]-4, [5]-10, [11], bl. [12], [15]-2[7]
      [sic], illus. [28], 29-284.   Green illus. wrps.   Intro. , pp.
      [15]-2[7], dated Dec. 15, 1895.

824   Russell, Henry B.   The Lives of William McKinley and Garret
      A. Hobart, Republican Candidates of 1896.   An Authorized,
      Impartial, Authentic, and Complete History....   Illustrated
      With Portraits and Full Page Engravings.   Hartford: A.
      D. Worthington & Co. ,   1896.

      Pf. [i], bl. [ii], t. [iii], [iv], [v], bl. [vi], vii-ix, bl. [x],
      xi-xii, xiii-xxxii, xxxiii, bl. [xxxiv], 35-546.   Buff coated
      wrps.   Pf. and 16 pls. inserted, other illus. in text.   Al-
      so noted in wrps. with illus. , p. [x] and p. [xxxiv].   Also
      noted in dark green cloth.

BRYAN, WILLIAM JENNINGS (Democratic)

825   Brown, John Howard.   Bryan, Sewall and Honest Money....
      Portraits of the Leaders in the Movement for the Restora-
      tion of Silver to Its Old Place as a Standard of Value.
      Platform, Speeches, Biographies....   New York: Derby
      and Miller Company,   1896.

Bl. [1], pf. [2], [3], [4], 5-9, bl. [10], 11-12, 13-193, bl.
[194]. Stiff buff wrps. , adv. on inner front and entire back,
front also noting Common Sense Library September, 1896.
Illus. in text. Sketches of Bryan and Sewall, pp. 13-40.

826 [Metcalfe, Richard L.] Life and Patriotic Services of Hon. William J. Bryan.... Also, the Life of Hon. Arthur Sewall....
Profusely Illustrated. [Omaha:] Edgewood Publishing Company Publishers [c1896.]

Pf. [1-2], t. [3], [4], [5-6], [7-8], [9-10], [11-12], 19-500.
Maroon cloth. Pf. and 15 pls. inserted. On t. , Richard
L. Metcalf. Also noted in aqua cloth.

827 Ogilvie, J. S. , ed. Life and Speeches of William J. Bryan.
Containing a Sketch of His Eventful Life.... Sketch of the
Candidate for Vice-President.... With an Introduction by
Col. A. C. Fisk.... New York: J. S. Ogilvie Publishing
Company, 1896.

Pf. [1-2], t. [3], bl. [4], fac. note [5], bl. [6], 7-8, 9-10,
[11], bl. [12], [13]-328, 11 pp. adv. , bl. p. Green coated
illus. wrps. , adv. on outer back. Pf. and 6 pls. inserted.
T. also notes The Peerless Series. No. 100. August,
1896.

*828 Stevens, Charles McClellan. Bryan and Sewall and the Great
Issue of 1896. New York: F. T. Neely, 1896.

303 pp. , front. , ports. Neely's Popular Library, No. 70.
Author's name spelled Stevans on t.

829 Sulzer, William. Life and Speeches of Hon. William J. Bryan.
With Biographical Sketch and Introduction. New York: J.
S. Ogilvie Publishing Company, 1896.

T. [i], bl. [ii], [iii], bl. [iv], [v], bl. [vi], [91]-98, [99]-
115, bl. [116], [117]-291, bl. [292]. Dark red leather
over bds. Sketch of life, pp. [99]-115; speeches, pp. [117]-
291.

PALMER, JOHN McAULEY (National [Gold] Democratic)

830 Campaign Text-Book of the National Democratic Party 1896.
Chicago and New York: National Democratic Committee,
1896.

T. [i], [ii], [iii-iv], [v-vi], 1-26, 1. 01-1. 99, 2. 00-[2. 12],
3. 01-3. 48, 4. 01-4. 16. Light blue wrps. P. [ii] notes
"Second Edition Revised"; sketches of Palmer and Buckner,
pp. 12-17.

1900

GENERAL WORKS

831   The Battle of 1900 an Official Hand-Book for Every American
      Citizen.   Issues and Platforms of All Parties With Portraits
      and Biographies of the Leaders Including the Lives of the
      Presidential Candidates.   Endorsed by the Parties.   Chi-
      cago: American Bible House [c1900.]

      Pub. prospectus.   Orange cloth.

832   The Battle of 1900....   [N. p. , c1900.]

      Flyleaf [1-2], bl. [3], f. [4], t. [5], [6], 7-8, div. t. [17],
      [18], 19-22, 23-24, 25-266, div. t. [267], bl. [268], 269-
      270, [271], bl. [272], 273-489, bl. [490], div. t. [491],
      492-519, bl. [520], div. t. [521], 522-544.   Orange cloth.
      F. and 58 pls. (in sigs.) inserted.

833   The Battle of 1900....   Norwich, Conn.:   Charles C. Haskell
      & Son [c1900.]

      As in entry 832.

834   Boyd, James P.   Men and Issues of 1900....   Together With
      the Lives of Candidates for President and Vice-President....
      [N. p. , c1900.]

      Bl. [1], f. [2], t. [3], [4], 5-9, 10-16, 17-19, [20]-703, bl.
      [704].   Blue cloth.   F. and 47 pls. inserted.   Also noted
      in 3/4 blue cloth with morocco backstrip.

835   _____.   Men and Issues of 1900....   Philadelphia, and Chi-
      cago: P. W. Ziegler & Co. [c1900.]

      As in entry 834.

836   Great Political Issues and Leaders of the Campaign of 1900....
      The Biographies and Portraits of All the Candidates for
      President and Vice-President....   Profusely Illustrated.
      Chicago: W. B. Conkey Company, 1900.

      Pf., t. [i], [ii], port. [iii-iv], [v]-vi, 9-14, [15], bl. [16],
      [17]-[660].   3/4 green cloth, red leather backstrip.   Pf.
      and 30 pls. inserted.

837   Moore, Rolland Bryant.   1900 Campaign Manual Containing the
      Constitution ... the Various Parties, Their Platforms and

Candidates.... New Britain, Conn.: R. B. Moore, Publisher [c1900.]

T. [1], [2], [3]-5, 6-7, 8-179, adv. [180-183], bls. [184-192]. Buff wrps. Very brief sketches of all the candidates; bl. pp. [184-192] have running head, "Memorandum."

838 Morris, Charles, and Ellis, Edward S. Great Issues and National Leaders.... With Party Platforms in Full and Lives of Candidates.... Assisted by I. T. Johnson.... Philadelphia: Fidelity Publishing Co. [c1900.]

F., t. [i], [ii], iii-iv, v-xi, bl. [xii], 17-527, bl. [528]. Bluish green cloth. F. and 30 pls. inserted, other illus. in text. At head of title, The Voter's Guide for the Campaign of 1900.

839 Prescott, Lawrence F. Living Issues of the Campaign of 1900.... Including the Platforms of All Parties and Biographies of the Presidential Candidates.... Chicago: Providence Publishing Co. [c1900.]

Pf., t. [i], [ii], [i]-iii, bl. [iv], v-vi, pl., I 17-203, illus. [204], 1-16, pl., II 1-139, illus. [140], 1-22, III [1]-208, A 209-233, illus. [234], B 235-242, D 243-258, E 259-261, F 262-286. Blue cloth. F. and 33 pls. inserted, other illus. in text.

840 _____ . Living Issues of the Campaign.... New York: R. S. Mighall & Company [c1900.]

As in entry 839, but letters of acceptance, pp. 1-16 and 1-22 conclude volume. Blue cloth, front noting Official Edition.

McKINLEY, WILLIAM (Republican)

841 Ellis, Edward S. From Tent to White House Or, How a Poor Boy Became President. New York: Street & Smith, Publishers [c1898, 1899.]

Adv. [1], bl. [2], t. [3], [4], [5], bl. [6], [7]-8, [11]-195, adv. [196], 7 ℓ ℓ. adv., pub. cat. [1]-16. Illus. wrps., adv. on outer back, front noting Medal Library No. 11.

842 Halstead, Murat. Victorious Republicanism and Lives of the Standard-Bearers McKinley and Roosevelt.... With Introduction by Senator Chauncey M. Depew.... Splendidly Illustrated With Many Half-Tone Views and Portraits. [N. p.] Republican National Publishing Co., Publishers [c1900.]

Flyleaf [1-2], pf. [3-4], t. [5], [6], 7-8, 9-11, 12-15, 16-17, 18-26, 27-562. Green cloth. Pf. and 23 pls. inserted.

843 Official Proceedings of the Twelfth Republican National Conven-
     tion.... Reported by M. W. Blumenberg, Official Report-
     er. Philadelphia: Press of Dunlap Printing Company
     [c1900.]

     Pf. (Lincoln), t. [1], [2], [3], bl. [4], pl., 5-188, pl.,
     189-191, bl. [192], [i]-vii, adv. [viii]. Brown cloth. Pf.
     and 11 pls. inserted. Life of McKinley, pp. 5-9; of Roose-
     velt, pp. 10-13; note on pub. tipped in at beginning.

BRYAN, WILLIAM JENNINGS (Democratic)

844 Life and Speeches of Hon. Wm. Jennings Bryan.   Illustrated.
     Baltimore: R. H. Woodward Company, 1900.

     Pf. [1-2], t. [3], [4], [5], bl. [6], [7]-9, bl. [10], [11]-
     12, bls. [13-14], [15], bl. [16], div. t. 17, bl. [18], 19-
     55, bl. [56] div. t. 57, bl. [58], 59-432, illus. [434],
     bls. [435-436], div. t. [437], bl. [438], 439-465, bl. [466].
     Blue green cloth. Pf. and 31 pls. inserted. Sketch of
     Bryan by Mary Baird Bryan, pp. 19-55; speeches, pp. 59-
     432; appendix, pp. 439-465.

845 [Metcalfe, Richard L.] Victorious Democracy Embracing Life
     and Patriotic Services of Hon. William J. Bryan the Fear-
     less and Brilliant Leader of the People.... And Concluding
     With the Life of Hon. Adlai E. Stevenson Candidate for
     Vice-President and the Democratic Issues of 1900 by A.
     J. Munson Author and Editor. Splendidly Illustrated With
     Half-Tone Portraits and Views. [N. p.] National Demo-
     cratic Publishing Co. Publishers [c1900].

     Flyleaf [1-2], ports. [3-4], t. [5], [6], 7-8, 9-10, 11-12,
     13-14, 15-562. Green cloth. Pf. and 23 pls. inserted.
     On t., Richard L. Metcalf.

846 _____. Victorious Democracy.... Chicago: The Dominion
     Company, Publisher Fine Books [c1900.]

     As in entry 845.

847 Newbranch, Harvey E. William Jennings Bryan a Concise But
     Complete Story of His Life and Services. Lincoln, Nebras-
     ka: The University Publishing Co., 1900.

     Pf., t. [i], [ii], [iii], bl. [iv], [1-2], [3], bl. [4], [5]-8,
     [9]-178. Grey cloth. Pf. and 8 pls. inserted.

848 The Second Battle or the New Declaration of Independence
     1776-1900. An Account of the Struggle of 1900 as Dis-
     cussed in Selections From the Writings of Hon. William J.
     Bryan and Others. Chicago: Issued by W. B. Conkey
     Company [c1900.]

Pf. , t. [1], [2], [3]-4, [5]-7, bl. [8], 9-571, 572-575, bl.
[576]. All copies examined rebound. Pf. and 23 pls. inserted. Life of Bryan, pp. 45-82.

WOOLEY, JOHN G. (Prohibition)

849 Mulvihill, W. Frank. The Prohibition Text Book for the Campaign of 1900.... Chicago: Dickie & Wooley, 1900.

T. [1], [2], port. [3], [4], port. [5], [6], 7-123, 124-126,
ℓ. adv. Lemon green illus. wrps. Illus. in text. Sketch
of Wooley, pp. 15-20; of Metcalf, pp. 21-24.

DEWEY, GEORGE (Republican)

850 Barrett, John. Admiral George Dewey a Sketch of the Man....
Illustrated. New York and London: Harper & Brothers
Publishers, 1899.

Pf. , t. [i], [ii], [iii], bl. [iv], v-[vi], vii-[ix], bl. [x], xi-
[xiii], bl. [xiv], div. t. [1], bl. [2], 3-[251], bl. [252],
div. t. [253], bl. [254], 255-[274], 275-[280], 2 ℓℓ. adv.
All copies examined rebound. Pf. and 23 pls. inserted.

851 Blagg, Robert L. Career and Triumphs of Admiral Dewey Being a Complete Biography of the Hero of Manila. Springfield, Ohio: Published by The Crowell & Kirkpatrick Co.
[c1899.]

Flyleaf [1-2], pf. , t. [3], [4], 5, 6-9, 10, 11-14, 15-177,
map 178, 179-264. Stiff aqua illus. wrps. pr. in blue,
entire back lacking in copies examined, front noting Farm
and Fireside Library. No. 175. September, 1899. Pf.
inserted, other illus. in text. "The Empire," pp. 179-264.

*852 Clemens, William Montgomery. Life of Admiral George
Dewey.... New York: Street & Smith [c1899.]

vi, 9-196 pp. Historical Series, No. 7.

853 Dewey, Adelbert M. The Life and Letters of Admiral
Dewey.... Embellished With Over Two Hundred and Fifty
Illustrations. Authorized Edition. New York: The Wool-
fall Company, MDCCCXCIX.

F. , t. [1], [2], [3], [4], 5-8, 9-14, 15-20, 21-538, 539-
559, bl. [560]. All copies examined rebound. Illus. in
text. T. pr. in red and black.

*854 Ellis, Edward S. The Life Story of Admiral Dewey.... [Phi-
ladelphia? c1899.]

ℓ., ix-xvi, 17-448 pp., incl. illus., pls., ports.; cld.
f., cld. pls.

855 Halstead, Murat. Life and Achievements of Admiral Dewey....
Chicago: The Dominion Company, Publisher Fine Books, 1899.

F., t., copyright on verso, 9, bl. [10], 11-14, 15-23, 24-
30, pl. [31-32], 33-35, bl. [36], 37-38, 39-452. 3/4 grey
green cloth, maroon leather corners, black leather backstrip. F. and 31 pls. inserted, map in text.

856 _____. Life ... of Admiral Dewey....   [N. p.] Our Pos-
sessions Publishing Co. [c1899.]

As in entry 855.

*857 Hamm, Margharita Arlina. Dewey the Defender; a Life Sketch
of America's Great Admiral. London, New York: F. T.
Neely [c1899.]

4 ℓ ℓ., [vii]-viii, [11]-187 pp., pls., ports.

858 Johnson, Rossiter. The Hero of Manila Dewey on the Missis-
sippi and the Pacific.... With Illustrations by B. West
Clinedinst and Others. New York: D. Appleton and Company, 1899.

Half title [i], adv. [ii], f., t. [iii], [iv], v, bl. [vi], vii,
bl. [viii], ix, bl. [x], 1-152, 3 ℓ ℓ. adv. All copies examined rebound. F. and 18 pls. inserted, one illus. in
text.

859 [Lawrence, W. J.] A Concise Life of Admiral Dewey U. S. N.
[Boston?] Published by J. F. Murphy [c1899.]

Cover title. [1]-62, adv. [63], bl. [64]. Stiff green illus.
wrps. pr. in blue and red, patriotic symbol on outer back.
Illus. in text. Title vignette. At foot of p. [1], "Copyright, 1899, By W. J. Lawrence."

860 Stickney, Joseph L. Life and Glorious Deeds of Admiral
Dewey.... Fully Illustrated With Photographs.... Chicago:
The Chas. B. Ayer Company [c1898.]

Pf., t. [5], [6], [7], bl. [8], 9-13, bl. [14], 2 pls., 15-
20, 21-22, 23-434, div. t. [435], [436-450]. All copies
examined rebound. Pf. and 38 pls. inserted.

861 What Dewey Did. A Brief History of the Hero of Manila....
New York: D. T. Mallett, Publisher [c1899.]

Unpaged, 23 ℓ ℓ. T. [1], [2], [3], bl. [4], [5-45], bl. [46].
Orange illus. wrps., triumphal arch on outer back. 3 pls.
inserted.

862   Williams, Henry L.   Taking Manila or in the Philippines With
      Dewey Giving the Life and Exploits of Admiral George
      Dewey, U. S. N.   New York: Hurst & Company Publishers
      [c1899.]

          Pf. , t. [1], [2], 5-228.   Red cloth.   Pf. and 19 pls. in-
          serted, other illus. in text.

863   Wyatt, Frank T.   Life of Dewey....   Illustrated With Pen
      Drawings and Half-Tone Engravings of Actual Scenes in the
      Great Struggle.   Chicago: W. B. Conkey Company [c1899.]

          Pf. , t. [1], [2], [3], [4-7], illus. [8], [9]-304.   Green
          cloth.   Pf. inserted, other illus. in text.

864   Young, Louis Stanley.   Life and Heroic Deeds of Admiral
      Dewey....   In Collaboration With Henry Davenport North-
      rop....   Philadelphia: National Publishing Co. [c1899.]

          Cld. f. , [i], bl. [ii], t. [iii], [iv], v-vi, vii-ix, bl. [x],
          pls. , 17-552.   All copies examined rebound.   Cld. f. and
          4 16 pp. sigs. of pls. inserted, other illus. in text.

865   _____ .   Life ... of Admiral Dewey....   Bay City, Mich. :
      The H. H. Taylor Publishing Co. [c1899.]

          As in entry 864, but text, pp. 17-504.   Blue cloth.   Cld.
          f. and 5 16 pp. sigs. of pls. inserted, other illus. in text.

1904

GENERAL WORKS

866   Bates, Lindon W. , Jr. , and Moore, Charles A. , Jr.   The
      Political Horoscope.   New York: Wynkoop Hallenbeck Craw-
      ford Co. [c1904.]

          T. [1], [2], 3-105, bl. [106], [107], bl. [108].   Red wrps. ,
          pub. note on inner front.   Brief sketches of Cleveland,
          Roosevelt, Parker, Root, Bryan, Taft, and Hearst, pp. 3-
          19.

867   Morris, Charles, and Ellis, Edward S.   Men and Issues of
      1904 Containing Intimate Biographies of the Presidential
      Candidates....   Magnificently Illustrated.   Philadelphia,
      Chicago, Toronto: The John C. Winston Co. [c1904.]

F., t., copyright on verso, 7-9, bl. [10], 11-16, 17-464.
Blue cloth.   F. and 23 pls. inserted.   Copies also noted
with above, but t. lacks imprint.   At head of both titles,
A Non-Partisan Handbook for the American Voter.

868   Rand, McNally & Co.'s Political Atlas a Compendium of Facts
and Figures, Platforms, Biographies, and Portraits....
Chicago, New York: Rand, McNally & Company, Publishers, 1904.

T. [1], 2-16.   Green coated wrps., adv. on inner front and
entire back.   Illus. in text.   At head of title, Special Edition for the North British and Mercantile Insurance Co.
Very brief sketches of Republican and Democratic candidates.

ROOSEVELT. THEODORE (Republican)

869   Andrews, Byron.   The Facts About the Candidate....   Illustrated by A. J. Klapp.   Chicago: Published by Sam Stone,
MCMIIII.

Unpaged, [224] pp.   Blue cloth.   Illus. in text.   Miniature
book, 2 1/4 x 1 3/4; preface dated May 1, 1904.   Copies
also noted in lemon canvas wrps., inner front noting Compliments of the New York Tribune.

*870   _____.   Livsskildring af Kandidaten....   Oversat af Anders
Mordt....   Illusteret af A. J. Klapp.   Chicago: S. Stone,
1904.

As in entry 869.

871   Garrison, E. E.   The Roosevelt Doctrine Being the Personal
Utterances of the President....   New York: Robert Grier
Cooke, 1904.

Cover title.   Half title [i], bl. [ii], pf. [iii], [iv], v-vi,
vii-viii, 1-181, bl. [182].   Green wrps. pr. in dark green.
Pf. inserted.   Brief sketch of Roosevelt by Albert Shaw,
pp. 1-9.

872   Halstead, Murat.   The Life of Theodore Roosevelt....   Profusely Illustrated.   Chicago, Akron, New York: The Saal-
field Publishing Co., 1902.

Pf. [i-ii], t. [iii], [iv], v-vi, vii-xii, xiii-xiv, xv-xvii, bl.
xviii, xix-xxi, bl. [xxii], 23-391, bl. [392].   All copies
examined rebound.   Pf. and 45 pls. inserted.   T. pr. in
red and black.

873   Handford, Thomas.   The Life and Sayings of Theodore Roosevelt....   Introduction by Charles Walter Brown....   Illustrated.   Chicago: M. A. Donohue & Co. [c1903.]

Half title [1], bl. [2], pf. , t. [3], [4], 5, 6-7, bl. [8], 9-
19, bl. [20], 21-242, 243-315, adv. [316], 2 ℓℓ. adv. Red
cloth. Pf. and 12 pls. inserted, other illus. in text. Intro. , pp. 9-19, dated June 1, 1903.

874 Howland, John A.   Triumphs of the Roosevelt Administration....
     With Introductions by Charles Dick ... and Chauncey M.
     Depew....   New York, Chicago: Republican Publishing
     Co. , 1904.

     Pf. , t. [1], [2], 3-10, pl. , 11-24, 25-209, bl. [210].   Tan
     cloth. Pf. and 11 pls. inserted.

875 Leupp, Francis E.   The Man Roosevelt a Portrait Sketch.   Il-
     lustrated. New York: D. Appleton and Company, MCMIV.

     Half title [i], bl. [ii], pf. , t. [iii], [iv], v-vii, bl. [viii],
     [ix], bl. [x], xi-xv, bl. [xvi], xvii, bl. [xviii], div. t. [1],
     bl. [2], 3-334, 335-341, bl. [342], 4 ℓℓ. adv. Red cloth.
     Pf. and 7 pls. inserted. Copyright, p. [iv], notes "Pub-
     lished, February, 1904"; preface, pp. v-vii, dated Jan. 1,
     1904.

876 Living Issues of the Campaign of 1904 Including Lives of
     Roosevelt and Fairbanks....   With an Introduction by Hon.
     Murat Halstead, the Famous Author.   Embellished With a
     Great Number of Superb Phototype Engravings. [N. p. ,
     c1904.]

     Cld. f. , t. [i], [ii], iii-iv, v-xv, bl. [xvi], xvii-xxiv, pls. ,
     17-350, 351-366, 367-384. Red cloth. F. and 3 16 pp.
     sigs. of pls. inserted, other illus. in text. Life of Roose-
     velt, pp. 17-350; of Fairbanks, pp. 351-366; the Republican
     Party, pp. 367-384.

877 Meyers, Robert C. V.   Theodore Roosevelt Patriot and States-
     man....   Beautifully Illustrated.   Philadelphia and Chicago:
     P. W. Ziegler & Co. [c1902.]

     Pf. [1], bl. [2], t. [3], [4], 5-8, 9-14, 15-16, 17-526.
     Red cloth. Pf. and 39 pls. inserted. T. added.

878 Miller, J. Martin.   The Official Handbook for All Voters.
     Leaders and Issues of the Campaign of 1904.   Containing
     the Biographies of All the Presidential Candidates....   Il-
     lustrated With Many Striking Photo-Engravings in Two
     Colors. [N. p. , c1904.]

     2 pf. , t. [1], [2], 3-6, 7-10, 11-12, 13-440 (i. e. [384]).
     All copies examined rebound. Pf. and 27 pls. inserted.
     T. misleading since this is really a biography of Roosevelt.
     Contents also misleading since p. 305 does begin with a
     sketch of Fairbanks, but the remainder of the text deals

with Democrats and other parties and not with Roosevelt's speeches and letters as listed.

879 _____ , ed. The Triumphant Life of Theodore Roosevelt Citizen Statesman President. . . . Lavishly Illustrated. . . . [N. p. , c1904.]

Pf. , t. [1], [2], 3-6, 7-10, 11-12, 13-303, bl. [304], 305-315, 316-330, 331-432. All copies examined rebound. Pf. and 23 pls. inserted. Life of Roosevelt, pp. 13-303; of Fairbanks, pp. 305-315; Roosevelt's letters, pp. .316-330; his speeches, pp. 331-432.

880 Morris, Charles. Our Presidents From Washington to Roosevelt. . . . Profusely Illustrated With Beautiful Color Plates, Half-Tones and Line Drawings. [N. p. , c1903.]

Cld. f. , t. [i], [ii], i-iv, v-vi, 17-248. All copies examined rebound (another copy reissued in 1905 bound in green cloth). Cld. f. and 10 pls. (2 cld.) inserted. Life of Roosevelt, pp. 238-248.

881 Official Proceedings of the Thirteenth Republican National Convention. . . . Reported by M. W. Blumenberg, Official Reporter. Minneapolis: Harrison & Smith Co. [c1904.]

T. [1], [2], [3], bl. [4], [5-8, 7 bl.], bl. [9-10], [11]-226, [227]-229, [230]-238, adv. [239], bl. [240]. Purple cloth. 25 pls. inserted. Life of Roosevelt, pp. [11]-22; of Fairbanks, pp. [23]-32.

882 Our Patriotic President His Life in Pictures Famous Words & Maxims Anecdotes Biography. . . . New York: The Columbia Press, Publishers, 1904.

Unpaged, 28 ℓℓ. T. [1], [2], [3], [4-56]. Buff illus. wrps. pr. in black, red and blue, with port. of Roosevelt looking to the left. Title vignette. Illus. in text. Author, Heinrich Charles?

883 Our Patriotic President. . . . New York: The Elite Art Press [1904.]

As in entry 883, but text [4-52] and wrp. with port. of Roosevelt looking straight ahead.

884 Perry, Frances M. A Life of Theodore Roosevelt. . . . New York: Published by J. M. Stradling & Company [c1903.]

Pf. , t. [1], [2], 3, 4, 5-126, pl. Green cloth, front noting Famous Americans' [sic] Series. Pf. and 3 pls. inserted.

885 Republican Campaign Text-Book 1904. Issued by the Republi-

can National Committee.   Milwaukee: Press of the Evening
Wisconsin Co. [1904.]

T. [i], bl. [ii], iii-iv, v-xx, xxi-xxiv, 1-549, bl. [550].
Purple wrps. Life of Roosevelt, pp. 248-264; of Fairbanks,
pp. 265-266.

886 Riis, Jacob A.   Theodore Roosevelt the Citizen....   Illustrated.
New York: The Outlook Company, MCMIV.

Flyleaf [i-ii], half title [iii], bl. [iv], pf. , t. [v], [vi],
[vii], bl. [viii], ix-x, xi-xii, div. t. [1], bl. [2], 3-449,
bl. [450], div. t. [451], bl. [452], 453-454, div. t. [455],
bl. [456], 457-464, 465-471, [472]. Brown cloth. Pf. and
16 pls. inserted. Copyright notes "Published March, 1904. "
Also noted in tan cloth stamped in maroon and noting "Reprinted March, 1904. "

887 Roosevelt and the Campaign of 1904 Including the Life of Fairbanks....   Philadelphia: National Publishing Company
[c1904.]

A reissue of entry 876.   Blue cloth.

888 Smith, Edward Garstin.   The Real Roosevelt....   New York:
Published by National Weekly Publishing Co. [c1904.]

Cover title [1], [2], 3-5, 6-63, adv. [64]. Stapled. Anti-
Roosevelt.

889 Stratemeyer, Edward.   American Boys' Life of Theodore
Roosevelt....   Illustrated From Photographs and With
Frontispiece by Charles Copeland.   Boston: Lee and Shep-
ard, 1904.

Half title [i], [ii], f. , t. [iii], [iv], v-x, xi-xvi, xvii, bl.
[xviii], 1-296, 297-311, bl. [312], 3 ℓℓ. adv. Green cloth.
F. and 15 pls. inserted. Preface, pp. v-x, dated May 2,
1904.

PARKER, ALTON B. (Democratic)

890 Campaign Text Book of the Democratic Party of the United
States, 1904.   Issued by Authority of the Democratic Na-
tional Committee.   [New York: The Metropolitan Printing
Company, 1904.]

[i]-ii, [iii]-viii, t. [1], [2], [3]-304, [305-307], bl. [308].
Green wrps. , citing above imprint. Sketches of candidates,
pp. [53]-65.

891 Campaign Text Book....   [New York: The Metropolitan Printing Company, 1904.]

T. [1], [2], [3]-353, [354-356], [i]-iii, [iv]-xi, bl. [xii].
Blue wrps., noting Second Edition.

892 Grady, John R. The Lives and Public Services of Parker and
Davis.... Embellished With a Large Number of Fine Por-
traits and Engravings. [Philadelphia? National Publishing
Company? c1904.]

T. [i], [ii], iii-iv, v, bl. [vi], 17-304. Red cloth. 2 16
pp. sigs. pls. inserted, other illus. in text. At head of
title, Only Authorized and Official Edition.

1908

GENERAL WORKS

893 Great Issues and National Leaders of 1908.... Illustrated
With ... Over 100 Pictures. [N. p., c1908.]

F. [1-2], t. [3], [4], 5-16, 17-480. All copies examined
rebound. F. and 20 pls. inserted, other illus. in text.
At head of title, The Voter's Non-Partisan Handbook and
Campaign Guide.

894 Rand, McNally & Co.'s Political Atlas a Compendium of Facts
and Figures, Platforms, Biographies, and Portraits....
Chicago, New York: Rand, McNally & Company, Publishers, 1908.

T. [1], 2-16. Green coated wrps., adv. on inner front
and entire back. Illus. in text. Brief sketches of Democratic and Republican candidates; at head of title, Special
Edition for the North British & Mercantile Insurance Co.

895 Salt, Mark H., ed. Candidates and the Issues. An Official
Handbook for Every American Citizen ... Including the
Lives of the Presidential Candidates.... [N. p., c1908.]

T., copyright on verso, 5-6, [7], [8-10], [11-14], [15-18],
pls., 33-430. Blue cloth. 5 16 pp. sigs. pls. inserted.

TAFT, WILLIAM HOWARD (Republican)

896 Davis, Oscar King. William Howard Taft the Man of the Hour
His Biography and His Views on the Great Questions of To-
day.... And a Sketch of the Nominee for Vice President....
Philadelphia: P. W. Ziegler Co. [c1908.]

Bl. [1], pf. [2], t. [3], [4], [5-6], [7-8], 9-11, bl. [12],
13-24, pl. [25-26], 27-406. Blue cloth. Pf. and 23 pls.
inserted.

897 Dunn, Robert Lee. William Howard Taft American. Boston:
The Chapple Publishing Company [c1908.]

T. [i], [ii], iii-vi, bl. [vii], illus. [viii], [1], bl. [2], [3]-
261, 262-263, bl. [264]. Tan cloth. Illus. in text.

898 Official Report of the Proceedings of the Fourteenth Republican
National Convention.... Reported by Milton W. Blumenberg, Official Reporter. Published Under the Supervision
of the General Secretary of the Convention. Columbus:
Press of F. J. Heer, 1908.

F., t. [1], [2], [3], bl. [4], [5], bl. [6], 7-241, 242-247.
bl. [248], 249-255, bl. [256]. All copies examined rebound.
F. and 28 pls. inserted. Sketch of Taft, pp. 7-18; of
Sherman, p. 19; appendix, pp. 242-247; index, pp. 249-255.

899 Patterson, Raymond. Taft's Training for the Presidency.
Boston: The Chapple Press, 1908.

T. [i], bl. [ii], 1-55, bl. [56]. White canvas-like wrps.

900 Republican Campaign Text-Book 1908. Issued by the Republican National Committee. Philadelphia: Press of Dunlap
Printing Company [1908.]

T. [i], bl. [ii], iii, bl. [iv], vi-xi, bl. [xii], 1-[548]. 3/4
leather with black cloth backstrip. Sketches of Taft, pp.
528-536; of Sherman, pp. 536a-536d. Also noted in mus-
tard coated wrps.

BRYAN, WILLIAM JENNINGS (Democratic)

901 Gale, Albert L., and Kline, George W. An Appreciation From
a Republican Viewpoint. Bryan the Man the Great Common-
er at Close Range.... St. Louis: The Thompson Publishing Company, 1908.

Pf., t. [1], [2], 3-4, 5, bl. [6], [7], [8], 9-191. Green
cloth. Pf. and 15 pls. inserted.

902 Metcalfe, Richard L. The Real Bryan Being Extracts From
the Speeches and Writings of "A Well-Rounded Man." Des
Moines: Personal Help Publishing Company, 1908.

F., t. [1], [2], 3-6, [7], bl. [8], 9-18, 19-22, 23-320.
Brown cloth. F. inserted. "What is the Explanation of
Bryan," pp. 9-18; an appreciation, pp. 19-22; speeches,
pp. 23-320.

DEBS, EUGENE V. (Socialist)

903 [Gale, Albert Liscomb.] Debs: His Life, Writings and
Speeches With a Department of Appreciation. Authorized.
Girard, Kansas: The Appeal to Reason, 1908.

Pf., t. [i], [ii], [iii-iv], [i]-ii, div. t. [iii], [iv], 1-515,
bl. [516]. All copies examined rebound. Pf. and 14 pls.
inserted. Intro., pp. [i]-ii dated Aug. 1, 1908; sketch of
Debs, pp. 1-76.

CHAFIN, EUGENE W. (Prohibition)

904 Headquarters of the National Committee of the Prohibition Party.... [N. p., 1908.]

[1]-64. Cream illus. wrps., sketch of Chafin on inner
front, of Watkins on inner back.

ROOSEVELT, THEODORE (Republican)

905 Cushing, Otho. The Teddyssey. New York: Life Publishing
Company, 1907.

[i], [ii], t. [iii], [iv], [v], bl. [vi], [vii], [8-29], bl. [30],
[31]. Brown paper bds., yellow cloth backstrip. Illus. in
text. Burlesque life in one line statements and illus. Title
vignette.

906 Douglas, George William. The Many-Sided Roosevelt an Anec-
dotal Biography. New York: Dodd, Mead and Company,
1907.

Half title [i], bl. [ii], pf., t. [iii], [iv], [v]-ix, bl. [x],
[xi], [xii], [1]-272. All copies examined rebound. Pf. inserted. Concludes with Roosevelt's statement against running for a third term. Copyright, p. [iv], "Published
March, 1907."

907 Langereis, H. H. D. Biographie Van Theodore Roosevelt, als
Burger, Staatsman en als President der Vereenigde Sta-
ten.... Geillustreerd. Grand Rapids, Mich.: Drukkerij
"De Huisvriend" en "Het Ideall," 1908.

Pf. [3-4], t. [5], bl. [6], [7]-113, bl. [114], port. [115-
116], [117]-120, [121]-124, [125]-126, [127], bl. [128], port.
[129], illus. [130]. Brown wrps. Pf. and 2 pls. inserted.

908 Levy, J. Leonard. The President and His Policies. A Sunday
Address Before the Rodeph Shalom Congregation. Pittsburgh: April 19th, 1908.

T. [i], bl. [ii], 1-26.   Brown wrps., adv. on inner front
and back, front noting Sunday Lecture, Series 7, No. 24.

909   Morgan, James.   Theodore Roosevelt the Boy and the Man.
New York: The Macmillan Company; London: The Macmillan Co., Ltd., MCMVII.

Half title [i], [ii], pf. [iii], [iv], [v], bl. [vi], vii, bl.
[viii], ix-x, xi-xii, div. t. [xiii], bl. [xiv], 1-320, 321-
324, ℓ. adv.   Red cloth.   Pf. and 24 pls. inserted.   Copyright notes "Published September, 1907. "

910   Riis, Jacob A.   Theodore Roosevelt the Citizen.   Illustrated.
New York: Grosset & Dunlap Publishers [c1907.]

Half title [i], bl. [ii], pf. [iii-iv], t. [v], [vi], [vii], bl.
[viii], ix-x, xi-xii, div. t. [1], bl. [2], 3-449, bl. [450],
div. t. [451], bl. [452], 453-454, 457-464, 465-471, bl.
[472].   Natural cld. cloth.   Pf. and 15 pls. inserted.
Copyright notes "Reprinted, May, 1907. "

1912

GENERAL WORKS

911   Great Leaders and National Issues of 1912 Containing the Lives
and Services of All Presidential and Vice-Presidential Candidates of All Parties....   A Magnificent Array of Portraits
and Pictures Including Portraits of All Candidates and Leaders of All Parties.   [N. p., c1912.]

Cld. f., t. [1], [2], 3-8, cld. pl., div. t. [9], cartoon
[10], I 11-40, pl., div. t. [41], cartoon [42], II 43-166,
div. t. [167], cartoon [168], III 169-195, div. t. [196], cartoon [197], IV 198-320.   Blue cloth.   F. and 20 pls. inserted, other illus. in text.

912   Great Leaders and National Issues of 1912....   [Philadelphia:
The J. C. Winston Company, c1912.]

As in entry 911.   At head of title here and in entry 911,
An Impartial People's Handbook.

913   Mowbray, Jay Henry.   Living Issues and Great Leaders Covering Every Phase of the Most Vital Questions of the Day Including Biographies of the Presidential Candidates....
Philadelphia: National Publishing Co. [c1912.]

Cld. f., t. [i], [ii], iii-iv, v-viii, [ix-xvi], 1-61, [1-96], [1-78], [1-90], [91-95], [350-352]. All copies examined rebound. F. and 3 16 pp. sigs. pls. inserted, other illus. in text. Imprint rubber stamped.

914 The Political Battle of 1912. Containing the Biographies of All the Presidential Candidates.... Editor-in-Chief Thomas H. Russell.... Illustrated With Many Striking Photo Engravings. [N. p., c1912.]

F., t. [1], [2], [3-4], 5-9, [10], 11-320. Blue cloth. F. and 15 pls. inserted.

WILSON, WOODROW (Democratic)

915 Bacon, Charles Reade. A People Awakened. The Story of Woodrow Wilson's First Campaign.... Garden City, N. Y.: Doubleday, Page & Company, 1912.

Half title [i], bl. [ii], pf., t. [iii], [iv], [v-vi], [vii], bl. [viii], [ix-x], div. t. [1], bl. [2], 3-226, [227], bl. [228]. Cream cloth. Pf. and 13 pls. inserted.

916 The Democratic Text-Book 1912. Issued by the Democratic National Committee, the Democratic Congressional Committee. [N. p., 1912.]

Cover title. [1]-424, 425-426, 427-432. Light green illus. wrps., inner front and back with comparison of Democratic and Republican platforms, outer back with port. and fac. signature of Thomas Marshall. Title vignette. Life of Wilson by William Bayard Hale, pp. 49-60; his record, pp. 61-65; life of Marshall, pp. 67-69; his record, pp. 70-71. Also noted in tan wrps.

917 Hale, William Bayard. Woodrow Wilson the Story of His Life. Garden City, N. Y.: Doubleday, Page & Company, 1912.

Half title [i], bl. [ii], pf., t. [iii], [iv], [v-vi], [vii], bl. [viii], div. t. [1], bl. [2], 3-233, bl. [234]. All copies examined rebound. Pf. and 3 pls. inserted.

918 Hosford, Hester E. Woodrow Wilson and New Jersey Made Over. New York: The Knickerbocker Press (G. P. Putnam's Sons) [c1912.]

Pf., t. [i], [ii], [iii], bl. [iv], v-vii, bl. [viii], ix-xvii, bl. [xviii], xix, bl. [xx], div. t. 1, bl. [2], 3-143, 144-152. Orange cloth. Pf. and 15 pls. inserted. Preface, pp. v-vii, dated Feb. 17, 1912; supplement, pp. 144-152.

919 _____. Woodrow Wilson His Career, His Statesmanship, and His Public Policies. Second Edition, Revised and En-

larged With a Preface by Thomas P. Gore.... With 16 Illustrations. New York and London: G. P. Putnam's Sons,
The Knickerbocker Press, 1912.

Half title [i], bl. [ii], pf. , t. [i], [ii], [iii], bl. [iv], v, bl.
[vi], vii-viii, ix, bl. [x], xi, bl. [xii], xiii-xxi, bl. [xxii],
xxiii-xxiv, div. t. [1], bl. [2], 3-223, 224-234. Blue
cloth. Pf. and 15 pls. inserted. Preface dated July 1912;
supplement, pp. 224-234. Running heads read "Woodrow
Wilson (verso) and New Jersey Made Over (recto). "

TAFT, WILLIAM HOWARD (Republican)

920 Official Report of the Proceedings of the Fifteenth Republican
National Convention.... Reported by Milton. W. Blumenberg, Official Reporter. Published Under the Supervision
of the General Secretary of the Convention. New York:
The Tenny Press [c1912.]

F. , t. [1], [2], 3, bl. [4], [5], bl. [6], 7-453, 454-460.
Green cloth. F. and 21 pls. inserted. Sketch of Taft, pp.
7-21; of Sherman, pp. 22-25.

921 Republican Campaign Text-Book 1912. Issued by the Republican National Committee. Philadelphia: Press of Dunlap
Printing Company [1912.]

T. [1], [2], 3-411, 412-416. Brown coated wrps. Sketch
of Taft, pp. 157-166; of Sherman, pp. 395-396.

922 Walker, Albert H. The Administration of William H. Taft, a
Historical Sketch. [New York: Albert H. Walker, 1912.]

Cover title. Preface, verso bl. , [1]-20. Cream wrps.
Number 1 of a series of 4, this being biographical.

ROOSEVELT, THEODORE (Progressive [Bull Moose])

923 Kullnick, Max. From Rough Rider to President.... Trans-
lated From the Original German by Frederick von Reith-
dorf.... Chicago: A. C. McClurg & Co. , 1911.

Half title [i], bl. [ii], t. [iii], [iv], v-vi, vii-viii, [ix], bl.
[x], 11-289, bl. [290]. Light green cloth. Pf. ? Copyright notes "Published April, 1911. "

924 Mowbray, Jay Henry. The Intellectual Giant. Roosevelt the
People's Champion for Human Rights ... Including Biographies of Roosevelt and Johnson, Candidates for President
and Vice-President.... Philadelphia: National Publishing
Co. [c1912.]

Cld. f. , t. [i], [ii], [iii]-iv, v-vi, 7-128, 1-64, [1-151], 346-352. All copies examined rebound. F. , 4 pp. sig. , 2 16 pp. sigs. pls. inserted, other illus. in text. Imprint rubber stamped.

925 Payne, George Henry. The Birth of the New Party or Progressive Democracy. Naperville, Ill. , Atlanta: J. L. Nichols & Company [1912.]

F. , t. [1], [2], 3-9, illus. [10], 11-16, pl. , 17-18, 19-[320] (352, 32pp. added for pls.). All copies examined rebound. F. and 16 pls. inserted, other illus. in text.

1916

GENERAL WORKS

926 [Ratcliffe, S. K.] Woodrow Wilson v. Hughes. The Men and the Presidential Issues, in The Manchester Guardian; American Number, October 3, 1916.

Pp. 18-19, signed S. K. R. , pr. in 4 cols.

WILSON, WOODROW (Democratic)

927 Brooks, Eugene C. Woodrow Wilson as President. Chicago, New York: Row, Peterson and Company [c1916.]

Half title [i], bl. [ii], pf. , t. [iii], [iv], 5-9, bl. [10], 11-12, 13-537, 538-572. Green cloth. Pf. inserted.

928 Creel, George. Wilson and the Issues. New York: The Century Co. , 1916.

Half title [i], bl. [ii], pf. , t. [iii], [iv], [v], bl. [vi], div. t. [1], bl. [2], 3-167, bl. [168]. Blue paper bds. , blue cloth backstrip. Pf. inserted. Copyright notes "Published, September, 1916. "

929 Ford, Henry Jones. Woodrow Wilson, the Man and His Work. A Biographical Study.... New York, London: D. Appleton and Company, 1916.

Half title [i], bl. [ii], pf. , t. [iii], [iv], [v], bl. [vi], [vii], bl. [viii], [ix], bl. [x], 1-[318], 319-[326], 327-[333], bl. [334]. Green cloth. Pf. and 3 pls. inserted. Preface, p. [v], dated March, 1916.

930 [Gounder, Howard M.] Woodrow Wilson, a Sketch Together
     With a Short Review of the Career of Thomas R. Marshall,
     Vice-President. With Illustrations. [N. p.] September,
     1916.

        T. [1], [2], [3]-19, bl. [20], port., [21]-22, bl. *l*. Cream
     illus. wrps. Illus. in text. Life of Marshall, pp. [21]-22.

HUGHES, CHARLES EVANS (Republican)

931 Official Report of the Proceedings of the Sixteenth Republican
     National Convention.... Reported By George L. Hart, Of-
     ficial Reporter. Published Under the Supervision of the
     General Secretary of the Convention. New York: The Ten-
     ny Press [c1916.]

        F., t. [1], [2], [3], bl. [4], pl., [5], bl. [6], pl., 7-299,
     300-308. Green cloth. F. and 22 pls. inserted. Life of
     Hughes by Robert H. Fuller, pp. 222-263; of Fairbanks by
     George B. Lockwood, pp. 264-272.

932 Ransom, William L. Charles E. Hughes the Statesman as
     Shown in the Opinions of the Jurist. New York: E. P.
     Dutton & Company [c1916.]

        Half title [i], bl. [ii], t. [iii], [iv], [v], bl. [vi], vii-xviii,
     xix-xx, xxi-xxiii, bl. [xxiv], div. t. [xxv], bl. [xxvi], 1-
     281, 282-345, bl. [346], 347-353, bl. [354]. Blue cloth.
     Preface, pp. vii-xviii, dated July 20, 1916.

933 Republican Campaign Text-Book 1916. Issued by the Republi-
     can National Committee. [N. p., 1916.]

        T. [1], 2, 3-424, 425-432. Green coated wrps. Sketch
     of Hughes, pp. 91-114; of Fairbanks, pp. 115-121.

1920

HARDING, WARREN G. (Republican)

934 Chapple, Joe Mitchell. Warren G. Harding the Man. Boston:
     Chapple Publishing Company, Limited, 1920.

        Pf., t. [1], [2], [3], [4], [5], bl. [6], 7-94. White paper
     bds., 7 7/16 x 4 3/4. Pf. and 7 pls. inserted.

935 _____ . Warren G. Harding.... Boston: Chapple Publishing Company, Limited, 1920.

Pf. t. [1], [2], [3], [4], div. t. [5], bl. [6], 7-128. White paper bds., 9 x 6. Pf. and 7 pls. inserted. Copies also noted with this collation, but measuring as in entry 934.

936 Official Report of the Proceedings of the Seventeenth Republican National Convention.... Reported By George L. Hart, Official Reporter. Published Under the Supervision of the General Secretary of the Convention. New York: The Tenny Press [c1920.]

F., t. [1], [2], [3], bl. [4], pl., [5], bl. [6], pl., 7-282, 283-292. Green cloth. F. and 25 pls. inserted. Sketch of Harding, pp. 241-247; of Coolidge, pp. 249-253.

937 Republican Campaign Text-Book 1920. Issued by the Republican National Committee. [N. p., 1920.]

T. [i], [ii], [1]-489, 490-496. White coated illus. wrps. Life of Harding, pp. [1]-8; of Coolidge, pp. [9]-15.

938 Schortemeier, Frederick E. Rededicating America. Life and Recent Speeches of Warren G. Harding.... With Foreword By Will H. Hays.... Indianapolis: The Bobbs-Merrill Company, Publishers [c1920.]

Pf., t. [1], [2], [3], bl. [4], [5-9], bl. [10], 11-33, 34-256. All copies examined rebound. Pf. inserted. Foreword, p. [3], dated Aug. 1, 1920; life, pp. 11-33; speeches, pp. 34-256.

939 Senator Warren G. Harding of Ohio. [Columbus: Published by Harding for President Club, 1920.]

Cover title. Unpaged, 8 ℓℓ. Ports. [1-2], [3-16]. Buff wrps. Illus. in text. At foot of p. [16], "Published by Harding for President Club Deshler Hotel, Columbus, Ohio [followed by officers]. "

940 What a Country Boy Did With 200 Pounds of Type. [New York: Publicity Department, Republican National Committee, 1920.]

Cover title. [1]-30, ports. [31-32]. Brown illus. wrps., copyright notice on inner front, compliments note on inner back, illus. on outer back. Title vignette. Illus. in text. Copies also noted with inner wrp. lacking compliments note from Republican National Committee.

COX, JAMES M. (Democratic)

941   Babson, Roger W.   Cox the Man.   New York: Brentano's, 1920.

> Pf., t. [i], [ii], iii, bl. [iv], [v], bl. [vi], 1-128.   Red cloth.   Pf. inserted.

942   Democratic Text Book 1920.   Issued by the Democratic National Committee; the Democratic Congressional Committee.   [N. p., 1920.]

> Cover title.   [1-2], 3-494, 495-504.   Light green illus. wrps.   Title vignette.   Life of Cox, pp. 99-104; of Roosevelt, pp. 105-107.   At head of title, Peace! Progress! Prosperity!

943   Morris, Charles E.   Progressive Democracy of James M. Cox. Indianapolis: The Bobbs-Merrill Company Publishers [c1920.]

> Half title, verso bl., t. [i], [ii], bl. ℓ. [iii-iv], v-vi, div. t. [vii], bl. [viii], [1]-106.   Grey paper bds.

COOLIDGE, CALVIN (Republican)

944   Calvin Coolidge a Man of Vision Not a Visionary.   [N. p., n. d., 1920?]

> Cover title [1], bl. [2], 3-15, [16].   Sewn.   Title vignette. Includes 10 reasons why Coolidge should be nominated.

945   Law and Order--Coolidge.   [Chicago: R. R. Donnelley & Sons Co., 1920.]

> Cover title.   Pf., i-iv, 1-59, [60].   Black coated leather. Pf. inserted.   Biog. sketch, pp. i-iv, dated "Chicago, June 8, 1920"; speeches, pp. 1-59.   Favorite son nominee; this work given to delegates to the Republican Convention.

HOOVER, HERBERT (Republican)

946   Kellogg, Vernon.   Herbert Hoover the Man and His Work. New York, London: D. Appleton and Company, 1920.

> Half title [i], bl. [ii], pf., t. [iii], [iv], [v], bl. [vi], vii-viii, [ix], bl. [x], 1-[280], div. t. [281], bl. [282], 283-[376].   All copies examined rebound.   Pf. inserted.   Appendices, pp. 283-[376].

947   Lane, Rose Wilder.   The Making of Herbert Hoover.   New York: The Century Co., 1920.

Half title [i], bl. [ii], pf. , t. [iii], [iv], v-vi, div. t. [1],
bl. [2], 3-15, bl. [16], 17-356.   Blue cloth.   Pf. inserted.

LOWDEN, FRANK O. (Republican)

948   Frank O. Lowden Governor of Illinois.   [N. p. , n. d. , 1920?]

Unpaged, 8 ℓℓ. Pf. [1], bl. [2], t. [3], [4-16].   Cream
wrps. , inner front reads "Prepared and Published by Friends
of Frank O. Lowden as a Well Merited Tribute to the Great
War Governor of Illinois. "   Illus. in text.

WOOD, LEONARD (Republican)

949   Hagedorn, Hermann.   That Human Being, Leonard Wood.   New
York: Harcourt, Brace and Howe, 1920.

T. [i], [ii], [1], [2], 3-126.   Grey paper bds.

950   Hobbs, William Herbert.   Leonard Wood Administrator, Sol-
dier, and Citizen....   With an Introduction by Henry A.
Wise Wood.   Illustrated.   New York and London: G. P.
Putnam's Sons, The Knickerbocker Press, 1920.

Half title [1], bl. [2], pf. , t. [3], [4], [5], bl. [6], 7-21,
bl. [22], [23], bl. [24], 25, bl. [26], 27, bl. [28], div. t.
29, bl. [30], 31-41, 42-253, bl. [254], 255-268, 269-270,
271-272.   All copies examined rebound.   Pf. and 12 pls.
inserted.   Foreword, pp. 7-21, dated October 27, 1919;
preface, p. [23], dated September 1, 1919; addendum, pp.
255-268; writings by Wood, pp. 269-270; about him, pp.
271-272.

951   Holme, John G.   The Life of Leonard Wood.   Illustrations
From Photographs.   Garden City, N. Y. :   Doubleday, Page
& Company, 1920.

F. , t. [i], [ii], [iii], bl. [iv], [v], bl. [vi], vii-xii, div. t.
[1], bl. [2], 3-228.   Dark blue cloth.   F. and 3 pls. inserted.   Intro. , pp. vii-xii, dated February 27, 1920; at
foot of p. 228, "The Country Life Press, Garden City, N. Y. "

952   Sears, Joseph Hamblen.   The Career of Leonard Wood.   New
York, London: D. Appleton and Company, 1920.

Half title [i], bl. [ii], pf. , t. [iii], [iv], [v], bl. [vi], [vii],
bl. [viii], div. t. [ix], bl. [x], 11-[273], bl. [274].   Blue
cloth.   Pf. and pl. inserted, pr. doc. in text.

953   Wood, Eric Fisher.   Leonard Wood Conservator of Americanism
a Biography.   Illustrated.   New York: George H. Doran
Company [c1920.]

Half title [i], bl. [ii], pf., t. [iii], [iv], [v], bl. [vi], vii-
viii, ix-xii, xiii, bl. [xiv], xv-xvi, div. t. [xvii], bl.
[xviii], 19-313, bl. [314], 315-344, 345-351 bl. [352].
Green cloth. Pf. and 11 pls. inserted. Appendices, pp.
315-344; index, pp. 345-351. Unbound advance copies also
noted.

1924

GENERAL WORKS

954 Gilbert, Clinton W. "You Takes Your Choice." New York &
London: G. P. Putnam's Sons, The Knickerbocker Press,
1924.

Half title [i], bl. [ii], t. [iii], [iv], v, bl. [vi], div. t. 1,
bl. [2], 3-234, div. t. 235, bl. [236], 237-255, bl. [256].
Blue cloth. Maps in appendix, pp. 237-255. Sketches of
Coolidge, Davis, LaFollette, Dawes, Bryan, and Wheeler.

COOLIDGE, CALVIN (Republican)

955 Bell, Edward Price. Coolidge: A Survey. The President's
Mind As Revealed in His Speeches and Official Actions.
[Chicago:] The Chicago Daily News Co., 1924.

T. [1], port. [2], 3-12. Brown wrps., adv. on inner back,
front noting The Chicago Daily News Reprints--No. 16.
Port. and fac. letter in text. Pr. in dbl. cols.

956 Calvin Coolidge a Man with a Vision But Not a Visionary. [N.
p., n. d., 1924?]

Cover title [1], [2], 3-14, bl. [15], [16]. Stapled. Title
vignette. "The Silent Man on Beacon Hill: An Appreciation
of Calvin Coolidge," by Bruce Barton (from the Woman's
Home Companion, March, 1920), pp. 3-14.

957 Green, Horace. The Life of Calvin Coolidge. Illustrated.
New York: Duffield & Company, 1924.

Half title [i], [ii], pf., t. [iii], [iv], [v], bl. [vi], [vii], bl.
[viii], [ix-x], div. t. [1], bl. [2], 3-224, 225-263, bl. [264].
Blue cloth. Pf. and 14 pls. inserted, 2 fac. letters in
text.

958   Hennessy, M. E.   Calvin Coolidge From a Green Mountain
       Farm to the White House.... Illustrated. New York &
       London: G. P. Putnam's Sons, The Knickerbocker Press,
       1924.

       Pf. , t. [i], [ii], [iii], bl. [iv], v-viii, ix-x, xl [sic], bl.
       [xii], div. t. 1, bl. [2], 3-187, bl. [188], 189-197, bl.
       [198], p. adv. , bl. p.   Blue cloth.   Pf. and 8 pls. in-
       serted.

959   Johnston, Thomas T.   Have Faith in Calvin Coolidge or From
       a Farm House to the White House. [Cedar Falls, Iowa:
       Woolverton Printing Company c1923.]

       Cover title. [1], [2], 3-44.   Brown wrps.   11 articles,
       pp. 3-44.

*960   Kinsley, Earle S.   Calvin Coolidge, Vermonter.... [Burling-
       ton, Vt. ? 1924.]

       14 pp. , pls. Address before the State Chamber of Com-
       merce, Burlington, March 24, 1924.

961   [Macdonald, Arthur.]   President Coolidge.   [N. p. , 1924.]

       Caption title.   363-373. Offprint from The Calcutta Re-
       view, August, 1924.

962   _____ .   Scientific Political Training of President Coolidge.
       [N. p. , 1924.]

       Caption title.   [1]-10, bl. ℓ. [11-12]. Green wrps. , upper
       left, outer front noting Overgedrukt ut "De Nieuwe Gids"
       Aflevering III-Maart 1924.

963   _____ .   Scientific Political Training of President Coolidge....
       Printed in the Congressional Record by Request of Senator
       Spencer, of Missouri, January 10, 1924.   Washington:
       Government Printing Office, 1924.

       Cover title [1], [2], 3-8. Sewn.

964   Official Report of the Proceedings of the Eighteenth Republican
       National Convention.... Reported by George L. Hart, Of-
       ficial Reporter. Published Under the Supervision of the
       General Secretary of the Convention. New York: The
       Tenny Press [c1924.]

       F. , t. [i], [ii], [iii], bl. [iv], pl. , [v], bl. [vi], pl. , 7-
       250, 251-256. Green cloth. F. and 24 pls. inserted.
       Sketches of Coolidge and Dawes, pp. 203-221; index, pp.
       251-256. Goldstamped leather copy belonging to Dawes
       also noted.

965 Republican Campaign Text-Book 1924. Issued By the Republi-
     can National Committee. [N. p. , 1924.]

     T. [1], [2], 3-426, 427-447, 448. White coated wrps.
     Sketch of Coolidge, pp. 3-10; of Dawes, pp. 11-20. List
     of the Republican National Committee, p. 448, continued on
     inner back of wrp.

966 Roberts, Kenneth L. Concentrated New England. A Sketch of
     Calvin Coolidge. Indianapolis: The Bobbs-Merrill Company
     Publishers [c1924.]

     Half title [i], bl. [ii], t. [iii], [iv], div. t. [1], bl. [2], 3-
     [58]. Red cloth.

967 Sawyer, Roland D. Cal Coolidge President. Boston: The
     Four Seas Company Publishers [c1924.]

     Half title [1], bl. [2], pf. , t. [3], [4], [5], bl. [6], 7-8,
     [9], bl. [10], 11-15, [16], div. t. [17], bl. [18], 19-119,
     120-128. Blue cloth. Pf. and 3 pls. inserted. Foreword,
     pp. 7-8, dated June 17, 1924; chronology, p. [16]; excerpts
     from speeches, pp. 120-128.

968 Washburn, R. M. Calvin Coolidge His First Biography. A
     Brief Biography of Calvin Coolidge From Cornerstone to
     Capstone. The ABC Edition. This Edition is Approved By
     Hon. William M. Butler of the Coolidge Pre-Convention Cam-
     paign. Boston: Published by The Roosevelt Club [c1924.]

     Half title, port. on verso, t. [1], [2], [3], bl. [4], [5-6],
     7-[48], illus. , capstone. Greyish blue illus. wrps. , inner
     front pr. C. C. , outer back pr. Calvin Coolidge, inner
     back with adv. Pf. and 5 pls. inserted. Copyright, p.
     [2] notes "First Edition. February, 1924. "

969 _____ . Calvin Coolidge His First Biography. . . . Boston:
     Published by The Roosevelt Club [c1924.]

     As in entry 968, except copyright, p. [2], notes "First Edi-
     tion. February, 1924 / Second Edition. April, 1924 (55th
     Thousand). "

970 _____ . Calvin Coolidge His First Biography. A Brief
     Biography. . . . The ABC Popular Edition. New York:
     Emerson, Forman & Fawcett, Inc. , Distributors [1924.]

     T. [1], port. [2], div. t. and copyright [3], port. [4], 5-
     47, adv. [48]. White wrps. Illus. in text. Copyright, p.
     [3], notes "Third Edition. June, 1924. "

971 _____ . Calvin Coolidge His First Biography. From Corner-
     stone to Capstone to the Accession. Boston: Small, May-
     nard and Company Publishers [c1923.]

Half title, [i], bl. [ii], f. , t. [iii], [iv], [v], bl. [vi], [vii],
bl. [viii], [ix], bl. [x], [xi], bl. [xii], [xiii], bl. [xiv],
[xv], bl. [xvi], div. t. [1], bl. [2], 3-150. Red cloth. F.
and 12 pls. inserted.

972 _____ . Calvin Coolidge. . . . Boston: Small, Maynard and
Company Publishers [c1923.]

As in entry 971, except copyright, p. [iv], also notes "Second Edition--November, 1923. "

973 _____ . Calvin Coolidge. . . . Boston: Small, Maynard and
Company Publishers [c1923.]

Half title, [i], bl. [ii], f. , t. [iii], [iv], [v], [vi], [vii], bl.
[viii], [ix], bl. [x], [xi], bl. [xii], [xiii], bl. [xiv], div. t.
[1], bl. [2], 3-169. Red cloth. F. and 17 pls. inserted.
Copyright, p. [iv], notes "Fourth Edition--June, 1924. "

974 Weeks, Eugene M. Have Faith in Coolidge! Boston: Seaver-
Howland Press, MCMXXIII.

Half title [1], bl. [2], bl. [3], port. [4], t. [5], [6], [7],
bl. [8], 9-24, [25], bl. [26]. Cream paper bds. Port.
tipped to p. [4]. Colophon, p. [25], notes 1, 500 copies pr. ,
of which 250 are a ltd. numbered ed.

975 Whiting, Edward Elwell. President Coolidge a Contemporary
Estimate. Boston: The Atlantic Monthly Press [c1923.]

Half title [i], bl. [ii], pf. , t. [iii], [iv], [v], bl. [vi], [vii],
bl. [viii], [ix]-xv, bl. [xvi], div. t. [1], bl. [2], [3]-204,
[205]-208. Blue cloth. Pf. and pl. inserted, one fac. in
text. Foreword, p. [v], dated Oct. 15, 1923.

976 Woods, Robert A. The Preparation of Calvin Coolidge: An
Interpretation. . . . Boston and New York: Houghton Mifflin
Company; Cambridge: The Riverside Press, 1924.

Half title [i], bl. [ii], t. [iii], [iv], [v], bl. [vi], div. t.
[vii], bl. [viii], [1]-280, [281]-283, [284], [285]-288. Blue
cloth. Notes, pp. [281]-283; author's chronology, p. [284];
index, pp. [285]-288. Copy noted in orange illus. wrps. ,
half title and index lacking.

DAVIS, JOHN W. (Democratic)

977 Democratic Campaign Book 1924. Issued by the Democratic
National Committee; the Democratic Congressional Committee. Washington [1924.]

Cover title. [1]-2, 3-349, 350-352. Blue coated illus.
wrps. , at head, Honesty At Home--Honor Abroad. Title

vignette.   Sketches of Davis and Bryan, pp. 47-86; index,
pp. 35; index, pp. 350-352.

978   Huntley, Theodore A.   The Life of John W. Davis.   Edited,
With a Compilation of Speeches, by Horace Green.   Illustrated.   New York: Duffield & Company, 1924.

Half title [i], [ii], pf. , t. [iii], [iv], [v-vi], [vii], bl. [viii],
[ix], bl. [x], xi, bl. [xii], xiii-xvi, div. t. [1], bl. [2], 3-
140, div. t. [141], bl. [142], 143-290, div. t. [291], bl.
[292], 293-295, bl. [296].   Blue cloth, pr. and illus. dj.
Pf. and 9 pls. inserted.   Life of Davis, pp. 3-140; his
speeches, pp. 143-290; appendices, pp. 293-295.

979   John W. Davis.   Biography and Record of John W. Davis,
Democratic Nominee for President.   Washington: Democratic National Committee [1924.]

Cover title [1], bl. [2], 3-31, bl. [32].   Stapled.   Title
vignette.   At head of title, Common Honesty Common Justice Common Courage.

980   Women's Democratic Campaign Manual 1924.   Issued by the
Democratic National Committee; the Democratic Congressional Committee.   Washington: [1924.]

Cover title.   Pf. , [1], bl. [2], [3], bl. [4], 5, bl. [6], 7-
142.   Cream wrps.   Pf. inserted, other illus. in text.
Sketches of the candidates, pp. 7-18.

LA FOLLETTE, Robert M. (Progressive)

981   The Facts La Follette-Wheeler Campaign Text-Book.   Chicago:
Published and Distributed by LaFollette-Wheeler Campaign
Headquarters [1924.]

T. [1], bl. [2], [3], illus. [4], [5]-17, illus. [18], [19]-29,
[30]-144.   Buff stiff wrps. , campaign officers on inner
front, a directory on entire back.   Illus. in text.   Life of
LaFollette, pp. [5]-17; of Wheeler, pp. [19]-29.

982   The Men for President for Vice President.   Chicago: La Follette-Wheeler Progressive Headquarters [1924.]

Cover title.   Unpaged, 2 ℓℓ. [1-4].   Fld.   Title vignette.
At head of title, Leaflet No. 1 "On Guard for the People";
at foot of title, "Fearless and Incorruptible. "

983   Warner, Arthur.   La Follette's Record.   New York: The Nation [1924.]

Cover title [1], [2], 3-21, cartoon 22, adv. 23, [24].
Stapled.   Title vignette.   One illus. in text.

McADOO, WILLIAM GIBBS (Democratic)

984 Synon, Mary. McAdoo the Man and His Times: A Panorama
     in Democracy. Indianapolis: The Bobbs-Merrill Company
     Publishers [c1924.]

          Half title [i], bl. [ii], pf. , t. [iii], [iv], [v], bl. [vi], div.
          t. [1], bl. [2], 3-[342], div. t. [343], bl. [344], 345-355,
          [356]. Green cloth. Pf. inserted. Index, pp. 345-355.

SMITH, ALFRED E. (Democratic)

985 Moskowitz, Henry. Alfred E. Smith an American Career.
     New York: Thomas Seltzer, 1924.

          Half title [i], bl. [ii], pf. , t. [iii], [iv], [v], bl. [vi], [vii],
          [viii], [ix-x], div. t. [1], bl. [2], 3-312. Green cloth with
          pr. and illus. dj. Pf. and 7 pls. inserted.

1928

GENERAL WORKS

986 Midgley, Wilson. Possible Presidents. London: Ernest Benn
     Limited [c1928.]

          Half title [1], bl. [2], t. [3], [4], [5], bl. [6], [7]-12, [13]-
          187, [188], 3 pp. adv. , bl. p. All copies examined re-
          bound. Includes sections on Coolidge, Hoover, Smith,
          Dawes, Lowden, Borah, Curtis, Reed, and Henry Ford.

987 Political Atlas for 1928. A Compendium of Facts and Figures,
     Platforms, Biographies and Portraits. The Men and the
     Issues of the Presidential Campaigns. Chicago, New York:
     Rand McNally & Company, 1928.

          T. [1], 2-16. Buff illus. wrps. , tbls. on inner front and
          back, outer back with "The Call to Citizenship. " Illus.
          and maps in text.

HOOVER, HERBERT (Republican)

988 Bernstein, Herman. Herbert Hoover the Man Who Brought
     America to the World. [New York: Herald-Nathan Press,
     1928.]

T. [1], [2], [3], bl. [4], 5-44.   Brown wrps.   Reprint in
pamphlet form of a series of articles pub. in the September
and October, 1925, issues of McClure's Magazine.

989   Biographical Sketch of Herbert Hoover, Reprinted From the National Cyclopedia of American Biography.   Washington: Republican National Committee, 1928.

Unpaged, 8 ℓℓ. Cover title [1], [2], port. [3], [4], [5-16].
Stapled.   Port. in text.

990   Chapple, Joe Mitchell.   Yes! I Am Going to Vote for Hoover!
For President Herbert Hoover.   Reasons Why....   [Boston:
The Chapple Press, c1928.]

T. [i], [ii], [iii], [iv], [v], illus. [vi], 1-[88].   Red coated
illus. wrps., pr. in white.   Title vignette.   Illus. in text.
At foot of p. [88], "The Chapple Press, Boston."

991   Chronological Biographical Sketch of Herbert Hoover Touching
the High-Spots in the Life and Activities of the Republican
Candidate for President of the United States.   Washington:
Republican National Committee, 1928.

Cover title [1], bl. [2], 3-15, bl. [16].   Stapled.   Title
vignette.

992   Cole, Cyrenus.   Herbert Hoover's Boyhood in Iowa.   Remarks
of ... In the House of Representatives, Tuesday, May 29,
1928.   The Story Back of the Organization of the Cedar
County (Iowa) Hoover Farm Club.   [Washington: Government
Printing Office, 1928.]

Caption title.   [1]-7, bl. [8].   Sewn.   At the foot of p. 7,
"U. S. Government Printing Office: 1928."

993   Crowther, Samuel.   The Presidency vs. Hoover.   Garden City,
N. Y.:   Doubleday, Doran and Company, Inc., 1928.

Half title [i], [ii], t. [iii], [iv], [v], bl. [vi], div. t. [1],
bl. [2], 3-286.   Tan cloth with brown coated pr. dj.   Copyright, p. [iv], notes "First Edition."

994   Hard, William.   The New Hoover.   In The American Review
of Reviews Edited By Albert Shaw, November [1928.]

Unpaged, 4 ℓℓ. Cover title [1], [2-8].   Stapled.   Title
vignette.   One illus. in text.   At foot of p. [2], "© The
Review of Reviews Corp. New York."; pr. in dbl. cols.

995   _____ .   The New Hoover.   Copyright 1928 by the Review
of Reviews Corporation.   Washington: Republican National
Committee, 1928.

Cover title [1], 2-16.   Stapled.

996 _____ .   Who's Hoover?   New York: Dodd, Mead and Company, 1928.

Half title [i], bl. [ii], t. [iii], [iv], [v], bl. [vi], vii-ix, bl. [x], [xi], bl. [xii], 1-274.   Green cloth.   Copies also noted with copyright, p. [iv], noting "Published, June 1928.   Second printing, July, 1928. " Also noted with buff pr. and illus. dj.

997 [Herter, Christian A.]   Herbert Hoover.   [N. p. , 1928.]

Cover title [1], [2], 3-11, bl. [12].   Stapled.   Port. in text.   At foot of p. [2], "Reprinted by Courtesy of The Christian Science Monitor"; text by Christian A. Herter.

998 _____ .   A Progressive Editor's Estimate of Herbert Hoover.   [N. p. , 1928.]

Cover title [1], 2-[6].   One sheet, 9 x 4, fld. twice.   Title vignette.   Caption title, p. 2, Hoover In Person By Christian A. Herter....

999 Hoover, Herbert.   Boyhood Days In Iowa. An Informal Address Before the Iowa Society of Washington.   [N. p. , Republican National Committee? 1928.]

Caption title.   Unpaged, 2 ℓℓ. [1-4].   Fld.

1000 _____ .   Hoover Recalls His Iowa Boyhood Days.   An Informal Visit With the Iowa Society of Washington, November 10, 1927.   Washington: Republican National Committee, 1928.

Unpaged, one sheet, $8\frac{1}{2}$ x 3 3/4, fld. accordion style, 8 pp.

1001 Howard, J. R.   Herbert Hoover's Record As a Friend of the American Farmer.   [N. p. , 1928.]

Cover title [1], bl. [2], 3-26, [27], [28].   Grey wrps. , inner front bl. [2], inner back, p. [27] with sources for statements, outer back, p. [28] with union seal.

1002 _____ .   Herbert Hoover's Record....   [N. p. , Republican National Committee, 1928.]

Caption title.   1-[16].   Stapled.   At foot of title here and in entry 1001, "Actions Speak Louder Than Words. "

1003 Introducing the Republican Candidates to New Jersey Voters. Facts About the National and State Candidates....   [N. p.]

Issued by New Jersey Republican State Committee,
MCMXXVIII.

Cover title [1], [2], 3-[16].   Stapled.   Illus. in text.
Sketches of Hoover and Curtis, pp. 3-9.

1004   Irwin, Will.   Herbert Hoover a Reminiscent Biography.   Il-
lustrated From Photographs.   New York: Grosset & Dunlap
Publishers;   Published by Arrangement with The Century
Company [c1928.]

Half title [i], bl. [ii], pf. , t. [iii], [iv], div. t. [1], bl.
[2], 3-315, bl. [316].   Green cloth.   Pf. and 7 pls. inserted.   First printing, March, 1928.   Copies also noted
with copyright, p. [iv], noting "Third Printing, June, 1928. "

1005   _____.   Herbert Hoover a Reminiscent Biography.   Illustrated.   Special Edition.   New York, London: The Century
Co. [c1928.]

Pf. , t. [i], [ii], [iii], bl. [iv], div. t. [1], bl. [2], 3-315,
bl. [316].   Red cloth with red pr. and illus. dj.   Pf. and
7 pls. inserted.   Copyright, p. [ii], noting "Special Edition
July, 1928. "   Copies also noted with citation, "Second Special Edition, July 1928. "

1006   Johnson, William.   That Man Hoover--He's Human.   [N. p. ,
1928.]

Single sheet offprint from article originally appearing in
Farm Life (Spencer, Indiana), Vol. 46, no. 1, January,
1928.

1007   Kellogg, Vernon.   The Outlook, an Illustrated Weekly of Cur-
rent Life.   Vernon Kellogg Tells What Hoover's Friends
Think of Him.   Reprinted From the Outlook Issues of October 19th and 26th, 1927.   [N. p. , 1928?]

Cover title.   1-[8].   White wrps. , front pr. in green on
yellow.   Illus. in text.   Pr. in triple cols.

1008   Official Report of the Proceedings of the Nineteenth Republican
National Convention....   Reported by George L. Hart, Official Reporter.   Published Under the Supervision of the
General Secretary of the Convention.   New York: The Tenny Press [c1928.]

F. , t. [1], [2], [3], bl. [4], pl. , [5-6], pl. , 7-311, 312-
319, bl. [320].   Green cloth.   F. and 23 pls. inserted.
Sketches of Hoover and Curtis, pp. 261-275.   Also noted in
3/4 brown leather with $\frac{1}{4}$ blue leather center panels, copy
belonging to Charles Curtis.

1009 Reeves, Earl. This Man Hoover. Part One. A Human In-
      terest Story.... Part Two. As a Man Thinks by Herbert
      Hoover (Compiled). New York: A. L. Burt Company Pub-
      lishers [c1928.]

          Pf., t. [1], [2], [3], bl. [4], div. t. [5] bl. [6], 7-171,
          bl. [172], div. t. [173], [174], 175-255, bl. [256]. Red
          cloth. Pf. and 3 pls. inserted. Life of Hoover, pp. 7-171;
          "As a Man Thinks," pp. 175-255.

1010 Republican Campaign Text-Book 1928. Issued by the Republi-
      can National Committee. [N. p., 1928.]

          T. [1], [2], 3-403 404-423, [424]. White coated wrps.,
          inner back with continuation of Committee members from
          p. [424]. Sketches of Hoover and Curtis, pp. 3-17.

1011 Swisher, J. A. Herbert Hoover's Boyhood. Iowa City: The
      Armstrong Publishing Company [1928.]

          Unpaged, 8 ℓℓ., final bl. Stapled. 2 pls. inserted. "Re-
          printed from The Palimpsest, 1928."

SMITH, ALFRED E. (Democratic)

1012 The Campaign Book of the Democratic Party. Candidates and
      Issues in 1928. New York: Published by the Democratic
      National Committee; the Democratic Senatorial Committee;
      the Democratic Congressional Committee [1928.]

          Cover title. [i], bl. [ii], iii-iv, [1]-403, 404-408, 409-412.
          Brown coated wrps., pr. on inner back. Sketches of Smith
          and Robinson, pp. 5-27.

1013 Costello, Jerry. The Life of Al Smith (Told in Forty-Eight
      Pictures). New York: The Avondale Press Incorporated
      [c1928.]

          T. [i], [ii], [iii], [iv], port. [v], illus. [vi], bl. [vii-viii],
          1-48. Green cloth. Illus. in text.

1014 Dickinson, Thomas H. The Portrait of a Man as Governor.
      With a Foreword by George Foster Peabody. New York:
      The Macmillan Company, 1928.

          Half title [i], [ii], t. [iii], [iv], v-vii, bl. [viii], div. t.
          [ix], bl. [x], 1-37, bl. [38]. 3/4 blue paper bds., blue
          cloth backstrip, gold pr. paper label on front. Copies also
          noted with orange dj pr. in blue.

1015 Doane, F. Clyde. From South Street to Albany. Alfred E.
      Smith. New York: Created, Printed, Published at The
      Riverside Press [c1928.]

T. [i], [ii], [iii], [iv], [v-vi], 9-97, adv. [98].   Leather.
Title vignette.   Illus. in text.   At head of title, Good Will
Ambassadors.

1016   Hapgood, Norman, and Moskowitz, Henry.   Up From the City
Streets: Alfred E. Smith. A Biographical Study in Con-
temporary Politics.   Illustrated.   New York: Harcourt,
Brace and Company [c1927.]

Pf., t. [i], [ii], [iii], bl. [iv], [v], bl. [vi], div. t. [1],
bl. [2], 3-340, 341-349, bl. [350], 2 bl. ℓℓ. Red cloth.
Pf. and 7 pls. inserted, facs. in text. Copyright, p. [ii],
notes "Published, November, 1927." Copies also noted
with copyright, p. [iv] (see below), noting "Second Printing,
November, 1927"; "Third Printing, January, 1928"; and
"Fourth Printing, March, 1928."

1017   _____ , and _____ . Up From the City Streets.... New
York: Grosset & Dunlap Publishers [c1927.]

As in entry 1016, except half title, [i], bl. [ii], pf., t.
[iii], [iv], [v], bl. [vi], [vii], bl. [viii] ... adv. [350], 5
11. adv. Brown cloth. Copyright, p. [iv], notes "Fourth
Printing, March, 1928."

1018   National Life Magazine. Al Smith. Al Smith's Life Story Illustrated. [N. p., 1928.]

Cover title [1], port. [2], [3], port. 4, 5-46, adv. 47, illus. [48]. Brown illus. wrps., being pp. [1-2] and 47-[48].
Illus. in text.

1019   Nations, Gilbert O. The Political Career of Alfred E. Smith.
Washington: The Protestant Militant Monthly for Thinkers
[c1928.]

T. [1], [2], 3, bl. [4], 5, bl. [6], 7-84. Cream wrps.
Anti-Smith.

1020   Pringle, Henry F. Alfred E. Smith a Critical Study. With
a Frontispiece by Wilfred Jones. [N. p.] Macy-Masius
Publishers, 1927.

Half title [i], bl. [ii], bl. [1], port. [2], t. [3], [4], [5],
bl. [6], [7], bl. [8], 9-10, div. t. [11], bl. [12], 13-391,
bl. [392], 393-402. Grey cloth, pr. gold labels on front
and backstrip. Pf. tipped to p. [2]. Copies also noted
with p. [4] citing, "Second Printing, September, 1927";
"Third Printing, November, 1927"; and "Fourth Printing,
July, 1928."

1021   Roosevelt, Franklin D. The Happy Warrior. Alfred E.
Smith, a Study of a Public Servant. Boston and New York:

Houghton Mifflin Company; Cambridge: The Riverside
Press, 1928.

Half title [i], bl. [ii], t. [iii], [iv], [v]-vi, div. t. [1], bl.
[2], [3]-40. Black cloth with pr. orange label on front,
back and backstrip; orange pr. dj.

1022   Taylor, Mack.   Alfred E. Smith.   A Psychological Analysis.
Fort Worth, Texas: Independent Publishing House [c1928.]

T. [i], [ii], port. [iii], bl. [iv], [v], [vi], [1]-87, bl. [88].
Green wrps. , pr. in red and green.   Illus. in text.

1023   What Everybody Wants to Know About Alfred E. Smith.   Issued by Democratic State Committee; Democratic Publicity
Bureau, Hotel Biltmore, New York City.   [New York?
1928.]

Cover title [1], bl. [2], 3-4, 5-30, 31-48.   Self wrps.
Port. in text.

COOLIDGE, CALVIN (Republican)

1024   Rogers, Cameron.   The Legend of Calvin Coolidge.   Garden
City, N. Y. : Doubleday, Doran & Company, Inc. , 1928.

Half title [i], [ii], t. [iii], [iv], [v], bl. [vi], div. t. [vii],
bl. [viii], 1-179, bl. [180].   Aqua cloth with pr. paper
labels in blue and red on front and backstrip; pr. dj.
First edition.   Concludes that Coolidge will not run.

1932

GENERAL WORKS

1025   The Mirrors of 1932.   Anonymous.   With 10 Cartoons by
Cesare.   New York: Brewer, Warren & Putnam, 1931.

Half title [i], bl. [ii], f. , t. [iii], [iv], [v], bl. [vi], div.
t. [1], bl. [2], 3-247, bl. [248].   Red cloth.   F. and 10
pls. inserted.   Burlesque treatment of 1932 Presidential
possibilities.   Copies also noted with copyright, p. [iv]
citing "Second Printing, July, 1931"; "Third Printing,
Aug. , 1931"; and "Fourth Printing, Dec. , 1931. " Pre-
sumed author, Clinton Wallace Gilbert? Ray Thomas
Tucker?

1026　Rand McNally Political Atlas for 1932.... Chicago, New
　　　York, San Francisco: Rand McNally & Company, 1932.

　　　T. [1], 2-16. White illus. wrps. Illus. and maps in text.
　　　Text pr. in blue.

ROOSEVELT, FRANKLIN DELANO (Democratic)

1027　Campaign Book of the Democratic Party. Candidates and Is-
　　　sues 1932. New York: Published by The Democratic Na-
　　　tional Committee; The Democratic Senatorial Committee;
　　　The Democratic Congressional Committee [1932.]

　　　Cover title. i, 2, 3-103, [104]. Off white wrps. Sketches
　　　of Roosevelt and Garner, pp. 5-20.

1028　Lindley, Ernest K. Franklin D. Roosevelt, a Career in Pro-
　　　gressive Democracy. New York: Blue Ribbon Books, Inc.
　　　[c1931.]

　　　Half title, [i], bl. [ii], pf. , t. [iii], [iv], [v], bl. [vi], div.
　　　t. [vii], bl. [viii], div. t. [ix], bl. [x], 11-344, div. t.
　　　[345], bl. [346], 347-379, bl. [380]. Blue cloth. Pf. in-
　　　serted.

1029　　　　. Franklin D. Roosevelt.... Indianapolis: The
　　　Bobbs-Merrill Company Publishers [c1931.]

　　　As in entry 1028. c1931 noting "First Edition. "

1030　Looker, Earle. This Man Roosevelt. New York: Brewer,
　　　Warren & Putnam, 1932.

　　　Half title [i], bl. [ii], pf. , t. [iii], [iv], bl. [vi], vii, bl.
　　　[viii], [ix], bl. [x], 1-228, 229-233, bl. [234]. Blue cloth.
　　　Pf. inserted.

1031　Roosevelt the Man. A Pictorial Biography of Franklin D.
　　　Roosevelt. [New York: Published by The Biography Pub-
　　　lishing Company c1932.]

　　　Cover title. 1, 2, 3-24. Illus. wrps. Title vignette.
　　　At foot of p. 2, publishing information and copyright notice.
　　　Edited by Warren B. Cody.

1032　Ross, Leland M. , and Grobin, Allen W. This Democratic
　　　Roosevelt, the Life Story of "F. D. " An Authentic Biogra-
　　　phy. Illustrated. New York: E. P. Dutton & Co. , Inc.
　　　[c1932.]

　　　Half title [i], bl. [ii], pf. , t. [iii], [iv], 5-6, [7], bl. [8],
　　　[9], bl. [10], div. t. [11], bl. [12], 13-278, div. t. [279],

bl. [280], 281-305, bl. [306], 307-312. Red cloth. Pf.
and 7 pls. inserted. First edition. First campaign biog.
written for 1932 election?

HOOVER, HERBERT (Republican)

1033 Charnley, Mitchell V. The Boys' Life of Herbert Hoover.
      Illustrated With Photographs. New York and London: Harp-
      er & Brothers Publishers, MCMXXXI.

      Half title [i], bl. [ii], pf., t. [iii], [iv], [v], bl. [vi], vii-
      viii, [ix], bl. [x], div. t. [1], bl. [2], 3-272. Purple
      cloth. Pf. and 6 pls inserted. First edition.

1034 Corey, Herbert. The Truth About Hoover.... With Illustra-
      tions. Boston and New York: Houghton Mifflin Company;
      Cambridge: The Riverside Press, 1932.

      Half title [i], bl. [ii], pf., t. [iii], [iv], [v]-vi, [vii], bl.
      [viii], [1]-318. Blue cloth. Pf. and 7 pls. inserted.

1035 Dexter, Walter Friar. Herbert Hoover and American Indi-
      vidualism. A Modern Interpretation of a National Ideal.
      New York: The Macmillan Company, 1932.

      Half title [i], [ii], pf., t. [iii], [iv], [v], bl. [vi], vii-viii,
      ix-x, div. t. [1], bl. [2], 3-248, 249-252, 253-256. Blue
      cloth. Pf. inserted. Copyright, p. [iv], notes "Published
      July, 1932"; bibliography, pp. 249-252; index, pp. 253-256.

1036 Emerson, Edwin. Hoover and His Times. Looking Back
      Through the Years.... Illustrated by Contemporary Car-
      toons. Garden City, N.Y.: Garden City Publishing Com-
      pany, Inc., 1932.

      Half title [i], [ii], illus., t. [iii], [iv], [v], bl. [vi], vii-
      viii, ix, bl. [x], xi-xiv, xv-xvi, div. t. [xvii], bl. [xviii],
      [1]-579, [580], div. t. [581], bl. [582], 583-595, bl.
      [596], 597-632. Blue cloth. Cartoon illus. in text. "First
      Edition" noted. Copies also noted lacking edition listing.

1037 Hamill, John. The Strange Career of Mr. Hoover Under Two
      Flags. Illustrated and Documented. New York: William
      Faro, Inc., 1931.

      F., t. [i], [ii], [iii], bl. [iv], [v-x], 13-366. Blue cloth
      with pr. paper label on backstrip. F. and 12 pls. in-
      serted, pr. in sepia. First edition.

1038 _____. The Strange Career of Mr. Hoover.... New
      York: William Faro, Inc., 1931.

F. , t. [i], [ii], [iii], bl. [iv], [v-vi], [vii-xii], div. t. , ver-
so bl. , 13-366, div. t. [367], bl. [368], 369-381, bl. [382].
Blue cloth as above.   F. and 12 pls. inserted, pr. in black.
Notes "Second Printing, October 13, 1931. " Copies also
noted citing "Third Printing, November 24, 1931"; "Fourth
Printing, December 1 [1931]" in green cloth; and "Tenth
Printing, January 30, 1932" in green cloth.   Anti-Hoover.

1039   Hoover, Herbert.   A Boyhood in Iowa.   With a Foreword by
Will Irwin.   New York: Aventine Press, 1931.

T. [1], [2], 3-10, div. t. [11], bl. [12], 13-[50], bl. [51],
[52].   Light green cloth.   Title vignette.   Illus. in text.
Foreword, pp. 3-10, dated October, 1931; colophon, p.
[52], notes 1, 000 copies pr.

1040   Liggett, Walter W.   The Rise of Herbert Hoover.   New York:
The H. K. Fly Company Publishers [c1932.]

Half title, verso bl. , pf. , t. [i], [ii], [iii], bl. [iv], v-vii,
bl. [viii], [ix], bl. [x], div. t. [1], bl. [2], 3-360, 361-
382.   Black cloth.   Pf. and 7 pls. inserted.   Appendix, pp.
361-382.   Unfavorable account.

1041   Marsh, William J. , Jr.   Our President Herbert Hoover.   New
Milford, Conn. :   William J. & Chas. Marsh, Pub. , 1930.

F. , bl. 1. , t. [i], [ii], 1-2, [3] bl. [4], [5], bl. [6], div.
t. [1], bl. [2], 3-45.   Blue paper bds. , blue cloth backstrip.   F. and pl. inserted, other illus. in text.   Note, p.
[3], "P. S. --Since printing my first 60 copies of this book
I have decided to let Doubleday, Doran & Co. , of Garden
City, print some more for me because they have bigger
presses, so this copy is printed in their print shop from
my type. " Issued by an 11-year-old.   Also noted in green
paper bds.

1042   _____ .   Why You Should Vote for President Hoover by
Bill Marsh Age 14 and Bub Marsh Age 12, Authors & Publishers of Our President Herbert Hoover.   First Edition.
100 Copies.   New Milford, Conn. :   William J. & Chas.
Marsh Publishers, 1932.

F. , t. [1], [2], [3], illus. [4], 5-10, 11-96.   Green cloth.
F. and 3 pls. inserted, other illus. in text.   Copies also
noted indicating on copyright p. [2] a later ed. issued by
The Norman W. Henley Pub. Co. , N. Y.

1043   Official Report of the Proceedings of the Twentieth Republican
National Convention. . . .   Reported by George L. Hart, Official Reporter.   Published Under the Supervision of the General Secretary of the Convention.   New York: The Tenny
Press [c1932.]

F., t. [1], [2], [3], bl. [4], pl., [5], bl. [6], pl., 7-277,
278-285, bl. [286]. Green cloth.   F. and 23 pls. inserted.
Sketch of Hoover, pp. 229-236; of Curtis, pp. 237-242.

1044 Text-Book of the Republican Party 1932. Issued by the Re-
      publican National Committee. [N. p., 1932.]

T. [i], bl. [ii], [1], [2], 3-271, 272-280, 281-283, 284-285,
[286]. White coated wrps. Title vignette. Sketch of
Hoover, pp. 3-10; of Curtis, pp. 11-16.

1045 Wood, Clement. Herbert Clark Hoover: An American Trag-
      edy. New York: Michael Swain, 1932.

Flyleaf, [1-2], half title [3], bl. [4], pf., t. [5], [6], [7],
bl. [8], [9], bl. [10], div. t. [11], bl. [12], 13-330. Blue
cloth with yellow pr. paper label on backstrip; dj in red,
illus. Anti-Hoover.

GARNER, JOHN NANCE (Democratic)

1046 Brown, George Rothwell. The Speaker of the House. The
      Romantic Story of John N. Garner. New York: Brewer,
      Warren & Putnam, 1932.

Half title [i], bl. [ii], pf., t. [iii], [iv], v, bl. [vi], div. t.
[1], bl. [2], 3-162. Light brown cloth. Pf. and 4 pls.
inserted.

1936

ROOSEVELT, FRANKLIN DELANO (Democratic)

1047 Brandeis, Erich. Franklin D. Roosevelt the Man. New York:
      Publishing Division, American Offset Corporation [c1936.]

T. [1], [2], [3], port. [4], 5-7, illus. [8], 9-43, illus.
[44], 45-55, bl. [56]. Orange paper bds. Illus. in text.

1048 The Democratic National Convention 1936. [N. p., 1936.]

Adv. [1-2], t. [3], adv. 4, [5], adv. 6, [7], adv. 8-[10],
port. [11], bl. [12], 13-20, 21-394. Illus. wrps., adv.
on inner front and entire back. 21 pls., fld. map, 2 facs.,
inserted, other illus. in text. Text pr. in dbl. cols.; life
of Roosevelt by Hendrik Willem Van Loon, pp. 13-20.

1049   Haber, Paul.   The House of Roosevelt.   New York: The Author's Publishing Company, MCMXXXVI.

T. [i], [ii], [iii], bl. [iv], [v], bl. [vi], [1]-89, bl. [90].
Off white wrps.   Copyright, p. [ii], notes "Published June,
1936. "   Anti-Roosevelt.

1050   _____ .   The House of Roosevelt.   Revised Edition.   Brooklyn: The Author's Publishing Company [c1936.]

Half title [1], [2], t. [3], bl. [4], [5], bl. [6], [7], bl. [8],
[9-12], 13-123, bl. [124].   Grey green cloth.   Illus. in
text.   Copyright, p. [2], "Published August, 1936. "

1051   Knowles, Archibald Campbell.   Franklin Delano Roosevelt the
Great Liberal.   Burlington, N. J. :   Enterprise Publishing
Co. [c1936.]

T. [1], [2], 3, bl. [4], 5-6, 7-64.   Green wrps. , adv. on
fld. over sections.   Wrp. also indicates cloth binding available.

LANDON, ALFRED M. (Republican)

1052   Comer, Burt.   The Tale of a Fox.   As Kansans Know Alfred
M. Landon.   Wichita: Burt Comer, Publisher [c1936.]

T. I, II, III-IV, V, VI, 1-89, div. t. [90].   Red illus.
wrps.   Foreword, pp. III-IV, dated July 4, 1936.   Anti-
Landon.

1053   Fowler, Richard B.   Deeds Not Deficits.   The Story of Alfred
M. Landon.   With an Introduction by William Allen White.
[N. p. , c1936.]

Half title [i], pf. [ii], t. [iii], [iv], i-vi, 1-89, bl. [90].
Brown wrps. pr. in red and brown.   Illus. in text.

1054   Hinshaw, David, ed.   Landon What He Stands for. . . .   The
Republican Candidate Interpreted by Henry J. Allen, John
Hamilton, Malcolm W. Bingay, Roy Roberts, Arthur Capper, Wm. Allen White.   New York: Mail & Express Publishing Co. [1936.]

T. [1], port. 2, 3-5, 6-48.   Buff illus. wrps.   Illus. in
text.

1055   Official Report of the Proceedings of the Twenty-First Republican National Convention. . . .   Reported by George L. Hart,
Official Reporter.   Published Under the Supervision of the
General Secretary of the Convention.   New York: The Tenny Press [c1936.]

T. [1], [2], [3], bl. [4], pl. , [5], bl. [6], pl. , 7-269, 270-276. Green cloth. 25 pls. inserted. Sketches of Landon and Knox, pp. 229-243.

1056   Palmer, Frederick. This Man Landon, the Record and Career of Governor Alfred M. Landon of Kansas. New York: Dodd, Mead & Company, 1936.

Half title [i], [ii], pf. , t. [iii], [iv], v-vi, div. t. [1], bl. [2], 3-245, bl. [246]. Orange cloth. Pf. inserted. Copies also noted with copyright, p. [iv], citing "Published, March, 1936 / Second Printing, March, 1936. "

1057   _____ . This Man Landon.... Revised and Enlarged Edition. New York: Dodd, Mead & Company, 1936.

Half title [i], [ii], pf. , t. [iii], [iv], [v], bl. [vi], vii-viii, div. t. [1], bl. [2], 3-323, bl. [324], 325-332. Orange cloth. Pf. , different than in entry 1056, inserted. Copyright, p. [iv], notes "Third Printing"; preface to 3rd ed. , p. [v].

1058   Text Book of the Republican Party 1936. Issued by the Republican National Committee. [N. p. , 1936.]

T. [1], [2], 3, port. [4], port. [5], [6], 7-151, bl. [152]. White wrps. , pr. in blue and red. Sketch of Landon, pp. 7-20; of Knox, pp. 21-25.

1059   Thornton, Willis. The Life of Alfred M. Landon. New York: Grosset & Dunlap Publishers [c1936.]

Half title [i], bl. [ii], pf. , t. [iii], [iv], v, bl. [vi], vii, bl. [viii], div. t. [ix], bl. [x], 1-174. Orange cloth. Pf. and 4 pls. inserted.

1060   White, William Allen. What It's All About: Being a Reporter's Story of the Early Campaign of 1936. New York: The Macmillan Company, 1936.

Half title [i], [ii], t. [iii], [iv], v-vii, bl. [viii], [ix], bl. [x], div. t. [xi], bl. [xii], 1-101, bl. [102], div. t. [103], bl. [104], 105-146. Orange cloth, with orange dj. Preface, pp. v-vii, dated August 20, 1936; life of Landon, pp. 38-66; appendices, pp. 105-146. "Published September, 1936. First Printing. "

1061   Why We Are Supporting Alfred M. Landon for President. By the Publicity Chairman, Landon-for-President Club of Northeast Johnson County, Kansas.... [N. p. , 1936.]

Cover title. [1]-32. Blue wrps. , inner front with "America" and copyright notice by Elizabeth Barr Arthur, adv. on inner back, poem by Tennyson on outer back. Port. in text.

BORAH, WILLIAM EDGAR (Republican)

1062 Johnson, Claudius O. Borah of Idaho. New York, Toronto:
Longmans, Green and Co., 1936.

Half title [i], bl. [ii], pf., t. [iii], [iv], [v], bl. [vi], vii-
viii, ix, bl. [x], xi-[xii], 1-500, 501-511, bl. [512]. Blue
cloth. Pf. and 7 pls. inserted. Copyright, p. [iv], notes
"First Edition"; preface, pp. vii-viii, dated February 12,
1936; index, pp. 501-511.

KNOX, FRANK (Republican)

1063 Beasley, Norman. Frank Knox American, a Short Biography.
Garden City, N. Y.: Doubleday, Doran & Company,
MCMXXXVI.

Half title [i], bl. [ii], pf., t. [iii], [iv], [v], bl. [vi], div.
t. [vii], bl. [viii], [1]-184. Blue cloth. Pf. inserted.
First edition.

1940

ROOSEVELT, FRANKLIN DELANO (Democratic)

1064 Flynn, John T. Country Squire in the White House. New
York: Doubleday, Doran and Company, Inc., 1940.

Half title [i], bl. [ii], t. [iii], [iv], v-vi, vii, bl. [viii],
div. t. [ix], bl. [x], [1]-131, bl. [132]. Blue cloth. Copyright, p. [iv], notes "First Edition"; note, pp. v-vi, dated
May 23, 1940. Anti-Roosevelt.

1065 _____. Country Squire.... New York: Doubleday, Doran
and Company, Inc., 1940.

Half title [i], bl. [ii], t. [iii], [iv], v-vi, vii, [1]-122.
Blue cloth. Lacks edition notation.

1066 Guffey, Joseph F. Roosevelt Again! Philadelphia: Franklin
[c1940.]

Half title [1], [2], t. [3], [4], [5], [6], 7-120. Blue cloth.
Also noted in blue coated wrps. pr. in red, white and blue,
outer back with port. and sketch of author.

1067   Ludwig, Emil.   Roosevelt, a Study in Fortune and Power.
       New York: The Viking Press, MCMXXXVIII.

       Half title [i], [ii], f., t. [iii], [iv], [v], bl. [vi], vii-xii,
       [xiii], bl. [xiv], [xv-xvi], div. t. [1], bl. [2], 3-344, div.
       t. [345], bl. [346], 347-350.   All copies examined rebound.
       F. and 8 pls. inserted.   Copyright, p. [iv], notes publica-
       tion as "June 1938. "   Also noted, but unexamined, as being
       published in 1940, New York: Garden City Publishing Com-
       pany.

1068   Ruskowski, Casimir W.   Is Roosevelt an Andrew Jackson?
       With an Introduction by Walter H. Hamilton.   Boston: Bruce
       Humphries, Inc.   Publishers [c1939.]

       Pf. [1], bl. [2], t. [3], [4], [5], [6], 7-9, bl. [10], div. t.
       [11], bl. [12], 13-65, bl. [66].   Maroon cloth.   Pf., pl.
       inserted.

WILLKIE, WENDELL (Republican)

1069   Chapple, Joe Mitchell.   Willkie and American Unity Including
       Face to Face With Presidents.   New York, Boston: Joe
       Mitchell Chapple Incorporated [c1940.]

       Half title [i], bl. [ii], t. [iii], [iv], [v], bl. [vi], vii-viii,
       ix-x, div. t. [1], bl. [2], 3-5, bl. [6], 7-166, div. t.
       [167], bl. [168], 169-242, [243], bl. [244].   Cream cloth.
       Face to face, pp. 169-242.

1070   Makey, Herman O.   Wendell Willkie of Elwood.   Elwood, Ind. :
       National Book Company [c1940.]

       Pf. [i], bl. [ii], t. [iii], [iv], [v], [vi], [vii-viii], pl. [ix],
       bl. [x], 1-290, [291], [292].   Blue cloth with illus. dj pr.
       in red, white and blue.   Pf. and 27 pls. inserted.

1071   Official Report of the Proceedings of the Twenty-Second Re-
       publican National Convention....   Reported by George L.
       Hart, Official Reporter.   Published Under the Supervision
       of Harold W. Mason, Secretary of the Convention.   Wash-
       ington: Judd & Detweiler, Inc. [1940.]

       T. [1], bl. [2], [3], bl. [4], pl., [5], bl. [6], pl., 7-408,
       409-418.   Green cloth.   33 pls. inserted.   Sketches of Will-
       kie and McNary, pp. 366-408.

1072   Wendell L. Willkie, Hoosier....   Vote to Put a Hoosier in
       the White House.   [N. p., 1940.]

       Cover title.   Unpaged, 2 ℓ ℓ.   [1-4].   Fld.   Title vignette.
       Illus. in text.   Brief sketch of Willkie, pp. [2-3].   Exam-
       ined in Xerox form only.

1073 Willkie, Wendell. Meet Mr. Willkie. A Selection of His
Writings on Present-Day Issues. With a Biographical Intro-
duction by Stanley Walker. Philadelphia: David McKay
Company [c1940.]

T. [1], [2], div. t. [3], bl. [4], [5], bl. [6], [7]-27, bl.
[28], [29], bl. [30], div. t. [31], bl. [32], [33]-62, bl. ℓ.
[63-64]. Yellow, white and blue illus. wrps. , Willkie port.
on front, illus. of Elwood High School on inner front, Mrs.
Willkie on inner back, Willkie waving on outer back. Biog.
intro. , pp. [7]-27; writings, pp. [33]-62. Abridged from
This Is Wendell Willkie. Copies noted with variant wrps. ,
Willkie sorting mail on front, climbing fence on inner front,
Mrs. Willkie sitting on inner back, Willkie standing by sign
on outer back.

1074 _____. This Is Wendell Willkie. A Collection of Speeches
and Writings on Present-Day Issues. With a Biographical
Introduction by Stanley Walker. New York: Dodd, Mead &
Company, 1940.

Half title [i], bl. [ii], pf. , t. [iii], [iv], [v], bl. [vi], [vii],
[viii], 1-37, bl. [38], div. t. [39], [40], 41-280. Blue
cloth. Pf. inserted. Copies also noted with copyright, p.
[iv], citing "Second Printing, August, 1940"; "Third Printing, August, 1940"; and "Fourth Printing, September, 1940. "

1075 _____. Wendell Lewis Willkie. Occasional Addresses and
Articles to Which Are Prefixed Biographical Sketches.
Stamford, Conn. : Printed at The Overbrook Press, 1940.

Half title [i], bl. [ii], pf. t. [iii], bl. [iv], [v], bl. [vi],
[vii-viii], div. t. [ix], [x], [i]-[x], [6]-57, bl. [58], div. t.
[59], [60], [61]-394. Natural cloth. Pf. inserted. Biog.
articles, pp. [i]-[x], [6]-57. T. pr. in red and black.

BROWDER, EARL R. (Communist)

1076 Campaign Book Presidential Elections 1940. New York:
Workers Library Publishers [1940.]

T. [1], [2], 3-122, 123, 124-128. Grey wrps. , pr. in red.
Sketches of Browder and Ford, pp. 3-5.

DEWEY, THOMAS E. (Republican)

1077 Hughes, Rupert. Attorney for the People: The Story of
Thomas E. Dewey. With Illustrations. Boston: Houghton
Mifflin Company; Cambridge: The Riverside Press, 1940.

Half title [i], bl. [ii], pf. , t. [iii], [iv], [v-viii], [ix]-x,
[xi], bl. [xii], [1]-350, [351]-361, bl. [362]. Orange cloth.
Pf. and 7 pls. inserted.

1078   Why Dewey Wins.   The Career of Thomas E. Dewey As Seen
       by the American Press.   New York: Published by Thomas
       E. Dewey Committee for Presidential Nomination [1940.]

       T. [1], [2], [3], bl. [4], [5], bl. [6], 7-8, 9-182, 183-189,
       bl. [190]. Illus. wrps. , pr. in red.   Cartoon illus. in text.

GARNER, JOHN NANCE (Democratic)

1079   James, Marquis.   Mr. Garner of Texas.   Indianapolis, New
       York: The Bobbs-Merrill Company [c1939.]

       Half title [1], bl. [2], pf. , t. [3], [4], [5], bl. [6], [7], bl.
       [8], div. t. [9], bl. [10], 11-145, bl. [146], div. t. [147],
       bl. [148], 149-158.   Red cloth, with pr. illus. dj.   Pf. and
       9 pls. inserted.

LA GUARDIA, FIORELLO H. (Republican)

1080   Limpus, Lowell M. , and Leyson, Burr W.   This Man La
       Guardia.   New York: E. P. Dutton & Co. , Inc. , 1938.

       Half title [1], bl. [2], f. , t. [3], [4], [5], bl. [6], [7], bl.
       [8], 9-11, bl. [12], 13-14, div. t. [15], bl. [16], 17-420,
       421-429, bl. [430].   Blue cloth.   F. and 15 pls. inserted.
       Copyright, p. [4], notes "First Edition. "

1944

ROOSEVELT, FRANKLIN DELANO (Democratic)

1081   Busch, Noel F.   What Manner of Man?   New York and Lon-
       don: Harper & Brothers Publishers [c1944.]

       Half title [i], bl. [ii], t. [iii], [iv], [v], bl. [vi], div. t.
       [vii], bl. [viii], 1-189, bl. [190], [191], bl. [192].   Cream
       yellow cloth.   Copyright, p. [iv], notes "First Edition. "
       Copies also noted with p. [iv] noting, "Second Edition. "

1082   Kingdon, Frank.   "That Man in the White House. "   You and
       Your President.   With a Message by Rex Stout.   New York:
       Arco Publishing Company [c1944.]

       Half title i, bl. ii, t. iii, iv, v, bl. [vi], div. t. vii, bl.
       [viii], ix-x, 1-173, bl. [174], 175, bl. [176], 177-178, car-
       toons 179-182.   Black cloth.   Illus. (cartoons) in text.

1083 _____ . "That Man in the White House. "... New York:
Arco Publishing Company [c1944.]

Reprint in stiff wrps., cartoons on inner back, [i-ii], [1]-
77, bl. [78], pr. in dbl. cols.

1084 Mackenzie, Compton. Mr. Roosevelt. Illustrated. New
York: E. P. Dutton & Co., Inc. [c1944.]

Half title [i], bl. [ii], t. [iii], [iv], [v], [vi], 7-10, 11-12,
13-16, pl., 17-238, div. t. [239], [240-247], 248-256.
Blue cloth. 43 pls. (12 cld.) inserted. First printing.
Other copies noted with copyright, p. [iv], citing "First
Printing, April 1944 / Second Printing, May 1944."

DEWEY, THOMAS E. (Republican)

1085 Hughes, Rupert. The Story of Thomas E. Dewey, Attorney
for the People.... [N. p.] Grosset & Dunlap, Publishers
by Arrangement with Houghton Mifflin Company, 1944.

Endpaper [i-ii], half title [iii], bl. [iv], bl. [v], pf. [vi],
t. [vii], [viii], [ix]-x, [1]-406. Blue cloth with pr., illus.
dj in red, white and blue. Pf. inserted.

1086 Official Report of the Proceedings of the Twenty-Third Republican National Convention.... Reported by George L.
Hart, Official Reporter. Published Under the Supervision
of Harold W. Mason, Secretary of the Convention. Washington: Judd & Detweiler, Inc. [1948.]

T. [1], [2], [3], bl. [4], pl., [5], bl. [6], 7-255, bl. [256],
257-264. Green cloth. 8 pls. inserted. Sketches of Dewey
and Bricker, pp. 247-255.

1087 Walker, Stanley. Dewey, an American of This Century. New
York, London: Whittlesey House, McGraw-Hill Book Company, Inc. [c1944].

Half title [i], bl. [ii], t. [iii], [iv], v-vi, div. t. [vii], bl.
[viii], 1-204, 205-350. Blue cloth with pr., illus. dj. 20
pp. sig. pls. inserted. Copies also noted listing "Third
Impression."

BRICKER, JOHN W. (Republican)

1088 Pauly, Karl B. Bricker of Ohio, the Man and His Record.
New York: G. P. Putnam's Sons [c1944.]

Half title [i], bl. [ii], pf., t. [iii], [iv], v-vi, vii, viii,
div. t. [1], bl. [2], 3-215, bl. [216]. Dark blue cloth

with pr. , illus. red and grey dj.   Pf. and 7 pls. inserted.
Pre-Convention biography.

WILLKIE, WENDELL (Republican)

1089   Hatch, Alden.   Young Willkie.   Illustrated With Photographs.
       New York: Harcourt, Brace and Company [c1944.]

       Half title [i], bl. [ii], pf. , t. [iii], [iv], [v], bl. [vi], vii-
       viii, [ix], bl. [x], [xi], bl. [xii], [xiii], bl. [xiv], div. t.
       [1], bl. [2], 3-224.   Navy blue cloth with yellow panels on
       front and backstrip.   Pf. and 11 pls. inserted.

1090   Sparks, C. Nelson.   One Man.   Wendell Willkie.   [N. p.]
       Published by Rayner Publishing Company,   1943.

       T. [1], [2], [3], [4], 5-48.   White wrps. , pr. in black and
       red.

1948

TRUMAN, HARRY S. (Democratic)

1091   Crane, John M.   The Pictorial Biography of Harry S. Tru-
       man, Thirty-Second President of the United States.   Phila-
       delphia: Distributed by Curtis Publishing Company,   1948.

       T. 1, f. [2], 3-32.   Illus. wrps. , chronology, illus. and
       credits on inner front, conclusion of text on inner back,
       quote on outer back.   Illus. in text.

1092   Democracy at Work, Being the Official Report of the Demo-
       cratic National Convention. . . .   [N. p. , 1948?]

       Pf. , t. [i], [ii], [iii], iv-xii, 1-568, 569, 570-574.   Blue
       cloth.   Pf. , pl. and one 24 pp. sig. pls. inserted, other
       illus. in text.   Sketches of Truman and Barkley, pp. 493-
       498.

1093   Helm, William P.   Harry Truman, a Political Biography.
       New York: Duell, Sloan and Pearce [c1947.]

       Half title [i], bl. [ii], t. [iii], [iv], v-vii, bl. [viii], div. t.
       [1], bl. [2], 3-235, bl. [236], 237-241, bl. [242].   Black
       cloth.   First edition.

1094   McNaughton, Frank, and Hehmeyer, Walter. Harry Truman, President. New York, Toronto: Whittlesey House, Mc-Graw-Hill Book Company [c1948.]

Half title [i], [ii], pf., t. [iii], [iv], v-vi, div. t. [1], bl. [2], 3-264, 265-294. All copies examined rebound. Pf. inserted.

1095   _____, and _____. This Man Truman. New York, London: Whittlesey House, McGraw-Hill Book Company [c1945.]

Half title [i], bl. [ii], cld. pf., t. [iii], [iv], [v], bl. [vi], [vii], bl. [viii], div. t. [ix], bl. [x], 1-219, bl. [220]. Dark blue cloth. Cld. pf. and 10 pls. inserted. First printing.

1096   Powell, Eugene. Tom's Boy Harry. The First Complete, Authentic Story of Harry Truman's Connection With the Pendergast Machine. Jefferson City, Mo.: Hawthorn Publishing Company [c1948.]

Pf., half title [i], bl. [ii], t. [iii], [iv], v, bl. [vi], vii-viii, ix-xi, bl. [xii], 1-170, div. t. 171, 172-194, 195-196. Blue cloth. Pf. and 6 pls. inserted. Preface, pp. ix-xi, dated Oct. 8, 1947.

1097   Schauffler, Edward R. Harry Truman Son of the Soil. Kansas City: Schauffler Publishing Company [c1947.]

T. [i], [ii], [iii-iv], pf. [v], bl. [vi], 1-99. Brown wrps. Pf. and 2 pls. in text. Copyright date rubber stamped.

WALLACE, HENRY A. (Progressive)

1098   Kingdon, Frank. An Uncommon Man. Henry Wallace and 60 Million Jobs. New York: The Readers Press, Inc. [c1945.]

Pf., t. [i], [ii], [1], [2-3], [4], 5-185, 186-187, cartoons 188-[190]. Black cloth. Pf. inserted, cartoons in text.

1099   Macdonald, Dwight. Henry Wallace, the Man and the Myth. New York: The Vanguard Press, Inc. [c1947, 1948.]

Half title [i], bl. [ii], t. [iii], [iv], [v], bl. [vi], [vii], bl. [viii], [ix], bl. [x], 11-181, bl. [182], ℓ., 183-187, bl. [188]. Cream cloth with dj in red, black, and white. Anti-Wallace.

1100   The Story of Henry Wallace. [New York: Published by National Wallace for President Committee, 1948.]

Cover title [1], [2], 3-13, [14], [15], [16]. Illus. self wrps., stapled. Title vignette. Illus. in text. Pub. information, p. [2].

1101 Wise, James Waterman. <u>Meet Henry Wallace.</u> New York:
Boni and Gaer, 1948.

Half title [1], bl. [2], t. [3], [4], [5-6], 7-8, 9-91, bl.
[92], [93-94], illus. [95], [96]. Illus. wrps. Illus. in
text. Pr. in dbl. cols.

GARNER, JOHN NANCE (Democratic)

1102 Timmons, Bascom N. <u>Garner of Texas: A Personal History.</u>
New York: Harper & Brothers Publishers [c1948.]

Half title [i], bl. [ii], t. [iii], [iv], fac. letter [v], bl.
[vi], [vii], bl. [viii], div. t. [ix], bl. [x], 1-294, [295], bl.
[296]. Black cloth. Cartoon illus. in text. Copyright, p.
[iv], notes "First Edition."

STASSEN, HAROLD E. (Republican)

1103 Stassen, Harold E. <u>Where I Stand.</u> Garden City, N.Y.:
Doubleday & Company, Inc., 1948.

Half title [i], bl. [ii], t. [iii], [iv], [v], bl. [vi], vii-viii,
[ix], bl. [x], div. t. [xi], bl. [xii], [1]-205, bl. [206].
Tan cloth with illus. dj pr. in white and black.

1952

EISENHOWER, DWIGHT D. (Republican)

1104 <u>Dwight D. Eisenhower--Richard M. Nixon the Choice of a Nation ... Highlights of the Lives of Great Americans.</u> [N.
p., n. d., 1952.]

Cover title. Comic book format, unpaged, 4 ℓℓ. [1-8].
Stapled; outer back reads <u>Elect the Men to Back "Ike."</u>
Title vignette. In color.

1105 Gunther, John. <u>Eisenhower the Man and the Symbol.</u> New
York, Evanston, and London: Harper & Row, Publishers
[c1951, 1952.]

Half title [i], [ii], t. [iii], [iv], [v], bl. [vi], vii, bl.
[viii], [ix], bl. [x], div. t. [xi], bl. [xii], 1-149, bl. [150],
151-169, bl. [170], 171-173, bl. [174], 175-180. Blue

cloth with pr. blue dj. Appendices, pp. 151-169; bibliography, pp. 171-173; index, pp. 175-180.

1106 Hatch, Alden. General Ike. A Biography of Dwight D. Eisenhower. Revised and Enlarged Edition. New York: Henry Holt and Company [c1952.]

T. [i], [ii], iii-iv, [v]-vi, div. t. [vii], bl. [viii], [1]-312, [313]-320. Tan cloth with illus. dj. Maps in text. Index, pp. [313]-320.

1107 Hicks, Wilson, ed. This Is Ike. The Picture Story of the Man.... Picture Research by Helen Faye. New York: Henry Holt and Company [c1952.]

Unpaged, 48 ℓℓ. Stiff illus. wrps., illus. on outer back. Title vignette. Illus. in text. Copyright notes "First Edition."; text concludes with picture credits and bibliography.

1108 McCann, Kevin. Man From Abilene. Garden City, N. Y. : Doubleday & Company, Inc. , 1952.

Half title [1], bl. [2], t. [3], [4], [5], bl. [6], 7-9, bl. [10], div. t. [11], bl. [12], 13-252. Grey cloth with illus. dj. T. pr. in blue and black. First edition.

1109 Pocket Biographies of the Republican Team.... [N. p. , Republican State (Connecticut) Central Committee, 1952.]

Cover title. Unpaged, 8 ℓℓ. Cover title [1], [2], [3], [4-15], [16]. Stapled. Title vignette. Illus. in text. T. pr. in red, white, and blue; sketches of Eisenhower and Nixon, pp. [4-7].

*1110 Russell, Don. Invincible Ike. The Inspiring Life Story of Dwight D. Eisenhower. Chicago: Successful Living Publications [1952.]

127 pp. , illus.

1111 Taylor, Allan. What Eisenhower Thinks. New York: Thomas Y. Crowell Company [c1952.]

T. [i], [ii], [iii-iv], [v-vi], 1-186. Red cloth with red illus. dj. 16 pp. sig. pls. inserted between pp. 90-91. Part I, pp. 1-38, basically biog.

STEVENSON, ADLAI E. (Democratic)

1112 Busch, Noel F. Adlai E. Stevenson of Illinois, a Portrait. New York: Farrar, Straus & Young [c1952.]

Half title [i], [ii], pf. , t. [iii], [iv], [1], bl. [2], 3-233,
bl. [234]. Red cloth. Title vignette. Pf. , 3 8 pp. sigs.
pls. (pp. 28-29; 92-93; 156-157) and one 12 pp. sig. pls.
(pp. 204-205) inserted.

1113 _____. Adlai E. Stevenson.... New York: Farrar,
Straus & Young [c1952.]

As in entry 1112, but acceptance speech, pp. 234-236; 12
pp. sig. pls. between pp. 220-221; illus. dj present.

1114 Crane, John M. The Pictorial Biography of Adlai Ewing
Stevenson. Foreword by John Hersey. Washington: American Historical Publications, 1952.

T. 1, 2-3, [4]-32. Illus. wrps. , illus. and quote on inner
front, chronology on inner back, state seal and quote on
outer back. Title vignette. Illus. in text.

1115 How to Win in '52. The Facts About the Democratic Road to
Prosperity, Peace and Freedom. Washington: Democratic
National Committee, 1952.

T. [i], ii, iii, iv-vi, 1-200, 201-217, bl. 218. Blue illus.
stiff wrps. pr. in red and black on white, cartoon on outer
back, ports. on inner front and back. Illus. in text. Index, pp. 201-217; "Speaker's Notes, " p. 218; sketches of
Stevenson and Sparkman, pp. 1-17.

1116 A Man Named Stevenson.... [Washington: Democratic National Committee, c1952.]

Cover title. Comic book format, unpaged, 8 ℓ ℓ. [1-16].
Stapled, inner front with Stevenson's record and pub. info. ,
inner back with Sparkman's record and c1952, outer back
with port. and blurb on Sparkman. Title vignette. In color.

1117 Martin, John Bartlow. Adlai Stevenson. New York: Harper
& Brothers Publishers [c1952.]

Half title, [i], bl. [ii], t. [iii], [iv], [v], bl. [vi], vii, bl.
[viii], div. t. [ix], bl. [x], 1-173, bl. [174], 175, bl.
[176]. 3/4 yellow cloth, black cloth backstrip with yellow
coated illus. dj. First edition.

1118 Meet the Candidates. Adlai E. Stevenson. [Washington:
Democratic National Committee, 1952.]

Cover title. Unpaged, 8 ℓ ℓ. [1-16]. Cld. illus. wrps. ,
outer back repeats cover title but substitutes port. and
John J. Sparkman. Title vignette. Illus. in text. Sketch
of Stevenson, pp. [1-11]; of Sparkman, pp. [12-15]; pub.
info. , p. [16].

1119   Stevenson, Adlai E.   Adlai Stevenson, the Man and His
       Views.... As Revealed In His Own Speeches and Writings.
       [N. p., Westbury Publications, Inc., 1952.]

       Cover title.   1-8.   White illus. wrps., inner front noting
       Volume 127, Number 5, Issue 1966, Washington, D. C.,
       August 4, 1952 New Republic, inner back with copyright no-
       tice, outer back noting Reprinted From the New Republic.
       Title vignette.   One illus. in text.   Includes Richard A.
       Meyer's "Adlai Stevenson--Growth of a Man."

1120   _____ .   Speeches of Adlai Stevenson.   With a Foreword by
       John Steinbeck and a Brief Biography ... by Debs Myers and
       Ralph Martin.   New York: Random House [c1952.]

       T. [1], [2], [3], [4], 5-8, 9-13, bl. [14], 15-128.   Stiff il-
       lus. wrps., info. about Stevenson on outer back.   Biog. in
       dbl. cols., pp. 9-13; first printing.

1121   The Stevenson Story.   Why Adlai Is Fitted to Be President....
       [N. p., n. d., 1952.]

       Cover title.   Comic book format, unpaged, 4 ℓℓ. [1-8].
       Stapled, outer back reading Back Your National Candidates.
       Title vignette.   In color.

TAFT, ROBERT A.   (Republican)

1122   Harnsberger, Caroline Thomas.   A Man of Courage, Robert
       A. Taft.   Foreword by Lloyd Bowers Taft.   Toronto, Chi-
       cago, New York: Wilcox and Follett Company [c1952.]

       Half title [i], pf. [ii], t. [iii], [iv], [v], [vi], vii-viii, ix-
       xi, xii, 1-353, 353-361, bl. [362], 363-370.   Orange cloth.
       Illus. in text.   At head of title, Living American Statesmen
       Series; notes, pp. 353-361; index, pp. 363-370.

1956

EISENHOWER, DWIGHT D.   (Republican)

1123   Beckhard, Arthur J.   The Story of Dwight D. Eisenhower.
       Illustrated by Charles Geer.   Enid Lamonte Meadowcroft
       Supervising Editor.   New York: Grosset & Dunlap Publish-
       ers [c1956.]

[i], port. [ii], t. [iii], [iv], v, bl. [vi], vii, bl. [viii], div.
t. [1], illus. [2], 3-180, adv. [181]. Illus. wrps. in color,
illus. on inner front and back. Illus. in text.

1124 Donovan, Robert J. Eisenhower the Inside Story. Illustrated.
      New York: Harper & Brothers, Publishers [c1956.]

      Half title [i], bl. [ii], [iii], t. [iv-v], [vi], [vii], bl. [viii],
      x-xvi, xvii-xviii, [xix], bl. [xx], div. t. [xxi], bl. [xxii],
      1-407, bl. [408], 409-423, bl. [424], [425], bl. [426]. 3/4
      blue cloth with dark blue cloth backstrip. 8 pp. sig. pls.
      inserted between pp. 74-75. Index, pp. 409-423; first edi-
      tion.

1125 Kornitzer, Bela. The Great American Heritage: The Story
      of the Five Eisenhower Brothers. New York: Farrar,
      Straus and Cudahy [c1955.]

      Half title [i], [ii], t. [iii], [iv], [v], bl. [vi], vii-viii, ix-
      xvii, bl. [xviii], div. t. [xix], bl. [xx], 1-331, bl. [332].
      Buff cloth with blue panels on backstrip. 32 pp. sig. pls.
      inserted between pp. 172-173. Copyright notice, p. [iv],
      notes "First Printing, 1955"; Foreword, pp. ix-xvii, dated
      April, 1955. Reprinted in paperback format, 1956, London:
      Collins (Comet Books).

1126 Pusey, Merlo J. Eisenhower the President. New York: The
      Macmillan Company, 1956.

      Half title [i], [ii], t. [iii], [iv], [v], bl. [vi], [vii], bl.
      [viii], 1-294, 295-300. Black cloth with yellow illus. dj.
      Copyright, p. [iv], notes "First Printing"; Preface, p. [v],
      dated January 12, 1956.

1127 Smith, Merriman. Meet Mister Eisenhower. Illustrated.
      New York: Harper & Brothers Publishers [c1955.]

      Half title [i], [ii], t. [iii], [iv], [v], bl. [vi], vii, [viii],
      ix-x, div. t. [xi], bl. [xii], 1-308. 3/4 blue cloth with
      black cloth backstrip and illus. dj.

1128 Snyder, Marty. My Friend Ike. By Marty Snyder With
      Glenn D. Kittler. New York: Frederick Fell, Inc., Pub-
      lishers, 1956.

      Half title [1], bl. [2], pf., t. [3], [4], [5], bl. [6], [7],
      bl. [8], [9]-237, bl. [238]. Blue cloth. Pf. inserted.

STEVENSON, ADLAI E. (Democratic)

1129 Ives, Elizabeth Stevenson, and Dolson, Hildegarde. My
      Brother Adlai. New York: William Morrow & Company,
      1956.

Half title [i], bl. [ii], f. , t. [iii], [iv], [v], bl. [vi], div.
t. [vii], bl. [viii], 1-308, [309], bl. [310]. Blue cloth.
F. inserted.

1130   The Ticket For You. Adlai Stevenson. [N. p. , Democratic
       National Committee? 1956.]

       Cover title. 1-9, [10]-[17]. Illus. wrps. in color, outer
       back as above but substituting port. and Estes Kefauver.
       Title vignette. Illus. in text.

JOHNSON, LYNDON BAINES (Democratic)

1131   Mooney, Booth. The Lyndon Johnson Story. New York:
       Farrar, Straus and Cudahy [c1956.]

       Half title, [i], bl. [ii], t. [iii], [iv], [v], bl. [vi], vii-x,
       div. t. [1], bl. [2], 3-178. Brown cloth with illus. dj.
       20 pp. sig. pls. inserted between pp. 84-85. Foreword,
       pp. vii-x, by Johnson; first printing.

KEFAUVER, CAREY ESTES (Democratic)

1132   Anderson, Jack, and Blumenthal, Fred. The Kefauver Story.
       New York: The Dial Press [c1956.]

       Flyleaf, [i-ii], half title [iii], [iv], t. [v], [vi], [vii]-xii,
       div. t. [1], bl. [2], [3]-240. 3/4 blue cloth, red cloth
       backstrip, illus. dj.

NIXON, RICHARD M. (Republican)

1133   Keogh, James. This Is Nixon. New York: G. P. Putnam's
       Sons [c1956.]

       Half title [1], bl. [2], t. [3], [4], [5], 6, 7, bl. [8], 9-10,
       div. t. [11], bl. [12], 13-191, bl. [192]. Brown cloth. 8
       pp. sig. pls. inserted between pp. 128-129.

1134   Toledano, Ralph de. Nixon. New York: Henry Holt and
       Company [c1956.]

       Half title [i], [ii], t. [iii], [iv], [5]-7, bl. [8], [9], bl.
       [10], [11]-188. Light blue paper bds. , grey cloth backstrip,
       white illus. dj pr. in blue and black. First edition.
       Copies also noted in grey paper bds. ; others noting "Second
       Printing, March 1956. "

1960

GENERAL WORKS

1135 Wells, John A.   The Voter's Presidential Handbook 1960.
[New York:]   McDowell, Obolensky Inc. [c1960.]

T. [1], [2], [3], [4-5], [6-10], 11-13, bl. [14], [15]-205,
206-207, 208.   All copies examined rebound.   Illus. in text.
Sketches of Nixon, Lodge, Humphrey, Johnson, Kennedy,
Symington, Rockefeller, Stevenson, and Edmund Brown.

KENNEDY, JOHN F. (Democratic)

1136 Burns, James MacGregor.   John Kennedy.   A Political Profile.   New York: Harcourt, Brace & Company [c1960.]

Half title [i], [ii], t. [iii], [iv], v-vii, bl. [viii], ix-x, div.
t. [1], [2], 3-284, 285-298, 299-309, bl. [310].   Green
cloth with illus. dj.   16 pp. sig. pls. inserted between pp.
118-119.   First edition.

1137 Dinneen, Joseph F.   The Kennedy Family.   With Illustrations.
Boston, Toronto: Little, Brown and Company [c1959.]

Bl. [i], [ii], half title [iii], bl. [iv], t. [v], [vi], [vii], bl.
[viii], [ix], bl. [x], [xi], bl. [xii], div. t. [1], bl. [2], 3-
238.   Black cloth.   4 pp. sig. pls. inserted between pp.
130-131.   Copyright, p. [vi], notes "Second Printing."

1138 Lasky, Victor.   John F. Kennedy.   What's Behind the Image?
Washington: Free World Press, Inc. [c1960.]

Half title [i], [ii], t. [iii], bl. [iv], [v], bl. [vi], [vii], bl.
[viii], div. t. [1], bl. [2], 3-300.   Stiff illus. wrps., ex-
cerpts from book on outer back.   Anti-Kennedy; a response
to Arthur Schlesinger's Kennedy or Nixon written in two
weeks; foreword, p. [v], dated October 26, 1960.

1139 McCarthy, Joe.   The Remarkable Kennedys.   New York: The
Dial Press, 1960.

[1], bl. [2], half title [3], bl. [4], t. [5], [6], [7], bl. [8],
9-190, bl. [191], [192].   All copies examined rebound.

1140 Martin, Ralph G. and Plaut, Ed.   Front Runner, Dark Horse.
Garden City, N. Y.: Doubleday & Company, Inc., 1960.

Half title [1], bl. [2], [3], bl. [4], t. [5], [6], [7], bl. [8],
[9]-10, [11], bl. [12], [13]-14, div. t. [15], bl. [16], [17]-

473, bl. [474].   Red cloth.   Kennedy vs. Symington.   First edition.

NIXON, RICHARD M. (Republican)

1141   Alsop, Stewart. Nixon & Rockefeller a Double Portrait.   Garden City, N. Y.: Doubleday & Company, Inc. , 1960.

Half title [1], bl. [2], t. [3], [4], [5]-11, bl. [12], [13], bl. [14], div. t. [15], bl. [16], [17]-240. Black cloth. First edition.

1142   Costello, William. The Facts About Nixon, an Unauthorized Biography. New York: The Viking Press, 1960.

Half title [i], bl. [ii], t. [iii], [iv], [v], bl. [vi], [vii], bl. [viii], ix-x, xi-xiii, bl. [xiv], div. t. [1], bl. [2], 3-290, 291-294, 295-297, bl. [298], 299-306. Natural cloth with illus. dj pr. in red, white, yellow, and black. Foreword, pp. xi-xiii, dated September 15, 1959; chronology, pp. 291-294; bibliography, pp. 295-297; index, pp. 299-306. Second printing, February, 1960.

1143   Kornitzer, Bela. The Real Nixon, an Intimate Biography. New York, Chicago, San Francisco: Rand McNally & Company [c1960.]

Half title [1], pf. [2], t. [3], [4], [5], [6], [7], bl. [8], 9-16, div. t. [17], illus. [18], 19-347, 348-352. Blue cloth with illus. dj. Illus. in text. Index, pp. 348-352; copyright, p. [4], notes "First Printing, March, 1960. "

1144   Mazo, Earl. Richard Nixon: A Political and Personal Portrait. New York: Harper & Brothers Publishers [c1959.]

Half title [i], bl. [ii], t. [iii], [iv], [v], bl. [vi], vii-viii, div. t. [ix], bl. [x], 1-300, 301-309, [310]. 3/4 red cloth, grey green cloth backstrip, illus. dj. Index, pp. 301-309; colophon, p. [310]; first edition.

1145 _____ . Richard Nixon: A Political and Personal Portrait. This Edition Has Been Specially Revised by the Author to Include New Material Covering Mr. Nixon's Recent Activities. New York: Avon Book Division, The Hearst Corporation [c1959, 1960.]
[1], bl. [2], t. [3], [4], [5], bl. [6], div. t. [7], bl. [8], 9-258, div. t. [259], bl. [260], 261-270. Stiff illus. wrps. Statements by Nixon, pp. 261-270.

1146   Nixon, Richard M. His Biography, Interviews, Nixon "Off the Record, " Recent Speeches, and His Statements Covering Important Issues of Our Day.... Washington: Issued by Nixon Volunteers [1960].

Portfolio containing 20 separate campaign items, one being a biog. sketch. Illus. portfolio case; cover title.

1147 Toledano, Ralph de. Nixon. Revised and Expanded Edition. New York: Duell, Sloan and Pearce [c1960.]

Half title [1], [2], t. [3], [4], [5]-8, [9], bl. [10], div. t., verso bl., [11]-244, [245]-250. Stiff wrps., illus., pr. white on red and black on white. Also noted in yellow cloth.

HUMPHREY, HUBERT H. (Democratic)

1148 Amrine, Michael. This Is Humphrey. The Story of the Senator. Garden City, N.Y.: Doubleday & Company, Inc., 1960.

Half title [1], bl. [2], t. [3], [4], [5], bl. [6], [7], bl. [8], div. t. [9], bl. [10], [11]-257, bl. [258], [259]-261, bl. [262]. Black cloth. Copyright, p. [4], notes "First Edition."

ROCKEFELLER, NELSON A. (Republican)

1149 Manchester, William. A Rockefeller Family Portrait From John D. to Nelson. With Illustrations. Boston, Toronto: Little, Brown and Company [c1958, 1959.]

Bl. [i], [ii], half title [iii], bl. [iv], t. [v], [vi], [vii], bl. [viii], ix-xv, bl. [xvi], [xvii], bl. [xviii], div. t. [1], bl. [2], 3-184. 3/4 green cloth with cream cloth backstrip. 8 pp. sig. pls. inserted between pp. 76-77. Copyright, p. [vi], notes "First Edition."

1150 Morris, Joe Alex. Nelson Rockefeller a Biography. New York: Harper & Brothers Publishers [c1960.]

Half title [i], bl. [ii], [iii], bl. [iv], t. [v], [vi], [vii], [viii], [ix], [x], [xi], bl. [xii], div. t. [xiii], bl. [xiv], 1-359, bl. [360], 361-369, bl. [370]. Blue cloth with illus. dj. 2 8 pp. sigs. pls. inserted between pp. 82-83 and 146-147. Copyright, p. [vi], notes "First Edition"; index, pp. 361-369.

1151 Poling, James, ed. A Political Self-Portrait: The Rockefeller Record. New York: Thomas Y. Crowell Company [c1960.]

Half title [i], bl. [ii], t. [iii], [iv], v-viii, ix-xi, bl. [xii], div. t. [1], bl. [2], 3-41, bl. [42], div. t. [43], bl. [44], 45-169, bl. [170], div. t. [171], bl. [172], 173-177, bl.

[178]. Grey green cloth with illus. dj pr. in black on yellow and white on blue. Sketch of life, pp. 3-41; speeches, pp. 45-169; prognosis, pp. 173-177.

SYMINGTON, WILLIAM STUART (Democratic)

1152 Wellman, Paul I. Stuart Symington, Portrait of a Man With a Mission. Garden City, N. Y.: Doubleday & Company, Inc., 1960.

Half title [1], [2], t. [3], [4], [5], bl. [6], [7], bl. [8], div. t. [9], bl. [10], 11-283, bl. [284]. Black cloth. Copyright, p. [4], notes "First Edition. "

WILLIAMS, G. MENNEN (Democratic)

1153 McNaughton, Frank. Mennen Williams of Michigan, Fighter for Progress. Preface by John D. Voelker.... New York: Oceana Publications, Inc. [c1960.]

F., t. [i], [ii], [iii], [iv], v-vi, vii-viii, 1-246, [247-248]. Green cloth with illus. dj. Foreword, pp. vii-viii, dated December 1959; index, pp. [247-248].

1964

JOHNSON, LYNDON BAINES (Democratic)

1154 Amrine, Michael. This Awesome Challenge. The Hundred Days of Lyndon Johnson. New York: G. P. Putnam's Sons [c1964.]

Half title [1], [2], t. [3], [4], [5], bl. [6], [7], bl. [8], 9-250, 251-272, 273-274, 275-283, bl. [284]. Blue cloth with illus. dj in red, white and blue.

1155 Haley, J. Evetts. A Texan Looks at Lyndon. A Study in Illegitimate Power. Canyon, Tx.: Palo Duro Press [c1964.]

T. 1, 2, 3, 4, 5-6, 7-10, 11-254, adv. 255-256. Stiff illus. wrps., sketch of author on outer back. Anti-Johnson.

1156 The Johnson Story. New York: Published by Macfadden-Bartell Corp., 1964.

T. 1, 2-3, 4-79, port. [80]. Illus. wrps., magazine format, adv. on inner front and entire back. Illus. in text.
Jack Podell, editorial director.

1157 Kluckhohn, Frank L. The Inside on LBJ. Derby, Conn.:
Monarch Books, Inc. [c1964.]

[1], [2], t. [3], [4], [5], bl. [6], 7-13, bl. [14], 15-191,
adv. [192]. Stiff wrps. At head of title, A Monarch Select
Book; published in May, 1964. Unfavorable.

1158 [McKinney, R. Kay.] LBJ. His Home and Heritage.
[San Angelo, Tx.: Anchor Publishing Company,
c1964.]

Cover title. 1-16. Stiff wrps., inner front with publishing
info. and copyright, map on outer back. Illus. in text.
Pr. in dbl. cols. Title vignette.

1159 _____. LBJ. His Home and Heritage. By R. Kay Mc-
Kinney. San Angelo, Tx.: Anchor Publishing Company,
1964.

T. [1], port. 2, 3-19, illus. 20. Wrps. as above, but inner front bl. Illus. in text. Pr. in dbl. cols.

1160 Mooney, Booth. The Lyndon Johnson Story. New York: Farrar, Straus and Company [c1956, 1963, 1964.]

Half title [i], bl. [ii], pf., t. [iii], [iv], [v], bl. [vi],
[vii], bl. [viii], ix-xvi, xvii-xviii, xix-xxii, [xxiii], bl.
[xxiv], 1-192, 193-198. Blue cloth with illus. dj.
Pf. and 10 pls. inserted. Foreword to this ed., pp.
xvii-xviii; Johnson's foreword to orig. ed., pp. xix-
xxii; address to Congress, November 27, 1963, pp.
193-198; "First Printing, 1962." "Revised and greatly
expanded version of the 1956 book originally written
by Mr. Mooney."

1161 Newlon, Clarke. L.B.J. The Man From Johnson City. Illustrated With Photographs. New York: Dodd, Mead &
Company [c1964.]

Half title [i], bl. [ii], t. [iii], [iv], v-vi, [vii], bl. [viii],
ix-x, 1-185, bl. [186], 187-[209], bl. [210], 211-213, bl.
[214]. Red cloth. 16 pp. sig. pls. inserted between
pp. 86-87. Appendices, pp. 187-[209]; index, pp.
211-213.

1162 1964 Democratic Fact Book. Washington: Published by the
Democratic National Committee [1964.]

T. [1], bl. [2], [3-8], 9-225, bl. [226] [227], bl. [228].
Stiff wrps. Life of Johnson by John Steinbeck, pp. 9-
17.

1163 Provence, Harry. Lyndon B. Johnson. A Biography. New
York: Fleet Publishing Corporation [c1964.]

Half title [1], bl. [2], t. [3], [4], [5], bl. [6], 7-170, div.
t. [171], bl. [172], 173-184, 185-192. Maroon cloth with
illus. dj. Appendix, pp. 173-184; index, pp. 185-192. Also noted in brown cloth.

1164 The Public Records of Lyndon B. Johnson and Hubert H.
Humphrey: The Lives, Votes and Stands of the 1964 Democratic Candidates. [Congressional Quarterly Special
Report, Part I of CQ Weekly Report, September 11,
1964.]

Cover title. 2057-2121. Stapled wrps., dbl. punched
for ring binder, contents on inner front [2056?],
conclusion of text inner back, p. 2121, adv. on
outer back [2122?]. 2 ports. in text. Pr. in dbl.
cols.

1165 Singer, Kurt, and Sherrod, Jane. Lyndon Baines Johnson,
Man of Reason. Minneapolis: T. S. Denison & Company,
Inc. Publishers [c1964.]

Half title [i], [ii], t. [iii], [iv], [v], bl. [vi], illus. [vii],
[viii], [ix-x], 11-373, 374-380, 380-384. Brown cloth with
illus. dj. Illus. and 16 pls. inserted. Chronology, pp.
374-380; index, pp. 380-384.

1166 White, William S. The Professional: Lyndon B. Johnson.
Boston: Houghton Mifflin Company; Cambridge: The Riverside Press, 1964.

Half title [i], [ii], t. [iii], [iv], [v], bl. [vi], [vii], bl.
[viii], div. t. [1], bl. [2], [3]-264, div. t. [265] bl. [266],
[267]-273. Orange cloth with illus. dj. Copyright,
p. [iv], notes "First Printing"; index, pp. [267]-273.
A Crest reprint, Greenwich: Fawcett, 1964, 176 pp.
also noted.

1167 Zeiger, Henry A. Lyndon B. Johnson: Man and President.
With a Foreword by James Tracy Crown.... New York:
Popular Library [c1963.]

[1], [2], t. [3], [4], [5]-6, [7]-125, bl. [126], div.
t. [127], bl. [128], [129]-143, bl. [144]. Stiff illus.
wrps., illus. on back. Copyright, p. [4], notes
"Published in December, 1963"; appendices, pp. [129]-
143.

GOLDWATER, BARRY M. (Republican)

1168 Barry M. Goldwater. Complete Life Story. [New York:
      Dell Publishing Co. , Inc. c1964.]

      Cover title. Comic book format, unpaged, 16 ℓ ℓ. Stapled
      illus. wrps. , chronology on inner front, port. of family
      on inner back, port. on outer front enlgd. with fac. signa-
      ture on outer back. In color.

1169 Bell, Jack. Mr. Conservative: Barry Goldwater. Garden
      City, N. Y.: Doubleday & Company, Inc. , 1962.

      Half title [1], [2], t. [3], [4], [5], bl. [6], [7], bl. [8], div.
      t. [9], bl. [10], 11-312. Cream yellow cloth. Copyright,
      p. [4], notes "First Edition. "

1170 _____. Mr. Conservative.... [N. p.] Macfadden-Bartell
      Corporation [c1964.]

      [1], [2-3], bl. [4], t. [5], [6], 7-239, adv. [240]. Stiff
      illus. wrps. , inner front and back bl.

1171 Cook, Fred J. Barry Goldwater Extremist of the Right. New
      York: Grove Press, Inc. , An Evergreen Black Cat Book
      [c1964.]

      [1], bl. [2], t. [3], [4], 5-6, 7-186, bl. ℓ. , 2 ℓ ℓ. adv.
      Stiff wrps. , about the book on outer back. First printing.
      Anti-Goldwater.

1172 Frommer, Arthur. Goldwater From A to Z: A Critical
      Handbook. [N. p. , c1964.]

      Half title [i], bl. [ii], t. [iii], [iv], [v-viii], [9]-18, div. t.
      [19], bl. [20], [21]-113, 114-115, [116-119], [120]. Stiff
      illus. wrps. Intro. , pp. [9]-18, primarily biog.; pp. [116-
      119] bls. with "Notes" as running heads; t. pr. in red and
      black.

1173 McDowell, Edwin. Barry Goldwater. Portrait of an Arizo-
      nan. Chicago: Henry Regnery Company, 1964.

      Half title [i], bl. [ii], t. [iii], [iv], [v], bl. [vi],
      [vii], bl. [viii], [ix], bl. [x], 1-262, 263-269, bl.
      [270]. Blue cloth. 16 pp. sig. pls. inserted be-
      tween pp. 86-87.

1174 Mattar, Edward Paul. Barry Goldwater. A Political Indict-
      ment. Riverdale, Maryland: Century Twenty One Limited
      [c1964.]

Half title [1], bl. [2], t. [3], [4], [5], bl. [6], [7]-8, [9]-10, [11]-12, [13]-20, div. t. [21], bl. [22], [23]-79, bl. [80], div. t. [81], bl. [82], [83]-[179], bl. [180], [181]-192.   Blue cloth.   Copyright, p. [4], notes "First Edition, September, 1964"; life, pp. [23]-79; the issues, pp. [83]-[179]; notes, pp. [181]-192.   Anti-Goldwater.

1175   Perry, James M.   Barry Goldwater.   A New Look at a Presidential Candidate.   Silver Spring, Maryland: Newsbook, The National Observer [c1964.]

[1], bl. [2], t. [3], [4], [5], bl. [6], [7], illus. [8], 9-137, illus. extending over to div. t. [138-139], 140-159, bl. (black coated) [160].   Yellow coated stiff wrps., illus. on inner front and back, about the "Newsbook" on outer back.   Sketch, pp. 9-137; speeches, pp. 140-159. Illus. in text.

1176   Portrait of Goldwater: The Contradictions of a Conservative. Washington: The New Republic [c1964.]

Half title [1], f. cartoons [2-3], bl. [4], t. [5], [6], [7], 8-61, cartoon [62-63], bl. [64].   Illus. wrps., copyright on inner front, adv. on inner back, about the book on outer back; pr. in red, white, and black.   A series of articles "Edited and published by the staff of The New Republic."; in dbl. cols. Anti-Goldwater.

1177   The Public Record of Barry Goldwater, His Stands, Statements and Key Votes on National and International Issues, and a Brief Biography.   [Congressional Quarterly Special Report, Part I of CQ Weekly Report No. 38, Sept. 20, 1963.]

Cover title   1593-1625.   Wrps., stapled, dbl. punched for ring binder, contents on inner front, inner back, p. 1625, adv. on outer back.   Port. in text.   Pr. in dbl. cols.

1178   The Public Record of Barry Goldwater....   [Congressional Quarterly Special Report, Part I of CQ Weekly Report No. 38, Sept. 20, 1963.]

Cover title [i], [ii], 1-33, adv. [34].   Note on p. [ii] cites "Second Edition: Oct. 11, 1963."

1179   The Public Records of Barry M. Goldwater and William E. Miller.   The Lives, Votes and Stands of the 1964

Republican Candidates. [Congressional Quarterly Special Report, Part I of CQ Weekly Report, July 31, 1964.]

Cover title. 1571-1631. Stapled wrps., punched for dbl. ring binder, contents on inner front, p. 1631 inner back, adv. on outer back. Ports. in text. Pr. in dbl. cols.

1180 Shadegg, Stephen. Barry Goldwater: Freedom Is His Flight Plan. Foreword by Clarence Budington Kelland. New York: Fleet Publishing Corporation [c1962.]

Half title [i], bl. [ii], t. [iii], [iv], v-vii, bl. [viii], ix-x, xi, bl. [xii], [xiii], [xiv], xv-xvi, div. t. [xvii], bl. [xviii], 19-302, 303-304. Silver grey cloth with illus. dj. 16 pp. sig. pls. inserted but figured in pagination. Copies also noted as above, but text, pp. 19-288, appendix, pp. 289-304.

1181 Shirey, Keith. Barry Goldwater. [N. p.] Harlequin Press [c1964.]

Cartoon f., t. [1], [2], [3-4], [5], bl. [6], [7], illus. [8], [9]-12, div. t., verso bl., 13-126, ℓ. adv., bl. ℓ., 5 ℓℓ., ℓ., bl. ℓ. Stiff wrps., illus., quotes on outer back. Cartoons in text. Biog. intro., pp. [9]-12; bibliography, 5 ℓℓ.; appreciation, about the author on verso, ℓ. Unfavorable.

1182 Shirey, Keith Faires. Barry Goldwater, His Political Philosophy. Los Angeles: Brewster Publications [c1963.]

T. [1], [2], [3]-4, [5], [6], [7], illus. [8], [9]-12, 13-82, [83]-92, [93], [94]. Stiff illus. wrps. Illus. in text. Biog. intro., pp. [9]-12.

1183 Wood, Rob, and Smith, Dean. Barry Goldwater. [New York: Avon Book Division, The Hearst Corporation c1961.]

[1], [2], t. [3], [4], [5], bl. [6], 7-136, div. t. [137], bl. [138], 139-175, adv. [176]. Stiff illus. wrps., illus. on inner front and back, about the book on outer back. 4 pp. sig. pls. inserted between pp. 88-89. Imprint info., p. [2].

ROCKEFELLER, NELSON A. (Republican)

1184 Desmond, James. Nelson Rockefeller, a Political Biography. New York: The Macmillan Company; London: Collier-Macmillan Limited [c1964.]

Half title [i], bl. [ii], t. [iii], [iv], [v], bl. [vi], [vii], bl. [viii], ix, bl. [x], [xi], bl. [xii], xiii-xv, bl. [xvi], 1-330. Black cloth. First printing.

1185   Gervasi, Frank. The Real Rockefeller. The Story of the Rise, Decline and Resurgence of the Presidential Aspirations of Nelson Rockefeller. New York: Atheneum, 1964.

Bl., books by author on verso, half title [i], bl. [ii], t. [iii], [iv], [v], bl. [vi], [vii], bl. [viii], [ix]-xii, [xiii], bl. [xiv], div. t. [1], bl. [2], [3]-262, [263]-271, [272]. Brown cloth with illus. dj pr. in black, red and blue on white. Index, pp. [263]-271; first edition.

1186   Josephson, Emanuel M. The Truth About Rockefeller "Public Enemy No. 1": Studies in Criminal Psychopathy. New York: Chedney Press, 1964.

T. [i], illus. [ii], iii-iv, v-vi, 1-272, 273-277, bl. [278]. Cream yellow stiff illus. wrps. Illus. (certificate) in text. Bibliography, pp. 273-277. Anti-Rockefeller.

1968

GENERAL WORKS

1187   Candidates 1968 the Public Records of Twenty-Three Americans Prominently Mentioned for the Presidency or Vice Presidency. Washington: A Publication of Congressional Quarterly, September, 1967.

T. [i], [ii], 1-130. Wrps., front in green, back cream pr. in green. Illus. in text. Includes Brooke, Chafee, Evans, Ford, Hatfield, Humphrey, Javits, Johnson, R. F. Kennedy, Kirk Jr., Lindsay, Love, Morton, Nixon, Percy, Reagan, Rhodes, Rockefeller, Romney, Shafer, Tower, Volpe, and Wallace. Reissued and revised, January 1968, text, pp. 1-136, and adding James M. Gavin and Eugene J. McCarthy. Both pr. in dbl. cols.

1188   Driscoll, James G. Elections 1968. Silver Spring, Maryland: Newsbook, The National Observer [c1968.]

T. [1], [2], [3], 4-156, illus. [157], [158], adv. [159], bl. [160]. All copies examined rebound. Illus. in text. Sketches of Nixon, Rockefeller, Reagan, Romney, and Percy.

1189 Schechter, William. Profiles for the Presidency. New York:
      Fleet Press Corporation [c1967.]

         Half title [i], [ii], t. [iii], [iv], [v], bl. [vi], vii-viii, ix-
         x, xi, bl. [xii], div. t. [1], bl. [2], 3-227, bl. [228].
         Grey cloth. Cartoon illus. in text. Sketches of Romney,
         Nixon, Reagan, Percy, Rockefeller, Johnson, Humphrey,
         and R. F. Kennedy. Foreword, pp. ix-x, dated Septem-
         ber 1967.

NIXON, RICHARD M. (Republican)

1190 Mazo, Earl, and Hess, Stephen. Nixon, a Political Portrait.
      New York, Evanston, and London: Harper & Row, Pub-
      lishers [c1968.]

         Half title [i], bl. [ii], t. [iii], [iv], [v], bl. [vi], vii-viii,
         div. t. [ix], bl. [x], 1-308, 309-316, 317-326. Blue
         cloth with illus. dj. Author's note, pp. vii-viii, dated
         May 31, 1968; appendix, pp. 309-316; index, pp. 317-326.

HUMPHREY, HUBERT H. (Democratic)

1191 Griffith, Winthrop. Humphrey a Candid Biography. New
      York: William Morrow & Company, 1965.

         Half title [i], bl. [ii], t. [iii], [iv], [v], bl. [vi], [vii],
         bl. [viii], [ix]-xii, div. t. [1], bl. [2], [3]-326, [327],
         bl. [328], div. t. [329], bl. [330], [331]-337, bl. [338].
         Blue cloth with illus. dj. 8 pp. sig. pls. inserted be-
         tween pp. 180-181. Index, pp. [331]-337.

1192 Hall, Perry D. The Quotable Hubert H. Humphrey. New
      York: Distributed by Grosset and Dunlap [c1967.]

         T. [i], [ii], div. t. [iii], bl. [iv], [v], bl. [vi], vii, bl.
         [viii], div. t. 1, bl. [2], 3-185, bl. [186], 187-188, div.
         t. [189], bl. [190], 191-196, 197, bl. [198]. Blue cloth.
         Biog. sketch, pp. 187-188.

1193 Martin, Ralph G. A Man for All People: Hubert H. Humph-
      rey. Captions and Commentary by Hubert H. Humphrey.
      Introduction by Adlai E. Stevenson III. New York: Gros-
      set & Dunlap Publishers [c1968.]

         Unpaged, 88 ℓℓ. Photographic essay. Stiff illus. wrps.

1194 Ryskind, Allan H. Hubert an Unauthorized Biography of the
      Vice President. New Rochelle, N.Y.: Arlington House
      [c1968.]

Half title [1], bl. [2], t. [3], [4], 5, bl. [6], [7], bl.
[8], 9-329, bl. [330], 331-333, bl. [334], 335-347, 348-
355, bl. [356]. Yellow cloth with illus. dj. Appendix,
pp. 331-333; notes, pp. 335-347; index, pp. 348-355.
Anti-Humphrey.

1195 Sherrill, Robert, and Ernst, Harry W.   The Drugstore Liberal.   New York: Grossman Publishers, 1968.

Half title [i], [ii], t. [iii], [iv], [v], bl. [vi], [vii], bl.
[viii], [1]-196, [197]-200. Blue cloth with dj. Index,
pp. [197]-200. Anti-Humphrey.

1196 That Man From Minnesota.   An Intimate Study of Hubert
Horatio Humphrey.   [N. p.] Joyce Press, 1965.

T. 1, 2, 3, 4, 5-115, 116-124, adv. 125-128. Stiff illus. wrps. Bibliography, pp. 116-124. Anti-Humphrey.

KENNEDY, ROBERT F. (Democratic)

1197 Bobby.   New York: Macfadden-Bartell Corporation, 1968.

T. [1], 2-[80]. Magazine format, illus. on inner front
and entire back, in color. Illus. in text. Jack J.
Podell, editorial director.

1198 Kimball, Penn.   Bobby Kennedy and the New Politics.   Englewood Cliffs, N.J.: Prentice-Hall, Inc. [c1968.]

Half title [i], bl. [ii], t. [iii], [iv], [v], bl. [vi], [vii],
bl. [viii], div. t. [ix], bl. [x], 1-203, bl. [204], 205-
214. Brown cloth. Index, pp. 205-214.

1199 Laing, Margaret.   The Next Kennedy.   New York: Coward-
McCann Inc. [c1968.]

Half title [i], t. [ii-iii], [iv], div. t. [v], bl. [vi], 7-310,
311-320. Red cloth with illus. dj. Index, pp. 311-320.

1200 Nicholas, William.   The Bobby Kennedy Nobody Knows.
Greenwich, Conn.: A Fawcett Gold Medal Book, Fawcett Publications, Inc. [c1968.]

Unpaged. Stiff illus. wrps. Illus. in text.

1201 Quirk, Lawrence J.   Robert Francis Kennedy, the Man and
the Politician. An Original Holloway House Edition.   Los
Angeles: Holloway House Publishing Co. [c1968.]

[1], bl. [2], bls. [3-4], t. [5], [6], bls. [7-8], [9], bl.
[10], 11-312, 313-316, 2 ℓℓ. adv. Stiff illus. wrps.

Copyright, p. [6], notes "First Printing 1968"; index, pp. 313-316.

1202   Schaap, Dick. R. F. K. [New York:] The New American Library [c1967.]

Half title [i], [ii], t. [iii], [iv], [v], [vi-vii], illus. [viii], div. t. [1], illus. [2], 3-[211], [212], [213], [214-216]. Green cloth. Copyright, p. [iv], notes "First Printing."

1203   . R. F. K. [New York:] A Signet Book, Published by The New American Library [c1967.]

[1], adv. [2], t. [3], [4], [5-6], [7], bl. [8], div. t. [9], bl. [10], 11-127, bl. [128]. Stiff illus. wrps. 16 pp. sig. pls. inserted between pp. 64-65. Copyright notes "First Printing, May, 1968 / Second Printing."

1204   Shannon, William V. The Heir Apparent. Robert Kennedy and the Struggle for Power. New York: The Macmillan Company; London: Collier-Macmillan Limited [c1967.]

Half title [i], bl. [ii], t. [iii], [iv], [v], bl. [vi], vii, bl. [viii], div. t. [ix], bl. [x], 1-293, 293-294, div. t. [295], bl. [296], 297-309, bl. [310]. Royal blue cloth with dj. Copyright, p. [iv], notes "Second Printing, 1967"; notes, pp. 293-294; index, pp. 297-309.

1205   Toledano, Ralph de. R. F. K. The Man Who Would Be President. New York: G. P. Putnam's Sons [c1967.]

Half title [1], [2], t. [3], [4], [5], bl. [6], div. t. [7], bl. [8], [9]-369, bl. [370], div. t. [371], bl. [372], [373]-381, bl. [382]. Black cloth with black dj pr. in red, white and gold. Copyright, p. [4], notes "Third Impression." Anti-Kennedy.

PERCY, CHARLES (Republican)

1206   Cleveland, Martha. Charles Percy: Strong New Voice From Illinois. A Biography. Jacksonville, Fla.: Harris-Wolfe & Co., Publishers [c1968.]

Half title [i], bl. [ii], t. [iii], [iv], [v], bl. [vi], [vii], bl. [viii], [ix], bl. [x], div. t. [1], bl. [2], 3-225, 226-228. Blue cloth. 8 pp. sig. pls. inserted between pp. 150-151. Author's note, p. [ix], dated June, 1968; epilogue by Brian Duff, pp. 226-228.

1207   Murray, David. Charles Percy of Illinois. New York, Evanston, and London: Harper & Row, Publishers [c1968.]

Half title [i], bl. [ii], t. [iii], [iv], [v], bl. [vi], vii-
viii, ix-x, div. t. [xi], bl. [xii], 1-174, 175-178.   Black
cloth with illus. dj.   8 pp. sig. pls. inserted between
pp. 52-53.   First edition.

REAGAN, RONALD (Republican)

1208   Boyarsky, Bill.   The Rise of Ronald Reagan.   New York:
Random House [c1968.]

Half title [i], t. [ii-iii], [iv], [v], bl. [vi], vii-viii, [ix],
bl. [x], div. t. [1], bl. [2], 3-263, bl. [264], 265-269,
bl. [270], [271], bl. [272].   Royal blue cloth with illus.
dj.   8 pp. sig. pls. inserted between pp. 148-149.

1209   Edwards, Lee.   Reagan, a Political Biography.   San Diego:
Viewpoint Books [c1967.]

T. [1], [2], [3]-4, [5], bl. [6], [7]-8, div. t. [9], bl.
[10], [11]-218, [219]-234, [235]-246, [247]-252, 2 ℓℓ. adv.
Stiff illus. wrps.   Copyright, p. [2], notes "First Printing, October 1967 / Second Printing, April 1968"; epilogue, pp. [219]-234; appendix, pp. [235]-246; index, pp.
[247]-252; tipped-in adv. between pp. 128-[129].

1210   Evans, M. Stanton.   The Reason for Reagan.   La Jolla,
Calif.:   La Jolla Rancho Press [c1968.]

T. [1], [2], 3-6, 7-61, bl. [62], ℓ. adv.   Stiff illus.
wrps., port. and sketch of author on outer back.   Copyright, p. [2], notes "First Printing, March 1968."

1211   Lewis, Joseph.   What Makes Reagan Run?   A Political Profile.   New York, Toronto, London, Sydney: McGraw-
Hill Book Company [c1968.]

Half title [i], bl. [ii], t. [iii], [iv], [v], bl. [vi], vii-xi,
bl. [xii], 1-204, 205-211, [212].   Blue cloth.   Index, pp.
205-211.

1212   Steffgen, Kent H.   Here's the Rest of Him.   Reno, Nevada:
Forsight Books [c1968.]

T. [i], [ii], [iii], bl. [iv], [v], bl. [vi], [vii-ix], [x], 1-
162, 163-172, ℓ. adv.   Stiff illus. wrps.   8 pp. sig.
pls. inserted between pp. 86-87.   Appendix, pp. 163-172.
Copyright, p. [ii], notes "First Printing, April, 1968."

ROMNEY, GEORGE (Republican)

1213   Angel, D. Duane.   Romney, a Political Biography.   New York:
An Exposition-Banner Book, Exposition Press [c1967.]

Half title [i], bl. [ii], t. [iii], [iv], [v], bl. [vi], [vii]-
ix, bl. [x], [xi]-xiii, bl. [xiv], [xv], bl. [xvi], div. t.
[1], bl. [2], 3-245, bl. [246], div. t. [247], bl. [248],
[249]-259, bl. [260], [261]-266. Grey cloth with illus.
dj. Notes, pp. [249]-259; index, pp. [261]-266; first edition.

1214 Harris, T. George. Romney's Way. A Man and an Idea.
Englewood Cliffs, N.J.: Prentice-Hall, Inc. [c1967.]

T. [i], [ii], [iii], bl. [iv], v-vi, vii-xiv, 1-259, bl. [260],
261-274. Charcoal grey cloth with illus. dj. Index, pp.
261-274.

1215 Mollenhoff, Clark R. George Romney Mormon in Politics.
New York: Meredith Press [c1968.]

Half title [i], [ii], t. [iii], [iv], [v], bl. [vi], vii-viii,
div. t. [1], bl. [2], 3-327, bl. [328], [329], bl. [330],
331-360. Dark blue cloth. Copyright, p. [iv], notes
"First Edition"; bibliography, p. [329]; appendices, pp.
331-360.

1216 Plas, Gerald O. The Romney Riddle. Detroit: The Berwyn
Publishers [c1967.]

[1], [2], t. [3], [4], [5], bl. [6], 7-10, 11-122, 123-126,
adv. [127], [128]. Stiff illus. wrps., quotes from reviews
on outer back. Copyright, p. [4], notes "First Printing,
November, 1967"; notes, pp. 123-126.

WALLACE, GEORGE C. (Democratic)

1217 Frady, Marshall. Wallace. New York, Cleveland: The
World Publishing Company [c1968.]

Half title [i], cartoon [ii], t. [iii], [iv], v-vi, vii-viii,
1-246. Pink cloth with black paper backstrip and illus.
dj. Unfavorable.

1218 George Wallace, Profile of a Presidential Candidate. Kil-
marnock, Va.: Published by MS, Inc. [c1968.]

[i], bl. [ii], t. [iii], bl. [iv], [v], illus. [vi], [1]-7, illus.
[8], [9]-162. Stiff illus. wrps., purchase info. on inner
front and back. Illus. in text. Text in question and
answer format; first edition. Later printing noted with
copyright, p. [iv], p. [vi] bl., "In Passing," pp. [vii-
viii], fac. letter, illus. on verso, pp. [ix-x] ... text,
[9]-148.

1972

GENERAL WORKS

1219 Candidates '72. Washington: Congressional Quarterly [c1971.]

   T. [i], [ii], [iii], bl. [iv], 1-87, 88-91, 92. Illus. wrps.
   Includes McGovern, Muskie, McCloskey, Humphrey, Jackson, McCarthy, Mills, Agnew, Kennedy, Lindsay, Wallace, Connally, Nixon, and "Other Prospective Candidates."

1220 Leek, Sybil. Astrological Guide to the Presidential Candidates. London, New York, Toronto: Abelar-Schuman
   [c1972.]

   Half title [i], bl. [ii], t. [iii], [iv], [v], vi-xiv, div. t.
   [1], bl. [2], 3-145, bl. [146]. Blue cloth. Charts in
   text. Includes Nixon, Bayh, Harris, Hughes, Humphrey,
   Jackson, Kennedy, Lindsay, McCloskey, McGovern,
   Muskie, Percy, and Wallace.

1221 Newman, Joseph, ed. Guide to the '72 Elections. Washington: Books by U. S. News & World Report [c1972.]

   Half title, verso bl., t., copyright on verso, contents,
   [9-10], [11], div. t. [12], 13-239, [240-247], 248-255,
   [256]. All copies examined rebound. Illus. in text.
   Biog. profiles of Nixon, McCloskey, Muskie, Humphrey,
   Kennedy, Jackson, McGovern, Lindsay, McCarthy, Mills,
   Chisholm, Yorty, and Wallace.

1222 _____ . U. S. News & World Report's Guide to the '72
   Elections. Washington: Books by U. S. News & World
   Report [c1972.]

   Half title [1], bl. [2], t. [3], [4], [5], [6], [7], illus.
   [8], 9-151, 152-159, adv. [160]. All copies examined
   rebound. Illus. in text. Adds sketches of Ashbrook and
   Hartke; pr. in dbl. cols.

NIXON, RICHARD M. (Republican)

1223 Allen, Gary. Richard Nixon, the Man Behind the Mask.
   Boston, Los Angeles: Western Islands [c1971.]

   Half title [i], bl. [ii], t. [iii], [iv], [v], bl. [vi], 1-424,
   425-433, bl. [434]. Brown cloth. Index, pp. 425-433.
   Anti-Nixon, written by a Conservative Republican.

1224 Hoyt, Edwin P. The Nixons, an American Family. New
York: Random House [c1972.]

Half title [i], [ii], t. [iii], [iv], [v], bl. [vi], [vii]-x, [xi]-
xii, div. t. [1], bl. [2], [3]-300, [301]-307, [308]. Red
cloth with white dj pr. in red and black. 16 pp. sig.
pls. inserted between pp. 148-149. Copyright, p. [iv],
notes "First Edition"; author's note, pp. [vii]-x, dated
December 1971; index, pp. [301]-307.

1225 Hughes, Arthur J. Richard M. Nixon. Illustrated With
Photographs. New York: Dodd, Mead & Company
[c1972.]

Half title [i], bl. [ii], t. [iii], [iv], [v], bl. [vi], vii-
viii, div. t. [ix], bl. [x], 1-169, bl. [170], 171-172, 173-
181, bl. [182]. Blue cloth. 2 16 pp. sigs. pls. inserted.
Bibliography, pp. 171-172; index, pp. 173-181.

1226 [Lurie, Leonard.] The Running of Richard Nixon. New
York: Coward, McCann & Geoghegan, Inc. [c1972.]

Half title [i], bl. [ii], [1], [2], t. [3], [4], [5], [6], [7],
bl. [8], [9-10], [11], bl. [12], div. t. [13], bl. [14], 15-
390, 391-395, bl. [396], div. t. [397], bl. [398], 399-
409, bl. [410]. 3/4 blue cloth, red cloth backstrip. 2 8
pp. sigs. pls. inserted. Bibliography, pp. 391-395; index, pp. 399-409. Unfavorable.

1227 Mazlish, Bruce. In Search of Nixon: A Psychohistorical In-
quiry. New York, London: Basic Books, Inc. [c1972.]

Half title [i], bl. [ii], t. [iii], [iv], v-viii, [ix]-x, div. t.
[1], bl. [2], 3-170, 171-179, bl. [180], 181-182, 183-187,
bl. [188]. Grey cloth. 10 pp. sig. pls. inserted between pp. 78-[79]. Notes, pp. 171-179; bibliography, pp.
181-182; index, pp. 183-187.

1228 Spaldine, Henry D. The Nixon Nobody Knows. Middle Vil-
lage, N.Y.: Jonathan David Publishers [c1972.]

Half title [i], pf. [ii], t. [iii], [iv], [v], bl. [vi], [vii],
bl. [viii], 1-451, bl. [452], 453-456. Blue cloth. Illus.
in text. Index, pp. 453-456. Review copy also noted
citing pub. date as September 27, 1972.

1229 Will the Real Richard M. Nixon Please Stand Up? [N. p.,
n. d., 1972?]

Cover title. Unpaged, 40 ℓℓ. text, 2 terminal ℓℓ. Stiff
white illus. wrps. Title vignette. Illus. in text. Burlesque, anti-Nixon.

McGOVERN, GEORGE (Democratic)

1230 Anson, Robert Sam. McGovern, a Biography. New York,
      San Francisco, Chicago: Holt, Rinehart and Winston
      [c1972.]

      Half title [i], bl. [ii], t. [iii], [iv], [v], bl. [vi], [vii],
      bl. [viii], ix-xiii, bl. [xiv], div. t. [xv], bl. [xvi], 1-292,
      293-303, bl. [304]. Royal blue cloth with illus. dj. 8
      pp. sig. pls. inserted between pp. 144-145. Copyright
      notes "First Edition."; preface, pp. ix-xiii, dated Novem-
      ber, 1971; index, pp. 293-303. Copies also noted with
      copyright, p. [iv], noting "Published, March, 1972 /
      Second Printing, May, 1972."

1231 MacLaine, Shirley, ed. McGovern, the Man and His Beliefs.
      New York: W. W. Norton & Company, Inc. [c1972.]

      Half title [i], bl. [ii], t. [iii], [iv], [v], bl. [vi], div. t.
      [vii], illus. [viii], 1-[132]. Blue cloth with blue dj, illus.
      and pr. in red, white and black. Illus. in text. Also
      noted in orange cloth. Imprint, New York: Artists &
      Writers for McGovern, 1972, 120 pp., noted, but unex-
      amined.

CHISHOLM, SHIRLEY (Democratic)

1232 Brownmiller, Susan. Shirley Chisholm, a Biography. Gar-
      den City, N.Y.: Doubleday & Company, Inc. [c1970,
      1971.]

      Bl. [1], [2], half title [3], bl. [4], t. [5], [6], [7], bl.
      [8], div. t. [9], bl. [10], 11-[144]. Blue cloth. 8 pp.
      sig. pls. inserted between pp. 72-73.

1233 Chisholm, Shirley. Unbought and Unbossed. Boston: Hough-
      ton Mifflin Company, 1970.

      Half title [i], bl. [ii], t. [iii], [iv], [v], bl. [vi], [vii],
      bl. [viii], [ix]-x, [xi]-xii, div. t. [1], bl. [2], [3]-177,
      bl. [178]. Black cloth. First printing.

JACKSON, HENRY M. (Democratic)

1234 Prochnau, William W., and Larsen, Richard W. A Certain
      Democrat. Senator Henry M. Jackson, a Political Biog-
      raphy. Englewood Cliffs, N.J.: Prentice-Hall, Inc.
      [c1972.]

      Half title [i], bl. [ii], t. [iii], [iv], [v], bl. [vi], [vii],
      bl. [viii], 1-351, bl. [352], 353-360. Black cloth with

illus. dj. 8 pp. sig. pls. inserted between pp. 178-179.
Index, pp. 353-360.

KENNEDY, EDWARD M.

1235 David, Lester. Ted Kennedy, Triumphs and Tragedies.
New York: Grosset & Dunlap, A National General Company, Publishers [c1971, 1972.]

Half title [i], bl. [ii], t. [iii], [iv], [v], bl. [vi], [vii-
viii], [ix], bl. [x], div. t. [xi], [xii], 1-274. Grey cloth
with dj. 2 8 pp. sigs. pls. inserted.

1236 Hersch, Burton. The Education of Edward Kennedy. A Family Biography. New York: William Morrow & Company,
Inc., 1972.

Half title [i], [ii], t. [iii], [iv], [v], bl. [vi], [vii]-x, [xi]-
xiii, bl. [xiv], [xv], bl. [xvi], [xvii], bl. [xviii], [1]-461,
bl. [462], [463]-496, [497]-500, [501]-510. Black cloth.
16 pp. sig. pls. inserted between pp. 270-271. Notes,
pp. [463]-496; bibliography, pp. [497]-500; index, pp.
[501]-510.

1237 Honan, William H. Ted Kennedy, Profile of a Survivor.
Edward M. Kennedy After Bobby, After Chappaquiddick,
and After Three Years of Nixon. [New York:] Quad-
rangle Books, A New York Times Company [c1972.]

Half title [i], bl. [ii], t. [iii], [iv], [v], bl. [vi], vii-[x],
xi-xii, div. t. [1], bl. [2], 3-174, 175-180. Blue cloth.
16 pp. sig. pls. inserted between pp. 84-85. Index, pp.
175-180. First printing.

McCLOSKEY, PETER (Democratic)

1238 Cannon, Lou. The McCloskey Challenge. New York: E.
P. Dutton & Co., Inc., 1972.

Half title [i], [ii], t. [iii], [iv], [v], bl. [vi], vii, bl.
[viii], ix-xiii, [xiv], 1-263, 264-272, [273], bl. [274].
Blue cloth. Index, pp. 264-272; first edition. Foreword,
pp. ix-xiii, dated August, 1971.

MUSKIE, EDMUND S. (Democratic)

1239 Lippman, Theo, Jr., and Hansen, Donald C. Muskie. New
York: W. W. Norton & Company, Inc. [c1971.]

Half title [1], bl. [2], t. [3], [4], [5], bl. [6], [7], bl.
[8], div. t. [9], bl. [10], 11-236, 237, bl. [238]. Blue

cloth.   8 pp. sig. pls. inserted between pp. 128-129.
Note on sources, p. 237; first edition.

1240 Muskie, Edmund S. Journeys. Garden City, N.Y.: Double-
      day & Company, Inc., 1972.

      Half title [i], bl. [ii], t. [iii], [iv], [v], bl. [vi], [vii],
      bl. [viii], [ix], bl. [x], div. t. [xi], bl. [xii], [1]-3, [4]-
      204. Black cloth. First edition.

1241 Nevin, David. Muskie of Maine. New York: Random House
      [c1972.]

      Bl. [i], [ii], half title [iii], bl. [iv], t. [v], [vi], [vii],
      bl. [viii], [ix], bl. [x], [xi], bl. [xii], div. t. [1], bl.
      [2], 3-233, bl. [234], div. t. [235], bl. [236], 237-238,
      [239], bl. [240]. Off white linen cloth with illus. dj.
      First printing. Afterword, pp. 237-238.

1976

GENERAL WORKS

1242 Candidates '76: Timely Reports to Keep Journalists, Scholars
      and the Public Abreast of Developing Issues, Events, and
      Trends. Washington: Congressional Quarterly, January
      1976.

      T. [i], [ii], [iii], bl. [iv], v-vi, 1-102, 103-105, bl. [106],
      107, 108-110. Illus. wrps., illus. on outer back. Illus.
      in text. Includes Ford, Reagan, Bayh, Bentsen, Carter,
      Church, Harris, Humphrey, Jackson, Kennedy, Muskie,
      Sanford, Shapp, Shriver, Udall, Wallace, and McCarthy;
      text generally in dbl. cols; intro., pp. v-vi, dated Novem-
      ber 1975.

CARTER, JAMES E. (Democratic)

1243 Carter, James E. Why Not the Best? Nashville: Broadman
      Press [c1975.]

      Half title [i], bl. [ii], t. [iii], [iv], [v], bl. [vi], [vii-
      viii], 9-[156]. Light orange cloth. Illus. in text.

1244 Collins, Tom. The Search for Jimmy Carter. [Waco, Tx.:
      Word Books, Publisher, c1976.]

Bl. [1], [2], t. [3], [4], [5], bl. [6], [7], illus. [8-11],
bl. [12], 13-191, [192]. Coated illus. wrps., about the
author on inner back. Illus. in text. P. [7] dated August 1976.

1245 Kucharsky, David. The Man From Plains. [New York,
Hagerstown, San Francisco, London: Harper & Row,
Publishers c1976.]

Half title [i], [ii], t. [iii], [iv], [v], [vi], vii-ix, bl. [x],
1-144, 145-146, 147-150. 3/4 green paper bds., blue
cloth backstrip. Title vignette. Pub. info., p. [ii]; copyright, p. [iv], notes "First Edition"; preface, pp. vii-ix,
dated July 4, 1976; bibliography, pp. 145-146; index, pp.
147-150.

1246 Norton, Howard, and Slosser, Bob. The Miracle of Jimmy
Carter. Plainfield, N.J.: Logos International [c1976.]

Half title [i], bl. [ii], t. [iii], [iv], [v], bl. [vi], vii, bl.
[viii], ix, bl. [x], xi-xii, 1-134. Red lacquered cloth.
8 pp. sigs. pls. inserted between pp. 70-71, preceded
and succeeded by bl. ℓℓ. Copyright, p. [iv], notes
"First Edition, June 25, 1976."

1247 Schram, Martin. Running For President. A Journal of the
Carter Campaign. New York: Published by Pocket Books
[c1976.]

[i], adv. [ii], t. [iii], [iv], [v], bl. [vi], vii-ix, bl. [x],
xi, bl. [xii], 1-255, bl. [256], 257-268, 269-276. Stiff
illus. wrps. 16 pp. sig. pls. inserted between pp. 148-
149. Copyright, p. [iv], notes "Pocket Book Edition published October, 1976"; pp. vii-ix, dated August 31, 1976;
appendices, pp. 257-268; index, pp. 269-276.

1248 Wheeler, Leslie. Jimmy Who? An Examination of Presi-
dential Candidate Jimmy Carter: The Man, His Career,
His Stands on the Issues. With a Foreword by James
W. Davis.... Woodbury, N.Y.: Barron's [c1976.]

T. [i], [ii], [iii], [iv]-v, [vi], vii-xiii, xiv-xvi, 1-170,
171-244, 245-256, 257-262, 263-270. Stiff illus. wrps.
32 pp. sig. pls. inserted between pp. 128-129, other illus. in text. Footnotes, pp. 245-256; bibliography, pp.
257-262; index, pp. 263-270. Cloth copies also noted,
xiv, 306 pp., 32 pp. pls.

FORD, GERALD R. (Republican)

1249 Aaron, Jan. Gerald R. Ford, President of Destiny. New
York: Fleet Press Corporation [c1975.]

Half title [1], bl. [2], t. [3], [4], [5], bl. [6], [7-8], div.
t. [9], bl. [10], 11-96, bl. p., 97-99, bl. [100], 101-103.
Red cloth. Illus. in text. Chronology, pp. 97-99; index,
pp. 101-103.

1250 Mollenhoff, Clark R. The Man Who Pardoned Nixon. New
      York: A Giniger Book Published in Association with St.
      Martin's Press, Inc.; London: St. James Press [c1976.]

      Half title [i], [ii], t. [iii], [iv], [v], [vi], [vii-viii], [1]-
      301, bl. [302], [303]-312. Red cloth. Index, pp. [303]-
      312.

1251 Reeves, Richard. A Ford, Not a Lincoln. New York and
      London: Harcourt Brace Jovanovich [c1975.]

      Half title [i], bl. [ii], t. [iii], [iv], [v], bl. [vi], vii, bl.
      [viii], ix-xi, bl. [xii], div. t. [1], bl. [2], [3], bl. [4],
      5-204, 205-212. 3/4 blue paper bds., burlap cloth back-
      strip, illus. dj. First edition.

CHISHOLM, SHIRLEY (Democratic)

1252 Haskins, James. Fighting Shirley Chisholm. New York:
      The Dial Press [c1975.]

      Half title [i], bl. [ii], [iii], pf. [iv], t. [v], [vi], [vii],
      bl. [viii], [ix], bl. [x], div. t. [1], bl. [2], 3-196, 197-
      200, 201-205, bl. [206], 207-211, bl. [212], [213], bl.
      [214]. Brown cloth. Illus. in text. P. [vi] notes "First
      Printing"; appendix, pp. 197-200; bibliography, pp. 201-
      205; index, pp. 207-211.

CONNALLY, JOHN B. (Republican)

1253 Ashman, Charles. Connally. The Adventures of Big Bad
      John. New York: William Morrow & Company, Inc.,
      1974.

      Half title [i], [ii], t. [iii], [iv], [v], bl. [vi], vii-viii, ix,
      bl. [x], [xi], bl. [xii], div. t. [xiii], illus. [xiv], 1-295,
      bl. [296], 297-305, bl. [306]. Blue paper bds., red
      cloth backstrip. Illus. in text. Index, pp. 297-305;
      foreword by Melvin Belli, pp. vii-viii. Anti-Connally.

1254 Crawford, Ann Fears, and Keever, Jack. John B. Connally,
      Portrait in Power. Austin, Tx.: Jenkins Publishing
      Company, 1973.

      Half title [i], pf. [ii], t. [iii], [iv], [v], bl. [vi], [vii]-x,
      [xi], bl. [xii], div. t. [xiii], illus. [xiv], [1]-433, bl.

[434], [435]-443, bl. [444], [445]-460. Silver coated
cloth. Illus. in text. Bibliography, pp. [435]-443; index,
pp. [445]-460; preface, pp. [vii]-x, dated September 15,
1973.

HUMPHREY, HUBERT H. (Democratic)

1255 Humphrey, Hubert H.   The Education of a Public Man.   My
Life and Politics.   Edited by Norman Sherman.   Garden
City, N.Y.:   Doubleday & Company, Inc., 1976.

Half title [i], bl. [ii], t. [iii], [iv], [v], bl. [vi], [vii]-ix,
bl. [x], [xi]-xiii, bl. [xiv], div. t. [1], bl. [2], [3]-438,
[439]-440, div. t. [441], bl. [442], 4 pp. pls. inserted.
[443]-495, bl. [496], [497]-513, bl. [514].   3/4 grey paper bds., black cloth backstrip.   6 4 pp. sigs. pls. inserted.   P. [iv] notes "First Edition"; acknowledgements,
pp. [439]-440, dated March 1976; notes, pp. [443]-495;
index, pp. [497]-513.

JACKSON, HENRY M. (Democratic)

1256 Ognibene, Peter J.   Scoop, the Life and Politics of Henry M.
Jackson.   New York: Stein and Day Publishers [c1975.]

Half title [1], bl. [2], t. [3], [4], [5], [6], [7], bl. [8],
9-11, bl. [12], 13-233, bl. [234], 235-240.   Orange paper
bds., blue cloth backstrip.   Index, pp. 235-240.   Anti-
Jackson.

KENNEDY, EDWARD M. (Democratic)

1257 Burns, James MacGregor.   Edward Kennedy and the Camelot
Legacy.   New York: W. W. Norton & Company [c1976.]

[1], [2], t. [3], [4], [5], bl. [6], [7]-8, [9]-10, [11]-16,
div. t. [17], bl. [18], [19]-340, div. t. [341], [342]-383,
bl. [384].   Green paper bds., maroon cloth backstrip.
4 sigs. pls. inserted, other illus. in text.   First edition.

1258 Lippman, Theo Jr.   Senator Ted Kennedy.   New York: W.
W. Norton & Company, Inc. [c1976].

Half title [i], [ii], t. [iii], [iv], [v], bl. [vi], [vii], bl.
[viii], [ix]-xi, bl. [xii], div. t. [xiii], bl. [xiv], [1]-282,
[283]-296.   Charcoal grey cloth.   8 pp. sig. pls. inserted
between pp. 160-161.   P. [iv] notes "First Edition"; author's note, pp. [ix]-xi, dated July 1975; index, pp. [283]-
296.

1259 Sherrill, Robert. The Last Kennedy. New York: The Dial
      Press, 1976.

      Half title [i], map [ii], t. [iii], [iv], [v], bl. [vi], vii, bl.
      [viii], ix-[x], div. t. [xi], bl. [xii], [xiii], bl. [xiv], 1-
      12, div. t. [13], bl. [14], 15-228, 229-230, 231-239, bl.
      [240]. Black cloth. Sources, pp. 229-230; index, pp.
      231-239; "First Printing 1976." Anti-Kennedy.

PERCY, CHARLES H. (Republican)

1260 Hartley, Robert E. Charles H. Percy. A Political Perspec-
      tive. Chicago, New York, San Francisco: Rand McNally
      & Company [c1975.]

      Half title [1], bl. [2], t. [3], [4], [5], [6], 7-[8], 9-239,
      240-247, bl. [248], 249-255, bl. [256]. Red cloth. 8
      pp. sig. pls. inserted. Notes on sources, pp. 240-247;
      index, pp. 249-255; first printing.

ROCKEFELLER, NELSON A. (Republican)

1261 Kramer, Michael, and Roberts, Sam. "I Never Wanted to
      Be Vice-President of Anything!" An Investigative Biog-
      raphy of Nelson Rockefeller. New York: Basic Books,
      Inc., Publishers [c1976.]

      Half title [i], bl. [ii], t. [iii], [iv], [v], bl. [vi], [vii],
      bl. [viii], ix-x, xi-xii, div. t. [1], illus. [2], 3-15, bl.
      [16], div. t. [17], bl. [18], 19-378, 379-407, bl. [408],
      409-420. Blue cloth. 2 8 pp. sigs. pls. inserted.
      Notes, pp. 379-407; index, pp. 409-420. Anti-Rockefeller.

ADDENDUM

1796

ADAMS, JOHN (Federalist)

1262 [Gardner, John.] A Brief Consideration of the Important Ser-
vices, and Distinguished Virtues and Talents, Which
Recommend Mr. Adams for the Presidency of the United
States. Boston: Printed by Manning & Loring, and to be
Sold by Joseph Nancrede, 1796.

Cover title [1], [2], [3]-31, bl. [32]. Sewn. P. 31 signed
"Aurelius"; originally pr. in the Columbian Sentinel.

1808

CLINTON, GEORGE (Democratic-Republican)

*1263 An Address to the People of the American States Who Choose
Electors ... to Which Is Added a Short Sketch of the Biography of Gen. George Clinton.... Washington City: 1808.

11, 2-54 pp., signed "Nestor." Sabin 430 (13741)

1264 Cragg, Saunders. George Clinton Next President, and Our
Republican Institutions Rescued From Destruction: Ad-
dressed to the Citizens of the United States: Or, James
Madison Unmasked. New York: Printed for the Author,
Henry C. Southwick, Printer, 1808.

Cover title [1], bl. [2], [3], bl. [4], [5]-40. Sewn.
Preface, p. [3]; p. 6 cited as 5.

PINCKNEY, CHARLES C. (Federalist)

1265 [Smith, William Lougtin.] A Letter, on the Approaching
Election of a President of the United States, Addressed
to the Citizens of South-Carolina. By a Native of
Charleston. Charleston: 1808.

Cover title [1], bl. [2], [3]-27, bl. [28]. Sewn. "Sketch of the Life and Character of General Charles Cotesworth Pinckney, " pp. 14-20.

1812

CLINTON, DEWITT (Federalist)

*1266 Letters to a Friend at Pittsburgh on the Character and Conduct of Dewitt Clinton. By Milo. New York: 1812.

15 pp. Sabin 13732.

1840

HARRISON, WILLIAM HENRY (Whig)

*1267 [Jackson, Isaac Rand.] Life of William Henry Harrison, the People's Candidate. Steubenville: J. & R. C. Wilson [1840?]

32 pp.

1852

PIERCE, FRANKLIN (Democratic)

*1268 Franklin Pierce's Leben und Wirken. Aufruf an die Deutschen Wahler. [N. p., n. d., 1852.]

8 pp. Sabin 62715.

SCOTT, WINFIELD (Whig)

*1269 Life of General Scott. [Columbus: Scott & Bascom, 1852.]

Caption title. 30 pp. Sewn. At foot of p. [1], "For Sale by Scott & Bascom, Columbus, Ohio."

1856

BUCHANAN, JAMES (Democratic)

*1270 Memoir of James Buchanan.... Philadelphia: C. Sherman & Son, 1856.

16 pp.   Issued by the Democratic State Central Committee
of Pennsylvania.   A separate printing from entry 354?

FILLMORE, MILLARD (American [Know-Nothing])

*1271 The Executive Acts of Ex-President Fillmore: With Reasons
       for His Election, and a Memoir of His Life and Adminis-
       tration.... And a Sketch of the Life of Andrew Jackson
       Donelson.... New York: Edward Walker, 1856.

       48 pp.   Sabin 24332.

PIERCE, FRANKLIN (Democratic)

*1272 [Bartlett, David Vandewater Golden.] The Life of Gen. Frank-
       lin Pierce, of New Hampshire, President of the United
       States.... Fifteenth Thousand. New York [etc.]: Miller,
       Orton & Mulligan, 1855.

       304 pp., port.

                              1884

CLEVELAND, GROVER (Democratic)

1273   Ferris, Geo. T. The Biography and Public Services of Hon.
       Grover Cleveland. Illustrated. New York and Chicago:
       H. S. Goodspeed & Co., 1884.

       Pf., t. [i], [ii], [iii]-iv, [v], [vi], [401 sic]-636, port.,
       [637-638], div. t. [639], [640], [641-642], [643], bl.
       [644], [645]-774. Maroon cloth. Pf., port., and 22 pls.
       inserted. At head of title, Authorized Edition; separate
       t. for life of Hendricks, pp. [645]-774; bound with The
       Biography ... of Hon. Samuel J. Tilden, the whole vol.
       being paged continuously. Also noted in red cloth.

                              1888

HARRISON, BENJAMIN (Republican)

1274   Boyd, James P. Biographies of Harrison and Morton. Phi-
       ladelphia: Franklin News Co., 1888.

       Cover title. Pf., [1]-54, 55-64, port., [1]-16. Blue
       green wrps., adv. on inner front and entire back. Pf.,
       pl. inserted. Cover also notes, The Franklin Library ...

Number 15, August, 1888; life of Harrison, pp. [1]-54;
convention proceedings, pp. 55-64; life of Morton, pp.
[1]-16.

1908

WATSON, THOMAS E. (People's Party [Populist])

*1275 The Life and Speeches of Thomas Edwards Watson.   Nash-
       ville: 1908.

       367 pp.

1916

GENERAL WORKS

*1276 Rand McNally Political Atlas ... the Men and the Issues of
       the Presidential Campaign of 1916.   Chicago, New York:
       Rand McNally & Company, Publishers, 1916.

       16 pp., illus.

1920

GENERAL WORKS

1277   Rand McNally Political Atlas ... the Men and the Issues of
       the Presidential Campaign of 1920.   Chicago, New York:
       Rand McNally & Company, Publishers, 1920.

       T. [1], 2-15, cld. maps 16.   Green wrps., tbls. on inner
       front and back, adv. on outer back, front also noting
       Compliments of E. Sondheimer Co.   Memphis, Tenn., pr.
       in red.   Illus. in text.   Text generally pr. in dbl. cols.

1928

HOOVER, HERBERT (Republican)

1278   Herbert Clark Hoover.   New York: James T. White & Co.,
       MCMXXVII.

       Unpaged, 14 ℓℓ.   Bl. [i], pf. [ii], t. [iii], [iv], [1-25],
       bl. [26], bl. ℓ.   Tan wrps.   Copyright, p. [iv], notes
       "From the National Cyclopedia of American Biography."

1936

GENERAL WORKS

*1279 Rand McNally Political Atlas for 1936.... New York, Chi-
cago [etc.]: Rand McNally & Company, 1936.

32 pp. On cover, Compliments of Stitt Ignition Company
... Columbus, Ohio.

1960

GENERAL WORKS

1280 Sevareid, Eric, ed. Candidates 1960. Behind the Headlines
in the Presidential Race. New York: Basic Books, Inc.
[c1959.]

Half title [i], [ii], t. [iii], [iv], [v]-viii, [ix], bl. [x],
div. t. [xi], bl. [xii], [1]-360, div. t. [361], bl. [362],
[363]-369, bl. [370]. Blue paper bds., white cloth backstrip. 8 pp. sig. pls. inserted between pp. 69-[70].
Copyright, p. [iv], notes "First Printing, September,
1959 / Second Printing, October, 1959"; index, pp. [363]-
369.

1972

PROXMIRE, WILLIAM (Democratic)

1281 Sykes, Jay G. Proxmire. Washington, New York: Robert
B. Luce, Inc. [c1972.]

Half title [i], bl. [ii], t. [iii], [iv], [v], bl. [vi], vii-viii,
ix-x, 11-256. Orange cloth. Foreword, pp. vii-viii,
dated January, 1972.

AUTHOR AND CANDIDATE INDEX

223

TITLE INDEX

233